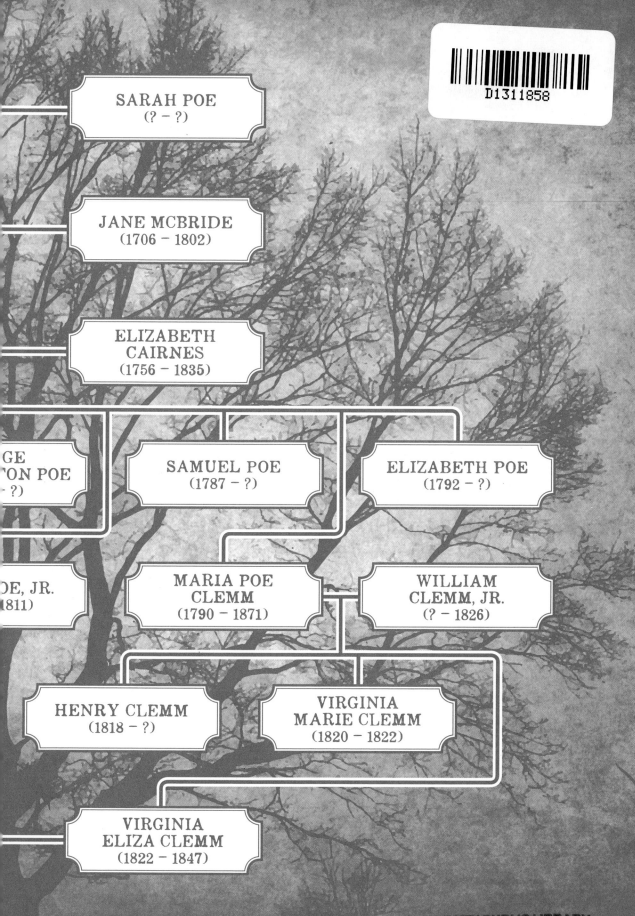

SARAH POE
(? – ?)

JANE MCBRIDE
(1706 – 1802)

ELIZABETH
CAIRNES
(1756 – 1835)

GE
ON POE
– ?)

SAMUEL POE
(1787 – ?)

ELIZABETH POE
(1792 – ?)

OE, JR.
811)

MARIA POE
CLEMM
(1790 – 1871)

WILLIAM
CLEMM, JR.
(? – 1826)

HENRY CLEMM
(1818 – ?)

VIRGINIA
MARIE CLEMM
(1820 – 1822)

VIRGINIA
ELIZA CLEMM
(1822 – 1847)

# EDGAR ALLAN POE

# EDGAR ALLAN POE

## THE STRANGE MAN STANDING DEEP IN THE SHADOWS

### CHARLOTTE MONTAGUE

**CHARTWELL
BOOKS**

"Words have no power
to impress the mind
without the exquisite
horror of their reality."

Edgar Allan Poe
(1809 – 1849)

# CONTENTS

# INTRODUCTION

Abraham Lincoln, Charles Baudelaire, Josef Stalin, Michael Jackson, and Bart Simpson, an unlikely group of people, all have one thing in common; they are or were fans of the nineteenth century American short story-writer, poet and critic, Edgar Allan Poe. The writer of 'The Raven' has legions of such fans across the world and his work has been translated into dozens of languages and is enjoyed probably even more today than it was a hundred and fifty years ago.

As if it was not enough that we are gripped by the brilliance of his stories, they are also easily translated into other media, so more than two hundred films have been made of his tales and of his tragic life. 'The Fall of the House of Usher', for example, has been filmed a dozen times, the first versions appearing in 1928, the most recent in 2006.

## A TRUE PIONEERING GIANT

Poe is viewed by many as the ultimate doomed romantic, a wild drunk whose last days are shrouded in sordid mystery, but whose achievements in the world of literature are staggering. He is widely recognized as the father of the modern short story, is the acknowledged inventor of the detective story, a pioneer of science fiction, a master of the horror story, the first writer of international stature to emerge from the United States and the first American writer to try to earn a living from his writing alone.

Without a doubt, he is a giant of American literature, but his life was a disaster, a tale of unremitting misery, constant poverty and repeated frustration and disappointment. To a certain extent, of course, Poe brought it on himself, as his friend, the writer James Russell Lowell said: 'One of the strange parts of his strange nature was to entertain a spirit of revenge towards all who did him a service ... He rarely, or never, failed to malign those who befriended him.'

Edgar Allan Poe, illustration by Edmund Dulac, 1912.

Time and time again, Poe turned on people who had helped him out, imploding in a haze of alcohol and indignation. More often than not, it ended with him out of work and scrabbling around for enough money on which he, his very sick wife and his mother-in-law could live.

It was, indeed, a tragic life. He and his two siblings lost their parents while young and were taken in by other families. Unfortunately for Poe, he enjoyed a dreadful relationship with his adoptive father, John Allan. After a luxurious, pampered childhood, he was abandoned very much to his own devices in his late teens, provided with inadequate funds to give a proper account of himself at university and remained unsupported by Allan in the desperate years following. A spell in the army ended disastrously, as did an effort to improve himself at West Point, the historic American military academy. From that point on, he staggered from one job to another and one bar to another, often wasting his prodigious talents on work unworthy of him.

## THE CHILDREN OF POE

Death seemed to stalk Poe throughout his life and not only did he lose his parents at a young age, he lost his first love, Jane Stanard, the mother of a friend, who provided much-needed emotional support to the young man, when she was only thirty-one. His adored wife Virginia fell victim to tuberculosis aged only twenty-four

and his brother Henry died of tuberculosis at the same age, his illness exacerbated by the same heavy drinking that blighted Edgar's life. There was tragedy, too, in Poe's mysterious death and he was unable to find peace afterwards, his reputation scandalously besmirched by a literary rival, leaving a stain on his character for many years.

But, at least we have the seventy-three wonderful, macabre stories and one novel that Poe left behind, filled with suspense and brilliantly twisted plots. He may have lived in poverty, but he changed American – and perhaps all – literature forever. As another master of horror, Stephen King, has said, we are all 'the children of Poe.'

'The Raven', illustration by Edmund Dulac, 1912.

## THE POE TOASTER

It may have begun as far back as the 1930s, some say. Every year in the early hours of January 19 – Edgar Allan Poe's birthday – a figure, known as the Poe Toaster, dressed head to foot in black, face hidden behind a scarf or a hood and carrying a silver-tipped cane, entered the Westminster Hall and Burying Ground at 519 West Fayette Street in Baltimore. He – it is presumed he was male – would make his way to the site of Poe's original grave, marked by a commemorative stone, where he would toast the dead writer with a glass of Martell cognac and place three red roses on the monument, always in a distinctive configuration and beside it he would leave the unfinished bottle of cognac. The roses represented Poe, his wife Virginia and her mother Maria Clemm but the significance of the cognac is unknown. Occasionally, he left a note and in 1993 it said 'The torch will be passed.' A note left in 1999 announced that the original Toaster had passed away and the tradition had been passed on to a 'son.' Other notes dealt with topical or sporting events. The tradition ended abruptly in 2009, the two hundredth anniversary of Poe's birth.

# PART 1
# ALONE IN HIS OWN IMAGINATION

From childhood's hour I have not been
As others were – I have not seen
As others saw – I could not bring
My passions from a common spring –
From the same source I have not taken
My sorrow – I could not awaken
My heart to joy at the same tone
And all I lov'd – *I* lov'd alone.

Edgar Allan Poe *from* 'Alone'

# CHAPTER 1

# THE SHAPE OF THINGS TO COME

Edgar Poe was born on January 19, 1809 in a boarding house near Carver Street in Boston, a city that later in life he would loath. His parents were both actors. His father, David Poe Jr. (1784 – 1811), had been born in Baltimore into a family that wanted him to become a lawyer, but the young man's interests lay elsewhere. He joined the Baltimore Thespian Group where, with other young men, he read and performed plays.

One night, while visiting Norfolk, Virginia, David went to the theater where he fell in love with the pretty nineteen year-old actress performing on stage. He and Eliza Arnold (1787 – 1811) were soon married and nine months later their first child William Henry Leonard Poe (1807 – 1831), known as Henry, was born. David's father, David Sr. (c. 1748 – 1818) was furious when he learned that not only had his son married an actor, at that time not considered a reputable profession, but that he had become one too, having joined his new wife's acting company.

## A WRETCHED ALONZO

David Poe was handsome and well-built, making him ideal for casting in juvenile and romantic roles but he was never as accomplished an actor as his wife, as one particularly scathing review, not long after they married, confirms: '... the lady was young and pretty, and evinced talent both as singer and actress; the gentleman was literally nothing.'

Another review written several years later, complained: '... a more wretched Alonzo have we never witnessed. This man was never destined for the high walks of drama;

a footman is the extent of what he ought to attempt ... his person, voice, and non-expression of countenance, all combine to stamp him – *poh*!' The lame pun on his name, with its allusion to chamber pots, would haunt him throughout his career. It would also be dragged out again during some of his son's numerous literary spats.

## WAXING LYRICAL

Eliza Arnold turned out to be no less talented than her mother who had been a fine actor and singer. Making her first stage appearance in Boston, aged nine, just three months after arriving in America, she won good reviews. Later that year she appeared in the David Garrick farce, *Miss in Her Teens*.

The Portland *Eastern Herald* was fulsome in its praise for her performance: 'Miss Arnold, in Miss Biddy, exceeded all praise. Although a miss of only nine years old, her powers as an Actress will do credit to any of her sex of maturer age.' A month later, a critic waxed lyrical about her performance, praising 'the powers of Miss Arnold to astonish us. Add to these her youth, her beauty, her innocence, and a character is composed which has not, and perhaps will not ever again be found in any theater.'

By the time David met Eliza, she was already a widow, her first husband, Charles Hopkins (? – 1805), also an actor, having died six months previously. She had married him in 1802 when she was only fifteen. By that time she was already an accomplished performer and she would play some three hundred roles during her theatrical career, including many major Shakespearian characters such as

Ophelia, Juliet and Cordelia, as well as pretty heroines in the farces and comedies of the time.

## TRAMPING THE BOARDS

The young couple's life was spent working in theaters in various towns up and down the East Coast but, money was tight and David's career was not thriving. Thus, Eliza could be found performing on a Boston stage just a week before the birth of their second child, Edgar. A month after the birth, she was tramping the boards once again.

If money had been tight with just one child, it was even worse with two. In February 1809, becoming increasingly desperate, David visited his cousin George Poe (1778 – ?) in Stockertown, fifty miles from Philadelphia. He told George he had not come to beg but would like to meet him the following day. George arrived for the meeting, but David failed to show, sending his cousin instead what George described as an 'impertinent note,' arrogantly and pathetically demanding money.

Understandably, George rejected David's overwrought appeal, forcing the Poes to deposit the five week-old Edgar with his grandparents, 'General' David Poe and his wife Elizabeth (1756 – 1835), in Baltimore so that they could carry on working. Then, in August, they placed Edgar in the care of an old nursemaid. His sister Rosalie (1810 – 1874), would join him there.

The children were described by a friend as '... thin and pale and very fretful. To quiet them their old nurse ... took them upon her lap and fed them liberally with bread soaked in gin, when they soon fell asleep.'

The nurse later acknowledged that she had 'freely administered to them gin and other spiritous liquors, with sometimes laudanum ... to make them strong and healthy ... or to put them to sleep when restless.' It is not difficult to see where Poe's later problems with alcohol came from.

The only known image of Eliza Arnold Poe, mother of Edgar Allan Poe.

# POE'S ANTECEDENTS

### EDGAR'S GREAT-GREAT-GRANDPARENTS

David Poe was a Protestant tenant-farmer from County Cavan in Ireland. He and his wife Sarah had four children – John (Edgar's great-grandfather), Alexander, Anne and Mary.

### EDGAR'S GREAT-GRANDPARENTS

John Poe married Jane McBride, and the couple had ten children – David Sr. (Edgar's grandfather), George, William, Robert, Samuel, Jane, Hester, John, Mary and James. John Poe and his family emigrated from Ireland to America, arriving in Lancaster County, Pennsylvania, around 1750.

### EDGAR'S GRANDPARENTS

David Poe Sr. married Elizabeth Cairnes who gave birth to seven children – John Hancock, William, George Washington, David Jr. (Edgar's father), Samuel, Maria, and Elizabeth. David Poe Sr. relocated to Baltimore in 1775, where he became the owner of a dry goods store. Four years later, he was appointed Assistant Deputy Quartermaster for the American Army and became well known during the American Revolution for paying for supplies with his own money. Such acts earned the respect and friendship of the Marquis de Lafayette, a French aristocrat and soldier fighting for the United States. David Poe Sr., a major, was given the honorary title of 'General' as a result. A title he proudly used for the rest of his life.

### EDGAR'S MATERNAL GRANDPARENTS

Henry Arnold married Elizabeth in London, May 1784. Not much is known about Henry, but Elizabeth was a successful actor, first taking the stage at the Theater Royal, Covent Garden, London in February 1791. In January 1796, Elizabeth, by this time a widow, arrived in Boston on the *Outram* with her daughter, Eliza. That same year, Elizabeth married actor, singer and pianist, Charles Tubbs, but is believed to have died around 1798, after which date her name no longer appears in American theatrical records.

## GIVING UP THE GHOST

The Poes' lives began to unravel, David Poe's theatrical career coming to an end with his last stage appearance in October 1809. By July 1811, he had abandoned his wife and young family and vanished. One can only speculate as to the reasons. He was a hard drinker and some say that he was possibly dismissed because of this.

The couple's unrelenting poverty must have played a part and David's failing career as an actor with poor performances and the hurtful reviews they engendered must also have contributed to his disillusion with life. He died five months later, around December 1811, in Norfolk, Virginia, but his son would inherit much from him in terms of habits and character.

Eliza was left in a very vulnerable position. She had three children to worry about, but worked in a profession that did not allow for family life and failed to provide financial security. She was constantly on the move from one theater to another and from one cheap guesthouse to another. It all took its toll and she made her last stage appearance on October 11, 1811, by this time very ill with tuberculosis, an illness with which Edgar would become sadly familiar in later years.

The Richmond Theater organized a benefit performance for her on November 29, the local newspaper, the *Enquirer*, making an appeal on her behalf: 'On this night, *Mrs Poe*, lingering on the bed of disease and surrounded by her children, asks your assistance and *asks it for the last time*.' Eliza finally gave up her struggle on December 8, aged just twenty-four. 'The stage has been deprived of one of its chief ornaments;' her obituary read. David and Eliza Poe had died within three days of each other.

## ARTISTIC FAMILY HERITAGE

At the time of his daughter-in-law's impoverished death, 'General' Poe was in no financial position to take responsibility for the children. Therefore, Rosalie was taken in by a

Richmond merchant, William Mackenzie, and his wife, while Edgar was welcomed into the household of a childless couple, John Allan (1779 – 1834) and his wife Frances, who lived above the store of the business in which John Allan was a partner, Ellis & Allan, general merchants, on the corner of Main and Thirteenth Streets in Richmond.

Edgar began a new life, but although he was too young to know and remember either his mother or his father, he remained staunchly proud of his artistic family heritage, writing later: 'The writer of this article is himself the son of an actress – has invariably made it his boast – and no earl was ever prouder of his earldom than he of his descent from a woman who, although well-born, hesitated not to consecrate to the drama her brief career of genius and of beauty.'

## THE ALLANS AND ENGLAND

Perhaps John Allan sympathized with the Poe children's situation, because he had himself been an orphan. Allan was born in Irvine on the west coast of Scotland, and, like many Scots, had decided to seek his fortune in the New World, emigrating to Richmond, Virginia, in 1795. In 1800, he entered into partnership with Charles Ellis, their business involving a variety of activities, including exporting Virginia tobacco. They also traded in old slaves who were hired out at coalmines where they were worked until they died.

John Allan, described as 'impulsive and quick-tempered ... rather rough and uncultured in mind and manner,' had been married since 1803 to Frances Valentine who, unfortunately, suffered from bad health and a nervous disposition. Perhaps because of his wife's poor health, Allan had relationships with a number of women, one of whom provided him with an illegitimate son, Edward Collier, who was a little older than Edgar Poe. The Allans never legally adopted Edgar although they did add their name to his, making him Edgar *Allan* Poe.

## MOVING RECITATIONS

Edgar wanted for nothing in the Allan household, doted on both by Frances Allan and her sister Nancy who also lived there. He was dressed in fine clothing and was described at the age of three as 'a lovely little fellow, with dark curls and brilliant eyes ... charming every one by his childish grace, vivacity and cleverness.' He was the apple of his adopted parents' eyes, often being shown off to visitors. From an early age Edgar had the ability to memorize and movingly recite passages of poetry – a talent that served him well throughout his life – and he would do so for guests standing on the dining room table, toasting the ladies, to the great amusement of all, in sweetened wine.

His relationship with John Allan, however, was nothing if not complicated and would blight Poe's life for years. Allan did not seem

John Allan, Poe's foster father.

sure how to treat him, one minute praising him to the hilt, the next chastising him for some oversight. Nonetheless, Edgar was sent to the best schools and taught how to behave as a young gentleman in polite society.

The War of 1812 between the United States and Britain brought a trade ban that did untold damage to Ellis & Allan's business. But, at the conclusion of the war, the British were anxious to re-establish trade ties. Allan decided to open a branch of the company in England and on June 23, 1815 he embarked with his family, including Nancy and Edgar, on the *Lothair* from Norfolk, Virginia, to Liverpool.

## THIS REVEREND MAN

The first months were spent visiting John's family in Scotland, but in October, they moved into lodgings at 47 Southampton Row in London. Six months later, Edgar was enrolled at a boarding school in Sloane Street in Chelsea run by the Misses Dubourg (a name Poe used later for the laundress who is a witness in his story, 'The Murders in the Rue Morgue'). In fall 1817, Allan established his family in better accommodation at 39 Southampton Row – the address Poe used for the narrator of his story 'Why the Little Frenchman Wears His Arm in a Sling'.

In 1818, now nine, Edgar moved to the Manor House boarding school in Stoke Newington (now part of north London), run by the Reverend John Bransby (1784 – ?). It cannot have been easy for the boy, recently uprooted from his native land and now separated from his parents and living in the strict regime that prevailed at Bransby's school. In his story 'William Wilson', set partly in Stoke Newington, he describes the routine:

*The morning's awakening, the nightly summons to bed; the connings, the recitations; the periodical half-holidays, and perambulations; the playground, with its broils, its pastimes, its intrigues ...*

Much to his chagrin, 'Dr' Bransby also appears in 'William Wilson':

*This reverend man, with countenance so demurely benign, with robes so glossy and so clerically flowing, with wig so minutely powdered, so rigid and so vast—could this be he who, of late, with sour image, and in snuffy habiliments, administered, ferule in hand, the Draconian Laws of the academy?*

A ferule is, of course, a cane used to administer punishment. The tenor of the discipline at Bransby's school, therefore, is evident. A later pupil at the school has shared with us Bransby's view of Edgar Allan Poe and his education. Of particular note is Bransby's opinion that Poe had been spoiled by John Allan's over-indulgence – not a view to which Poe would have subscribed, one imagines.

*When he left it he was able to speak the French language, construe any easy Latin author, and was far better acquainted with history and literature than many boys of a more advanced age who had greater advantages than he had had. I spoke to Dr. Bransby about him two or three times during my school days ... Dr. Bransby seemed rather to shun the topic, I suppose from some feelings with regard to his name being used distastefully in the story of 'William Wilson'. In answer to my questions on one occasion, he said 'Edgar Allan (the name Poe was known by at school) was a quick and clever boy and would have been a very good boy if he had not been spoilt by his parents', meaning the Allans; 'but they spoilt him, and allowed him an extravagant amount of pocket-money, which enabled him to get into all manner of mischief—still I liked the boy.—poor fellow, his parents spoilt him!' At another time he said, 'Allan was intelligent, wayward, and wilful.'*

Even John Allan was pleased with his adopted son's progress, however. Writing home to Richmond in several letters in 1818 and 1819, he said: 'Edgar is a fine Boy and I have no reason to complain of his progress

... [He] is growing wonderfully, & enjoys a good reputation and is both able & willing to receive instruction.' This view would soon change, however.

## HIS IMAGINATIVE POWERS

Her health having deteriorated during the family's stay in England, Frances Allan anticipated the voyage back to America with

Composite photo of Frances Allan and Rosalie Poe, Edgar Allan Poe's foster mother and sister.

some trepidation. Things had not worked out entirely as John Allan had hoped and he was keen to cut his losses. Therefore, on June 20, 1820, they set off from Liverpool on the *Martha*, arriving thirty-one days later in New York.

The sojourn in England had undoubtedly been of benefit to the eleven year-old Edgar. He had received a better education thus far than any of his Richmond contemporaries and had seen something of the world. In the fall of that year he enrolled at the school of Joseph Clarke, an irascible Irish bachelor who was also a good classical scholar. He learned mathematics and read the great writers of classical literature. Clarke described his talented pupil:

> *As to Edgar's disposition and character as a boy, though playful as most boys, his general deportment differed in some respects from others. He was remarkable for self-respect, without haughtiness, strictly just and correct in his demeanor with his playmates, which rendered him a favorite even with those above his years. His natural and predominate passion seemed to me, to be an enthusiastic ardor in everything he undertook; in his difference of opinion with his fellow students, he was very tenacious, and would not yield till his judgment was convinced. As a scholar he was ambitious to excel, and tho' not conspicuously studious always acquitted himself well in his classes. His imaginative powers seemed to take precedence of all his other faculties, he gave proof of this, in some juvenile compositions addressed to his young female friends. He had a sensitive and tender heart, and would strain every nerve to oblige a friend.*

## DANGEROUS ADVENTURES

He reserved particular praise for Edgar's poetry and, in fact, even John Allan was impressed by it. When Edgar was still only eleven, Allan sought advice from Clarke on publishing the poetry, but the teacher advised him not to pursue the matter for fear that it would turn the boy's head. Edgar's next school was William Burke's which he entered in April 1823, aged fourteen. There, he studied Latin, Greek, Italian and French, Geography and Grammar.

The Allans were living at this time in the home of John Allan's business partner, Charles Ellis. Edgar would take part in dangerous adventures with Charles's son,

Mrs Jane Stanard (1793 – 1824).

Thomas, who described him in the fondest terms: 'No boy ever had a greater influence over me than he had. He was, indeed, a leader among boys; but my admiration for him scarcely knew bounds.' Another friend, a classmate who would become Colonel James Preston, was less charitable about the nature of Edgar's character. Preston pointed out that the profession of his late parents carried a good deal of social stigma for the boy, as did his status as an adopted son:

> [He] *was self-willed, capricious, inclined to be imperious, and though of generous impulses, not steadily kind or even amiable ... Of Edgar Poe it was known that his parents were players, and that he was dependent upon the bounty that is bestowed upon an adopted son. All this had the effect of making the boys decline his leadership; and on looking back on it since, I fancy it gave him a fierceness he would otherwise not have had.*

It is little wonder that Edgar became increasingly isolated as he grew older. He was a victim of a tragic childhood, felt socially inadequate due to his parents' profession, and the Allans refusal to legally adopt him to give him a proper place in the world. He had also enjoyed a different type of upbringing to his classmates, had lived in England and, to make matters worse, he wrote poetry.

## DOOMED ON DESPERATE SEAS

Jane Stanard (1793 – 1824), the mother of Edgar's friend Robert, was the first love of his life. When there were troubles at home – which there often were – he turned to Jane for consolation. Like many of the women in Edgar Allan Poe's life, however, she died young, aged thirty-one. He suffered greatly, having terrible nightmares and spending most nights hiding under the bed covers. From Jane's death came the beautiful elegiac love poem, 'To Helen', the name changed for poetic effect. He compares her beauty to the ancient vessels that carry home the exhausted warrior and towards the end of the poem, he gazes on the unattainable, perfect Jane/Helen.

> *On desperate seas long wont to roam,*
> *Thy hyacinth hair, thy classic face,*
> *Thy Naiad airs have brought me home*
> *To the glory that was Greece,*
> *And the grandeur that was Rome*
>
> *Lo! in yon brilliant window-niche*
> *How statue-like I see thee stand,*
> *The agate lamp within thy hand!*
> *Ah, Psyche, from the regions which*
> *Are Holy-land!*

Soon, however, Edgar's ardent young heart was fluttering again. In 1825, a year after Jane Stanard's death, he fell for and became secretly engaged to his fifteen year-old neighbor, Sarah Elmira Royster (1810 – 88). It was a relationship doomed from the start, however. Elmira's father, believing the couple to be too young, intercepted the letters that Edgar sent her from university. She believed he had simply forgotten her and became engaged to another young man. She described Poe as:

> *... a beautiful boy—Not very talkative. When he did talk though he was pleasant but his general manner was sad—He was devoted to the first Mrs Allan and she to him ... [he] was very generous ... He had strong prejudices. Hated anything coarse and unrefined. Never spoke of his [birth] parents. He was kind to his sister as far as in his power. He was warm and zealous in any cause he was interested in, very enthusiastic and impulsive.*

Later she admitted: 'I married another man, but the love of my life was Edgar Poe. I never loved anyone else.'

Poe and Elmira would rekindle their relationship many years later, shortly before his death, but for the moment, all he had was the inspiration for his poem 'Song' which deals with her marriage to another. In the poem he catches her eye on her wedding day and glimpses a 'burning blush' that suggests she is perhaps still in love with him.

*I saw thee on thy bridal day—*
*When a burning blush came o'er thee,*
*Though happiness around thee lay,*
*The world all love before thee:*

## JOHN ALLAN'S DARK MOODS

Problems with his adoptive father really began in November 1824. Allan's view of Edgar was ambiguous. He believed he was a very good poet and he was occasionally full of praise for him: 'Edgar is wayward and impulsive ... for he has genius ... he will someday fill the world with his fame.' But still Edgar felt that he had not been sufficiently encouraged by Allan in his poetic endeavors. Allan was a man who did not suffer fools gladly, he was irascible, hot-tempered and could exhibit cruelty towards

his son. William Mackenzie, who had taken in Rosalie Poe, spoke of how 'when angry with Edgar [Allan] threatened to turn him adrift and that he never allowed him to lose sight of his dependence on his charity.'

Contributing to John Allan's dark moods was the perilous state of his business and the devastating economic depression that started in 1819, eventually, in 1824, forcing him to end his partnership with Charles Ellis. By this time, he had completely turned against the fifteen year-old Edgar, failing utterly to understand the boy who, with his mood swings and attempts to assert his independence, was really only behaving as many teenagers do. Allan expressed his frustration with the boy in a letter to Edgar's older brother Henry, written in November 1824:

> *... he does nothing and seems quite miserable, sulky & ill-tempered to all the Family. How we have acted to produce this is beyond my conception—why I have put up so long with his conduct is a little less wonderful. The boy possesses not a Spark of affection for us, not a particle of gratitude for all my care and kindness towards him. I have given him a much superior Education than ever I received myself. If Rosalie had to relie on any affection from him, God in his mercy preserve her.—I fear his associates have led him to adopt a line of thinking & acting very contrary to what he possessed when in England ... Had I done my duty as faithfully to my God as I have to Edgar, then Death, come when he will, had no terrors for me.*

Was this antipathy more than just a failure to understand teenage angst? Some suggest that Edgar blotted his copybook by siding with Frances Allan regarding her husband's infidelities, which were many. Or did he just resent the fact that Edgar was growing beyond his control, establishing his independence as he got older?

Everything was about to change for John Allan, however. With his business collapsing and his future looking increasingly bleak, he had a remarkable stroke of luck. In March

Sarah Elmira Royster, allegedly adapted from a drawing by Poe himself.

1825, his uncle, William Gault, one of the wealthiest men in Virginia, passed away, leaving Allan a couple of hundred thousand dollars. Of course, this should also have been very good news for Edgar who stood to inherit some of Allan's fortune, but that would depend on his relationship with his adoptive father. Unfortunately, when he went to university, it deteriorated even further.

## CHAOS REIGNS

In February 1826, having just turned seventeen, Edgar Allan Poe entered the University of Virginia at Charlottesville which was the brainchild of United States Founding Father, Thomas Jefferson (1743 – 1826). Poe was provided with inadequate funds by Allan and within a week of his arrival on campus, was requesting more money.

The university had opened only the previous March and chaos reigned. The central rotunda, containing a library, around which the institution was based, was only half-built and the library's books had still to be catalogued. The rules were strict, but generally ignored. Tobacco, wine, liquor, servants, horses, dogs and guns were banned. Gambling and dueling were prohibited but were rife, and students became wild and even violent.

Eventually, in 1840 a professor was killed while trying to intervene in a disturbance. Of the students who enrolled between 1825 and 1850 only around a third lasted longer than a year, only a quarter lasted two years and just ten per cent made it to the end of the three-year course. Things calmed down towards the end of the century.

Ominously, Poe chose room 13 of his dorm and tried to settle into this new life. He enrolled in two classes – Ancient Languages and Modern Languages. They presented little problem for him and he was reported to be able to go to classes without a great deal of preparation, spending no more than a few minutes on the work before delivering a superb recitation, a tribute to his intellect and memory.

In December 1826, Poe faced exams and the frightening prospect of being personally examined in each subject for several hours by two former Presidents of the United States – James Madison (1751 – 1836) who had followed Thomas Jefferson in the role of the university's rector, and James Monroe (1758 – 1831). Edgar achieved high scores in both his subjects.

## THAT INVISIBLE SPIRIT OF WINE

He was nicknamed 'Gaffy' after reading aloud to his fellow students a short story featuring a character by that name. One classmate remembered him at university: 'My impression was, and is, that no one could say that he *knew* him. He wore ... a sad, melancholy face always, and even a smile, for I don't remember his ever having laughed heartily, seemed forced.' This view of the young Poe echoed Elmira Royster's earlier thoughts about him.

But he was described by another student as 'a pretty wild young man,' probably because of his interest in sports and the fact that he could jump twenty feet in the long jump. Another, however, recalled him as a 'sober, quiet and orderly young man,' and recalled that his 'deportment was uniformly that of an intelligent and polished gentleman.'

His classmate, Miles George (1807 – ?), provides the most compelling description of Poe at university and perhaps gives an inkling of the beginnings of his later problems:

*[He] was fond of quoting poetic authors and reading poetic productions of his own, with which his friends were delighted and entertained; then suddenly a change would come over him; he would with a piece of charcoal evince his versatile genius by sketching upon the walls of his dormitory, whimsical, fanciful and grotesque figures, with so much artistic skill, as to leave us in*

*doubt whether Poe in future life would be Painter or Poet—He was very excitable & restless, at times wayward, melancholic and morose, but again—in his better moods frolicksome, full of fun & a most attractive and agreeable companion. To calm and quiet the excessive nervous excitability under* *which he labored, he would too often put himself under the influence of that 'Invisible Spirit of Wine.'*

Another student recalled how Poe would try to get drunk as quickly as possible:

### Edgar Allan Poe
### by Samuel Stillman Osgood

This 1845 portrait lacks the compelling intensity of the later daguerreotype images, and several of Poe's contemporaries complained that it 'scarcely resembles him at all.' Nevertheless, it was widely used as the standard image of the writer for nearly twenty years after his death.

*Poe's passion for strong drink was as marked and as peculiar as that for cards. It was not the taste of the beverage that influenced him; without a sip or smack of the mouth he would seize a full glass, without water or sugar, and send it home with a single gulp. This frequently used him up ... Poe was particularly fond of playing cards—seven-up and loo being his favorite games. He played in such an impassioned manner as to amount to almost an actual frenzy. All of his card playing and drinking he did under a sudden impulse ... He would always seize the tempting glass ... and without the least apparent pleasure swallow the contents, never pausing until the last drop had passed his lips. One glass at a time was about all that he could take.*

And, indeed, throughout his life, Edgar Allan Poe had the capacity to get drunk on just one glass. Could his low tolerance for alcohol be evidence of a physiological condition? We will never know.

## SPIRALING OUT OF CONTROL

During his time at university, his card playing brought problems. He confessed to the university librarian William Wertenbaker that his gambling debts had spiraled out of control. Wertenbaker recalls:

*He spoke with regret of the large amount of money he had wasted and of the debts he had contracted during the Session ... He estimated his indebtedness at $2,000, and though they were gaming debts he was earnest and emphatic in the declaration, that he was bound by honor to pay at the earliest opportunity, every cent of them. He certainly was not habitually intemperate, but he may occasionally have entered into a frolick.*

However, his card playing at Virginia was used to fuel one of his greatest stories, 'William Wilson'.

The problem for Edgar at university was that he was perceived as the heir to one of the richest men in the state but Allan had sent him to university without sufficient funds to justify this belief. When he found out about the gambling debts, he refused to pay them and, worse still, refused to provide Edgar with any further support.

He removed him from university and brought him back to work in the finance department of Ellis & Allan which was, at that time, being wound up. Needless to say, Poe was bitter, a bitterness that he explained in a letter written to Allan four years later:

*I will boldly say that it was wholly and entirely your own mistaken parsimony that caused all the difficulties in which I was involved while at Charlottesville. The expenses of the institution at the lowest estimate were $350 per annum ... I had, of course, the mortification of running in debt for public property—against the known rules of the institution, and was immediately regarded in the light of a beggar. You will remember that in a week after my arrival, I wrote to you for some more money, and for books.—You replied in terms of the utmost abuse—if I had been the vilest wretch on earth you could not have been more abusive than you were because I could not contrive to pay $150 with $110.*

*In this manner debts were accumulated, and money borrowed from Jews in Charlottesville at extravagant interest—for I was obliged to hire a servant, to pay for wood, for washing, and a thousand other necessities. It was then that I became dissolute, for how could it be otherwise? ... I applied to James Gault [the adopted son of William Gault]— but he, I believe, from the best of motives refused to lend me any—I then became desperate and gambled—until I finally involved myself irretrievably ... You would not let me return because bills were presented you for payment which I never wished nor desired you to pay. Had you let me return, my reformation had been sure — as my conduct the last 3 months [at university] gave every reason to believe.*

# CHAPTER 2

# GOING FROM BAD TO WORSE

It is difficult to understand why, after providing Edgar with a good education in England, Allan should inhibit his further development by depriving him of sufficient funds to get through university. Perhaps he was trying to teach him a lesson about money – he had got through without having money and so should Edgar.

He had been accused already of spoiling the boy; perhaps he was trying to reverse this and force him to stand on his own two feet. He may even have been jealous of the relationship that Edgar had with his wife or it may simply have been jealousy of the advantages Edgar was being given. The boy was obviously of a much more able intellect than Allan and perhaps he wanted him to fail so that he could remain his superior.

## EATING THE BREAD OF IDLENESS

It was when he returned to Richmond in late December 1826 that Poe learned that Elmira's father had been intercepting his letters to her. Life became unbearable for the now eighteen year-old young man, disappointed both in his prospects and in love.

On March 19, 1827, he wrote a letter to John Allan filled with recrimination, indignation, demands for money and threats of suicide. He complained that even Allan's household slaves no longer had any respect for him. It was a rehearsal for many such letters he would send in the next few years and probably served to alienate Allan from his adopted son even more.

*My determination is at length taken—to leave your house and endeavor to find some place in this wide world, where I will be*

Portrait of Edgar Allan Poe, painted by J. A. McDougall, in New York City, about 1846. The artist was a friend of Poe and other literary men of that time. Whilst the image cannot be authenticated beyond all question, there is strong circumstantial evidence to suggest that it was indeed painted from life.

*treated—not as you have treated me ... Since I have been able to think on any subject, my thoughts have aspired, and they have been taught by you to aspire, to eminence in public life—this cannot be attained without a good Education ... But in a moment of caprice— you have blasted my hope because forsooth I disagreed with you in an opinion ... I have heard you say ... that you had no affection for me. You have moreover ordered me to quit your house, and are continually upbraiding me with eating the bread of idleness, when you yourself were the only person to remedy the evil by placing me to some business.— You take delight in exposing me before those whom you think likely to advance my interest in the world. You suffer me to be subjected to the whims & caprice, not only of your white family, but the complete authority of the blacks ... [I hope] to place myself in some situation where I may not only obtain a livelihood, but lay by a sum which one day or another will support me at the University ... Send me I entreat you some money immediately.—If you fail to comply with my request—I tremble for the consequence.*

In a letter sent the following day, Allan refused to help. 'I taught you to aspire,' he wrote, 'even to eminence in public life, but I never expected that Don Quixote, Gil Blas ... & such works were calculated to promote the end ... The charge of eating the bread of idleness, was to urge you to perseverance and industry in receiving the classics, in perfecting yourself in the mathematics, mastering the French.' He seems to have missed the fact that Poe's results at university were exemplary.

Poe wrote back that he was roaming the streets of Richmond, exhausted. For four days he lived thus, refusing stubbornly to put upon any of his friends in Richmond. Finally, on March 24 he traveled to Norfolk where he embarked on a coal ship for Boston. There he worked for a month in a waterfront warehouse before finding short-term employment as a clerk and reporter for the commercial news-paper, the *Weekly Report*.

## ASSIGNED TO BATTERY H

At the end of May, unemployed again, he decided to enlist in the American army for five years. Using the name 'Edgar A. Perry', he gave his occupation as clerk and his age as twenty-two, although he was still only eighteen. The record shows that he was five feet eight, had gray eyes, brown hair and a fair complexion. He had gone even further down in social class, from university student to ordinary soldier, but at least he would have some security, a monthly wage – only five dollars, but a regular wage, nonetheless – and his basic necessities.

It was better than the uncertainty and anxiety he had experienced in the few months since he had left Richmond. Of course, his intellect and the fact that he was educated were not lost on his superiors and he was allotted more interesting work. He was assigned to Battery H of the First Artillery, stationed at Fort Independence in Boston Harbor as company clerk, and he also worked as an assistant in the commissariat department. His work involved lots of routine paperwork but he also wrote letters for the officers, prepared payrolls and was a messenger between his company and regimental headquarters.

## A KINGDOM FOR A BROKEN HEART

Despite the travails of the recent past, Poe had never stopped writing poetry, both at university and while he worked for his father. While working in Boston, he decided to have his poems printed, and in July 1827, *Tamerlane and Other Poems* by 'a Bostonian' was published.

It seems likely that it was published anonymously simply because he was still trying to avoid his creditors from university. One Virginia debt collector presumed that he had most probably run off to join a foreign revolutionary cause. 'Poe has gone off entirely,' he wrote, 'it is said, to join the Greeks. He had as well be there as anywhere else, I believe, for he appears to be worthless.'

Forty pages long and really no more than a chapbook, *Tamerlane and Other Poems* passed completely unnoticed by the literary press and establishment. He did not help, however, by apologizing in the preface for the poor quality of the work. 'The greater part of the Poems which compose this little volume, were written in the year 1821 – 2, when the author had not completed his fourteenth year.'

His poem 'Tamerlane' follows in the footsteps of Johnson's *Rasselas*, Beckford's *Vathek* and Voltaire's *Zadig* in dealing with the exotic orient. It is an allegory of his love for Elmira that has been thwarted by his poetic ambition. The fourteenth century Turkic warlord Tamerlane has given up love of a beautiful peasant girl, Ada, for the pursuit of power and on his deathbed he expresses regret at his decision to exchange the creation of 'a kingdom for a broken heart.' The remainder of the poems in the slim volume deal with the topics of youthful poetry – lost love and lost youth.

## HEAVENS! MY HAND DOES TREMBLE

After six months in Boston, Poe's unit was ordered to Fort Moultrie on Sullivan's Island in Charleston Harbor. It was a rough passage to the island and one of the ships carrying the troops was lost in the storm. On arrival, they found a barren landscape of nothing but sea and sand which would later become the setting for his story, 'The Gold Bug' – 'No trees of any magnitude are to be seen. Near the western extremity, where Fort Moultrie stands, and where some miserable frame buildings, tenanted, during summer, by fugitives from Charlestown dust and fever, may be found, indeed, the bristly palmetto.' And it would also appear in his stories 'The Oblong Box' and 'The Balloon-Hoax.'

Meanwhile, he continued writing and revising his poems, some of which appeared in magazines. To fool the debt collectors Edgar used his brother's name, Henry, on some of the poems that appeared in the *North American* magazine. Henry's name was also appended to a short prose work, 'A Fragment', that appeared in the November 3, 1827 issue of *North American*, but it reads like nothing else written by Henry and could well be the first piece of fiction published by his brother. It is a first-person account narrated by a desperate man about to shoot himself in the head:

> *Heavens! my hand does tremble—No! tis only the flickering of the lamp ... No more— the pistol—I have loaded it—the balls are quite new—quite bright—they will soon be in my heart—Incomprehensible death— what art thou?*

## MIND-NUMBINGLY DULL

Poe remained at the dreary Fort Moultrie for a soul-destroying eighteen months, during which he was promoted to artificer, a soldier with particular skills relating to artillery, for which his pay was doubled to ten dollars a month. But, he knew that he was in a dead end job; there was no prospect of further advancement. He was never going to become an officer and the work was mind-numbingly dull and repetitive. When he approached his superior to find out how he could get out of serving the remaining three and a half years of his five-year enlistment, Lieutenant Howard told him that, as he was still a minor – Poe had confessed to his real age – he would be allowed to leave if he could obtain John Allan's permission.

Poe wrote to Allan in November 1828 – his first letter to him in some time – explaining the situation and enclosing a report that detailed his exemplary behavior while in the service –'His habits are good and interly [sic] free from drinking.' Allan, true to form, was quite happy for Edgar to remain in the army, out of harm's – and his – way. He wrote that

Edgar 'had better remain as he is until the termination of his enlistment.'

Refusing to let it lie, Poe wrote again to Allan, trying everything in his power to obtain the necessary permission. He told him that the best years of his life would be thrown away by remaining in the army and as usual threatened dire consequences, that he might be 'driven to more decided measures if you refuse to assist me.' Unmoved, Allan did not even reply. He wrote for a third time after his battery relocated to Fortress Monroe at Old Point Comfort, near Hampton, Virginia, ending dramatically 'If you determine to abandon me—here take I my farewell.— Neglected—I will be doubly ambitious, & the world shall hear of the son whom you have thought unworthy of your notice.' Again, there was no response.

## FINALLY FREE

On January 1, 1829, he attained the highest rank open to him – regimental sergeant major. Nonetheless, a month later he was once again working on his exit. But there was about to be a crisis at home. On February 28, Frances Allan died aged forty-three. Poe was granted leave but arrived a day late for her funeral. At least, however, her death achieved a reconciliation of sorts between John Allan and his adopted son, demonstrated by the fact that in his next communication Edgar reverted to his childhood address to Allan – 'My Dear Pa'.

Finally, Allan gave permission for Poe to leave the army. In those days, however, the custom was that when one soldier left, he should pay for a substitute to take his place. Instead of waiting for a recruit to arrive on the scene, the impatient Poe agreed to pay an ex-soldier seventy-five dollars to enlist in his place. He gave the man twenty-five dollars and an I.O.U. for the remaining fifty, something he would later regret. On April 15, 1829, he was finally free of the army.

Interestingly, Poe blotted out these years in the army by inventing a story about joining an expedition to help the Greeks who were at the time oppressed by the Ottoman Empire. He spun a yarn about how he got into difficulties while traveling to St Petersburg and was rescued by the American Minister to Russia, Henry Middleton (1770 – 1846). It remained in his biography for years after his death.

## GOING TO WEST POINT

At the end of 1829, Poe published another book of poems, *Al Aaraaf, Tamerlane, and Minor Poems,* and this time the paper cover proudly bore his name. The contents included revised versions of poems from his 1827 volume as well as the first 264 lines of his unfinished poem, 'Al Aaraaf'. Complete with footnotes, astronomical discoveries by Tycho Brahe and Koranic notions, this complex poem came across as fairly pretentious and received mostly negative reviews, although some critics saw potential in his work. The great critic, John Neal (1793 – 1876), wrote, 'If the young author now before us should fulfill his destiny ... he will be *foremost* in the rank of *real* poets.'

For fourteen months after leaving the army, Poe lived at his cousin's house in Baltimore, spending his time reading, writing and trying to find work. He was at least able to see his brother Henry, but life was tough. He wrote to John Allan that he was 'without one cent of money—in a strange place ... my grandmother is extremely poor and paralytic. My aunt Maria if possible still worse & Henry entirely given up to drink & unable to help himself, much less me.'

Still no relief came from Allan who merely continued to berate him for past mistakes. As well as asking for money, Poe also requested Allan's help in getting him into West Point, America's prestigious military academy. He managed to solicit a letter of recommendation from Colonel Worth, commander of Fortress Monroe but Allan's letter to the Secretary of War, rather than support Poe's acceptance to the college, raked up the problems of the past:

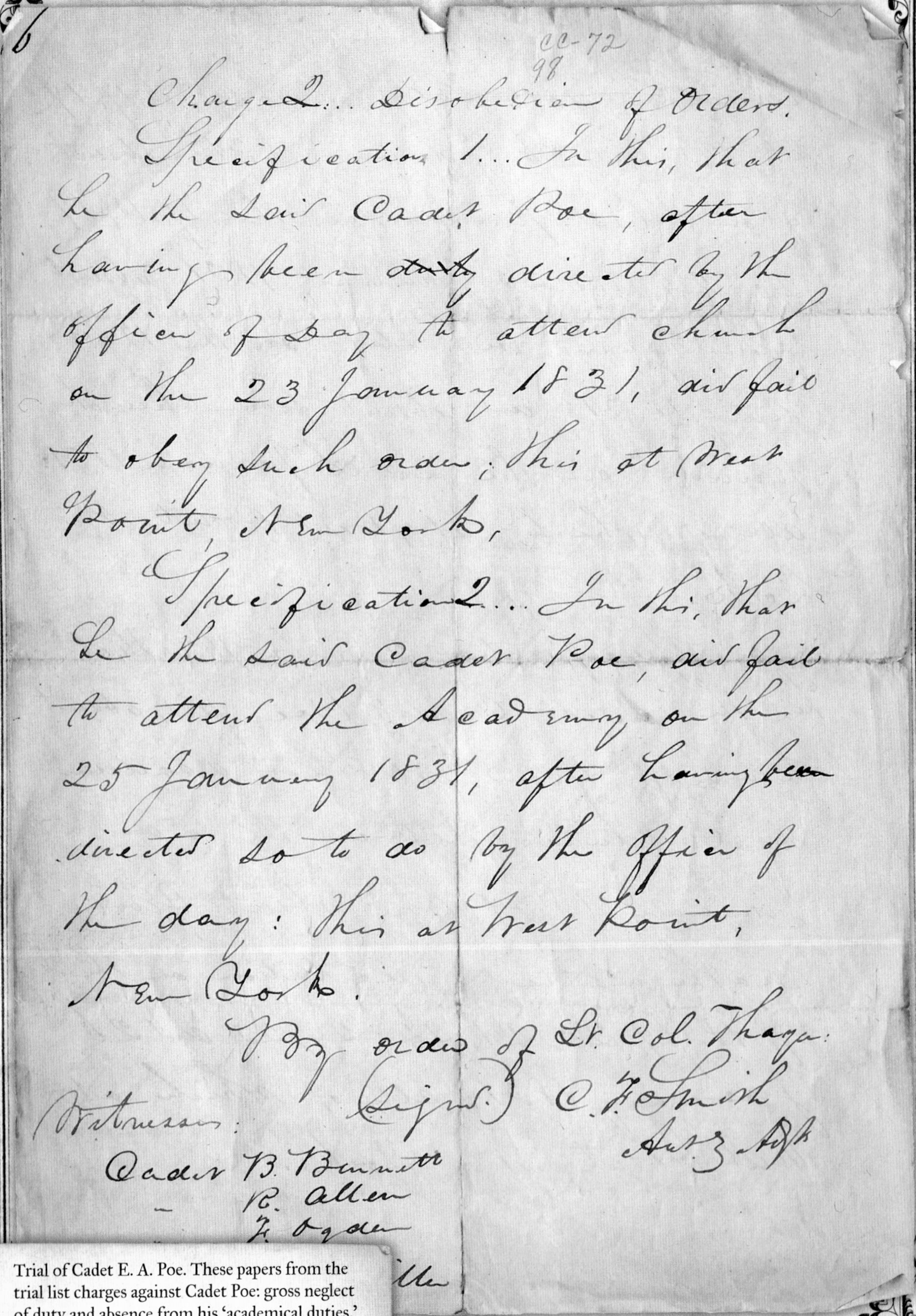

CC-72
98

Charge 2... Disobedience of Orders.

Specification 1... In this, that he the said Cadet Poe, after having been duly directed by the officer of Day to attend church on the 23 January 1831, did fail to obey such order; this at West Point, New York,

Specification 2... In this, that he the said Cadet Poe, did fail to attend the Academy on the 25 January 1831, after having been directed so to do by the officer of the day; this at West Point, New York.

By order of Lt. Col. Thayer.
(Signed) C. F. Smith
Asst Adjt

Witnesses:
Cadet B. Bennett
— R. Allen
— F. Ogden

Trial of Cadet E. A. Poe. These papers from the trial list charges against Cadet Poe: gross neglect of duty and absence from his 'academical duties.' On March 6, 1831, Poe was dismissed from West Point by sentence of court-martial.

*He left me in consequence of some Gambling at the university at Charlottesville, because (I presume) I refused to sanction a rule that the shopkeepers & others adopted there, making Debts of Honor of all indiscretions.—I have much pleasure in asserting that He stood his examination at the close of the year with great credit to himself. His History is short. He is the Grandson of Quartermaster-General Poe of Maryland ... Frankly, Sir, I declare that He is no relation to me whatever ... I do request your kindness to aid this youth in the promotion of his future prospects ... Pardon my frankness; but I address a soldier.*

Fortunately, letters from others were in a more positive vein and on June 20, 1830, having sailed through the entrance exam, he enrolled at West Point.

With its rigorous discipline, and spartan conditions, West Point must have reminded Poe somewhat of his schools in England. Cadets were forbidden 'to drink, play cards or chess, gamble, use or possess tobacco, keep any cooking utensils in their room, participate in any games, read novels, romances, or plays, go off the post, bathe in the river, or play a musical instrument.'

## A RELICT OF THE BLACKEST HEART

He was disappointed to learn that his Army experience counted for little and instead of being given a commission long before the end of his course, he now realized he would have to put in the full four years. The rigid and stultifying routine – awake at sunrise, classes until four in the afternoon, drills followed by supper and then still more classes until bedtime – drove him once more to the bottle.

Meanwhile, he delighted his fellow cadets by writing vicious, mocking verses about the instructors at West Point. His unhappiness was evident. One classmate wrote: 'He would often write some of the most vicious doggerel. I have never seen a man whose hatred was so intense.'

He ignored the rules, continuing to drink and read his beloved poetry. One classmate remembered his 'wayward and capricious temper [that] made him at times utterly oblivious to the ordinary routine of roll-call, drills, and guard duties. These habits subjected him often to arrest and punishment, and effectually prevented his learning or discharging the duties of a soldier.'

Another remembers him as 'a slovenly, heedless boy, very eccentric, inclined to dissipation, [who], of course, preferred making verses to solving equations.' Even so, he did well in his courses. At the end of his first half-year he was third out of a class of eighty-seven in French and seventeenth in mathematics.

There was another reason for him to be feeling depressed. On October 5, 1830, John Allan remarried. His second wife was Louisa Patterson of Elizabeth, New Jersey and she and Allan would have three children together. To Edgar, any chance of his inheriting from John Allan disappeared. Allan had been providing for him at West Point, but as before, the funds he sent were barely adequate to live on.

As Poe wrote bitterly to him in January 1831: 'You sent me to W. Point like a beggar. The same difficulties are threatening me as before at Charlottesville—and I must resign.' He resolved to leave the academy and began to deliberately flout the rules, not attending classes, disobeying orders and failing to arrive on the parade ground. Finally, on March 6, 1831, he was expelled. He wrote again to Allan:

*I am obliged once again to recur to you for assistance.—It will however be the last time that I ever trouble any human being.—I feel that I am on a sick bed from which I will never get up ... I, as I told you, neglected my duty when I found it impossible to attend to it, and the consequences were inevitable— dismissal. I have been dismissed—when a single line from you would have saved it.—The whole academy have interested themselves on my behalf because my only crime was being sick ... I shall never rise from my bed—besides a most violent cold on my lungs, my ear discharges blood and matter continually.*

It was a letter to which Allan responded angrily, describing it to a friend as: 'a precious relict of the Blackest Heart & deepest ingratitude, alike destitute of honor & principle. Every day of his life has only served to confirm his debased nature.—Suffice it to say my only regret is in Pity for his failings—his Talents are of an order that can never prove a comfort to their possessor.'

He was forecasting, in other words, that Poe had the capacity to be destroyed by his own genius. John Allan was now finished with his adopted son.

## DOOM IS THE THEME

Before he left West Point, Edgar Poe's superintendent allowed him to raise money from his fellow cadets to produce a new book of his poetry. Of the 232 in the class 131 donated $1.25 each but the resulting volume, 500 copies of which were printed, was not the book of witty doggerel composed at the academy that they had hoped for. Instead, *Poems* – dedicated to the 'United States Corps of Cadets' – contained revisions of some of his Romantic works as well as half a dozen new, shorter poems. The production was tawdry, '... a miserable production mechanically,' as one classmate described it, 'bound in green boards and printed on inferior paper, evidently gotten up on the cheapest scale.' A disappointed cadet scribbled in his copy 'This book is a damned cheat.'

Doom is the theme of several of the poems – 'The Sleeper', 'The Valley of Unrest' and 'The City in the Sea'. In 'The Sleeper', he engages with a theme that would remain with him, the death of a beautiful woman. Poe thought this poem one of his best, writing to an admirer: 'In the highest quality of poetry, it is better than 'The Raven'—but there is not

one man in a million who could be brought to agree with me in this opinion.'

A huge influence on Poe at this time was the English Romantic poet, Samuel Taylor Coleridge (1772 – 1834), and that influence is apparent in *Poems*. 'Of Coleridge I cannot speak but with reverence,' he wrote in the preface of the book, 'His towering intellect! His gigantic power! ... In reading his poetry I tremble, like one who stands upon a volcano, conscious, from the very darkness bursting from the crater, of the fire and the light that are weltering below.'

## RESORTING TO HORROR

He was back living in Baltimore but in August 1831 was dealt a blow when his brother Henry died, aged twenty-four. He had been ill for some time, mainly as a consequence of his alcoholism. The Baltimore house belonged to his father's widowed sister, 41 year-old Maria Clemm who had married a prominent Baltimore widower, William Clemm in 1817, and the couple had three children, one of whom died in infancy.

Unfortunately, when William Clemm died in 1826, his fortune had disappeared, leaving Maria and her daughter poor and unprotected. By the time Poe joined their household in 1831, Maria was taking in sewing and having occasional lodgers in her small house. Poe became close with her nine year-old daughter, Virginia (1822 – 1847) but they lived a hand-to-mouth existence. To make matters worse, Poe was once more in debt, having borrowed $80 to help his late brother. With debtors' prison staring him in the face he sent a letter to John Allan who wrote a cheque but took a month to send it, despite numerous desperate letters from Poe.

He was determined to launch a career as a writer and had begun composing satirical horror pieces, some of which he entered in a competition in the *Philadelphia Saturday Courier* in January 1832. He did not win but the *Courier* thought them of enough merit to publish anyway. 'Metzengerstein' was the first Edgar Allan Poe story to appear in print.

## GHOSTS OF BURIED CENTURIES

Other stories that appeared were the comic short story, 'Bon-Bon', originally submitted as 'The Bargain Lost', which consists of an exchange between Pierre Bon-Bon who thinks he is a profound philosopher and the Devil. 'A Decided Loss' sees its narrator undergo a number of horrific experiences including twice being autopsied while alive and having his nose chewed off by cats. It was an intentional send-up of the sensationalist 'predicament tales' that appeared in *Blackwood's Edinburgh Magazine*.

Despite the appearance of these stories in print, however, Poe did not receive much, if anything, by way of payment. His letters to John Allan were by this time not even being answered and he was forced to work for a spell at a local brickyard.

Soon, however, he heard of another competition. In June 1833, the Baltimore magazine, the *Saturday Visitor* trumpeted that it was 'desirous of encouraging literature' and, to this end, was staging a short story competition with a prize of $50 for the winning tale. Poe submitted a number of stories, but the one the judges liked best was 'Ms. Found in a Bottle', a story that is supposed to have been found on a manuscript inside a bottle that has been thrown into the sea by a mariner in trouble.

## THE MAN IN BLACK

The editor of the *Saturday Visitor* who delivered the prize personally to the delighted Poe, could see immediately that the money was much needed. 'He carried himself erect and well, as one who had been trained to it. He was dressed in black ... not a particle of white was visible. Coat, hat, boots and gloves had evidently seen their best days, but so far as mending and brushing go, everything had been done apparently, to make them presentable. On most men his clothes would have looked shabby and seedy, but there was something about this man that prevented one from criticizing his garments. The impression made, however, was that the award in Poe's favor was not inopportune.'

Of course, for Poe it was about more than the money. He saw it as respect for his abilities as a writer and it vindicated his belief that he could devote his life to his craft. One of the judges, the novelist, John Pendleton Kennedy (1795 – 1870), persuaded Poe to work on a collection of stories, to be called *Tales of the Folio Club*. Sadly, despite interest from the *Saturday Visitor* and a Philadelphia publisher, nothing came of it.

## SAVE ME FROM DESTRUCTION

On March 27, 1834, John Allan passed away, an extremely wealthy man. He owned eight houses and had shares in banks and gold mines but in his will, as might be expected, there was not even a mention of Edgar. He had written desperately a year previously, begging for Allan's help. 'I am perishing, absolutely perishing for want of aid. And yet I am not idle—nor addicted to any vice—nor have I committed any offense against society which would render me deserving of so hard a fate. For God's sake pity me, and save me from destruction.'

There was no response and Edgar had decided to confront Allan in person. On February 14, 1834, he had turned up on the doorstep of his adoptive father's house. According to Poe's childhood friend, Thomas Ellis, Louisa Allan opened the door to find him.

*A man of remarkable appearance stood there, & without giving his name asked if he could see Mr Allan. She replied that Mr Allan's condition was such that his physicians had prohibited any person from seeing him except his nurses. The man was Edgar A. Poe, who was, of course, perfectly familiar with the house. Thrusting her aside & without noticing her reply, he passed rapidly upstairs to Mr Allan's chamber, followed by Mrs Allan. As soon as he entered the chamber, Mr Allan raised his cane, & threatening to strike him if he came within his reach, ordered him out.*

Poe now entered a very dark period. He tried with John Pendleton Kennedy's help to find employment as a teacher but was unsuccessful. On one occasion, Kennedy invited him to dinner but Poe declined the invitation 'for reasons of the most humiliating nature [in] my personal appearance.'

# AMERICAN MAGAZINE PRODUCTION

Technology and transport developments meant that in the 1830s America's magazine industry was entering a period of rapid expansion. German engineer, Andreas Friedrich Bauer, invented the first functional steam printing press with his colleague Friedrich Koenig and the pair had sold it to *The Times* in London in 1814. It was capable of producing 1,100 impressions an hour but by 1818 their machines could turn out 2,400 pages an hour. This made periodicals not only quicker to print, but also cheaper. At the same time, the development of America's road and rail infrastructure meant that distribution to magazine subscribers across the nation was both easier and quicker. There was an explosion of new titles as a result.

Koenig's 1814 steam-powered printing press.

# JOHN PENDLETON KENNEDY

John Pendleton Kennedy was born in Baltimore in 1795, son of an Irish immigrant merchant and the daughter of a wealthy Virginia family that went bankrupt in 1809. Well educated for his time, Kennedy graduated from Baltimore College in 1812. In 1814, during the War of 1812 against the British, he enlisted in the army, joining the 5th Baltimore Light Dragoons, fighting in several battles and demonstrating courage on at least one occasion when he carried a wounded comrade to safety.

Having begun his literary career with an anonymously produced magazine called the *Red Book* in 1819, he published the novel *Swallow Barn, or a Sojourn in the Old Dominion* in 1832. *Horse-Shoe Robinson*, a historical romance of the American Revolution, followed in 1835 and proved very popular, being adapted for the stage a number of times. Kennedy was a friend of a number of leading literary figures of the time, including James Fenimore Cooper, Charles Dickens, Washington Irving and William Thackeray.

He was also prominent in Whig politics, elected to the Maryland House of Representatives in 1820 and the United States House of Representatives in 1838. In 1852, he became Secretary of the Navy and he was proposed as Vice-Presidential running mate to Abraham Lincoln but was not selected.

He was a great source of help and encouragement to Poe as he tried to establish a literary career and wrote of him:

> *I then got him employment with Mr White, in one department of the editorship of the Southern Literary newspaper at Richmond. His talents made that periodical quite brilliant while he was connected with it. But he was irregular, eccentric and querulous, and soon gave up his place for other employments of the same character in Philadelphia and New York. His destiny in those places was as sad and fickle as in Richmond. He always remembered my kindness with gratitude, as his many letters to me testify.*

John Pendleton Kennedy died aged seventy-four on August 18, 1870.

# METZENGERSTEIN

Set in Hungary, the story opens with a description of the age-old rivalry between two families – the Metzengersteins and the Berlifitzings. The narrator explains that the rivalry seems to have evolved from an 'ancient' prophecy: 'A lofty name shall have a fearful fall when, as the rider over his horse, the mortality of Metzengerstein shall triumph over the immortality of Berlifitzing'.

Frederick, Baron of Metzengerstein, has been orphaned when young and, at eighteen, inherits the family fortune. He abuses his wealth and power, exhibiting great cruelty. Four days after he comes into his inheritance, the stables of the Berlifitzings burn down and everyone immediately blames Frederick although at no point does the story indicate whether he was actually responsible. Later that day, as he stares at a tapestry of 'an unnaturally colored' horse and its fallen rider who has been killed by the 'dagger of Metzengerstein,' the horse moves.

> To his extreme horror and astonishment, the head of the gigantic steed had, in the meantime, altered its position. The neck of the animal, before arched, as if in compassion, over the prostrate body of its lord, was now extended, at full length, in the direction of the Baron. The eyes, before invisible, now wore an energetic and human expression, while they gleamed with a fiery and unusual red; and the distended lips of the apparently enraged horse left in full view his gigantic and disgusting teeth.

As he opens the door to leave the room, the Baron's shadow falls exactly on the spot where the murder has occurred in the tapestry. Outside, Frederick spies his men handling a horse just like the one in the tapestry. It has been found in his stables, they tell him, and the letters 'W.V.B.' are branded on its forehead, the initials of William Von Berlifitzing.

Frederick decides to claim the horse as his own but at that moment a page arrives to inform him that a small piece of the tapestry is missing. Later, he learns that William Berlifitzing has died in the stable fire, trying to save one of his horses. Frederick and the horse with the brand on its forehead become inseparable and he is the only one who can handle it. He rides it constantly every day, neglecting the affairs of his house and estate. As he becomes increasingly reclusive, people begin to suspect he is sick or that he has gone mad.

One night, he rides the horse into the forest and in his absence Castle Metzengerstein catches fire. The crowd that gathers to watch the fire see the horse and rider return but the animal is clearly uncontrollable.

> One instant, and the clattering of hoofs resounded sharply and shrilly above the roaring of the flames and the shrieking of the winds—another, and, clearing at a single plunge the gate-way and the moat, the steed bounded far up the tottering staircases of the palace, and, with its rider, disappeared amid the whirlwind of

*The young Metzengerstein seemed rivetted to the saddle of that colossal horse.* Illustration for 'Metzengerstein' by Arthur Rackham, 1935.

# MS. FOUND IN A BOTTLE

The unnamed narrator of this maritime tale, embarks as a passenger on a cargo ship from Batavia, nowadays known as Jakarta, in Indonesia. After a few days at sea, the ship is becalmed before being struck by a storm. The ship capsizes and everyone but the narrator and an old Swedish man are thrown overboard into the sea. The ship is driven south by the storm towards the South Pole.

Eventually it collides with a gigantic black galleon of 'nearly four thousand tons' under full sail. When the two vessels collide, the narrator is thrown onto the rigging of the other ship. He hides but finds that it is pointless because the aged crew do not see him anyway when they pass. They are like 'the ghosts of buried centuries.' He steals writing materials and begins to keep a journal, the manuscript of the title, planning to throw it into the sea in the hope that it will be found. Meanwhile, the ship continues to plot a course southward, the men on board anxious to reach their destination.

'It is evident that we are hurrying onwards to some exciting knowledge—some never-to-be-imparted secret, whose attainment is destruction.' And on the faces of the crew he notices 'an expression more of the eagerness of hope than of the apathy of despair.' Eventually, the ship reaches Antarctica and goes to its doom.

*Oh, horror upon horror! the ice opens suddenly to the right, and to the left, and we are whirling dizzily, in immense concentric circles, round and round the borders of a gigantic amphitheater, the summit of whose walls is lost in the darkness and the distance. But little time will be left me to ponder upon my destiny—the circles rapidly grow small—we are plunging madly within the grasp of the whirlpool—and amid a roaring, and bellowing, and shrieking of ocean and of tempest, the ship is quivering, oh God! and—going down.*

*A wilderness of foam ... swept the entire decks from stem to stern.* Illustration for 'Ms. Found in a Bottle' by Arthur Rackham, 1935.

# CHAPTER 3

# INTO THE STRANGE AND MYSTIC

One of the new magazines that emerged in the 1830s was the *Southern Literary Messenger*, a monthly of sixty-four double-column pages, 'Devoted to Every Department of Literature and the Fine Arts'. It was first published in August 1834 by Thomas Willis White (1788 – 1843). John Pendleton Kennedy persuaded Poe to submit a few stories to the fledgling magazine, and he obliged with 'Berenice' and 'Morella'.

Kennedy helped Poe's cause by sending Thomas Willis White a letter about him: 'He is very clever with his pen—classical and scholar-like. He wants experience and direction, but I have no doubt he can be made very useful to you. And, poor fellow! He is *very* poor ... highly imaginative and a little given to the terrific.'

## SOPHISTICATED REALISM

The economical, and beautifully atmospheric 'Berenice' appeared in the March 1835 issue of the *Messenger*. It is a forest of em-dashes used by Poe for punctuation as well as for dramatic effect and follows the Gothic tradition then popular in America and Great Britain but Poe's imagery is more sophisticated and realistic than the run-of-the-mill Gothic horror story.

Its main theme is revealed at the start when Egaeus asks himself and the reader, 'How is it that from beauty I have derived a type of unloveliness?' It was the first time that Poe used monomania – a pathological obsession in an otherwise sound mind – a device that he would return to a number of times in his stories.

## PARADISE LOST

Fearing, perhaps, for White's reaction to these grim tales, Poe wrote to him: 'The ludicrous heightened into the grotesque: the fearful colored into the horrible: the witty exaggerated into the burlesque: the singular wrought out into the strange and mystical. You may say all this is bad taste. I have my doubts about it ... But whether the articles of which I speak are, or are not in bad taste is little to the purpose. To be appreciated you must be *read*, and these things are invariably sought after with avidity.'

Poe knew and understood the market and believed that the magazine's circulation would bear out what he thought, that what the public said it appreciated and what it actually bought were, in fact, two entirely different things. He went on in his letter to point out that the sensational tales in *Blackwood's* were the work of some well-known literary figures.

White was impressed by the young writer, especially when he refused to promote the *Messenger* in other magazines with which he was associated. He offered him a job although the exact title on offer was vague. The duties were various, such as acting as secretary to White, dealing with correspondence, making sure contributors delivered their promised articles and writing reviews and other material to pad out the magazine.

Indeed, Poe would churn out thousands of such column inches in his time at the *Messenger*. But, he was paid $15 a week and, although a modest wage, to the down-at-heels Edgar Poe, this was paradise, especially as his seventy-nine year-old grandmother would die in July 1835, removing her annual pension from the already lean coffers of his household.

# BERENICE

A studious young man named Egaeus is raised in a large, gloomy mansion with his beautiful doomed cousin Berenice. He is an obsessive individual while she is a victim of a degenerative illness that occasionally puts her into a cataleptic state, a 'trance very nearly resembling positive dissolution.' Seeing her one afternoon as he sits reading in the library, he focuses on her teeth and for days he sits in the library thinking about them, imagining himself holding them and examining them from every angle. At length, he hears a commotion outside and learns that Berenice has died.

Later, back in the library again, he awakes as if from a dream knowing he has done something but ignorant of what it is. A 'shrill and piercing shriek of a female voice' is ringing in his ears. In front of him is a 'little box of ebony.' At that moment there is a knock at the door and a servant informs him that Berenice's grave has been violated during the night. The servant points to the narrator's garments that are 'muddy and clotted with gore.' There is also a spade leaning against the wall. The tale ends with a grisly discovery:

> With a shriek I bounded to the table, and grasped the ebony box that lay upon it. But I could not force it open, and in my tremor it slipped from out my hands, and fell heavily, and burst into pieces, and from it, with a rattling sound, there rolled out some instruments of dental surgery, intermingled with many white and glistening substances that were scattered to and fro about the floor.

Illustration for 'Berenice' by Harry Clarke, 1919.

This brought a temporary halt to his own creative writing – 'Having no time upon my hands, apart from my editorial duties, I can write nothing worth reading,' he wrote to a reader of the magazine. He was right because his most recent work was a faintly outlandish tale entitled 'The Unparalleled Adventure of One Hans Pfaall'. This tells how an indebted Dutch bellows-mender flees his creditors by flying a hot-air balloon all the way to the moon. Poe followed up on the hoax in further installments but was upstaged by the 'Great Moon Hoax' that was enthralling readers of the *New York Sun*.

## BLINDED WITH TEARS

Poe had to move to Richmond to work on the magazine, leaving behind Maria and Virginia and his grandmother (who had only a few months to live). He was earning a wage at last but his spirits were no better, as he wrote to Kennedy: 'I am suffering under a depression ... I am still miserable in spite of the great improvement in my circumstances.'

The depression brought an illiberal consumption of alcohol. His condition did not go unnoticed by White who, in a letter to a friend, described Poe as '... unfortunately rather dissipated ... I should not be at all astonished to hear that he has been guilty of suicide.'

His emotional crisis continued. He was lonely in Richmond, separated from the Clemms and to make matters worse, he had learned that his well-off cousin, Neilson Poe (1809 – 1884), had invited Virginia to live with his family. Poe was now seriously of a mind to marry Virginia and was concerned that Neilson, who opposed this liaison, was trying to come between him and the girl, offering to become her guardian and to introduce her into polite society.

On August 29, Edgar opened up his heart in a moving letter to Maria, declaring that he loved Virginia and was worried that he was going to lose her because he could not provide the financial security and entrée into society that his cousin could. He begged that Virginia decline Neilson's invitation and added the customary threats of dire consequences if she did not.

*I am blinded with tears while writing this letter.—I have no wish to live another hour. Amid sorrow, and the deepest anxiety your letter reached [me]—and you know how little I am able to bear up under the pressure of grief. My bitterest enemy would pity me could he now read my heart ... I love, you know I love Virginia passionately, devotedly. I cannot express in words the fervent devotion I feel towards my dear little cousin—my own darling ... [I would find happiness] in making you both comfortable & in calling her my wife.—But the dream is over. O God have mercy on me. What have I to live for? Amongst strangers with not one soul to love me.*

*The tone of your letter wounds me to the soul.—O Aunty, Aunty you loved me once—how can you be so cruel now? ... Are you sure she would be more happy [with Neilson]? Do you think any one could love her more dearly than I? ... Virginia, My love, my own sweetest Sissy, my darling little wifey, think well before you break the heart of your cousin. Eddy.*

## DEALING WITH THE DEMONS

At the end of September, Poe was in turmoil and drinking heavily, leading White to fire him from the *Messenger*. He traveled to Baltimore to plead in person with Maria and Virginia. White, meanwhile, wrote to him, warning him of the consequences of his behavior and generously offering to let him live at his house while he dealt with his demons. He even promised to reinstate him in his role if he would agree to stop drinking. 'If you should come to Richmond again,' he wrote, 'and again should be an assistant in my office, it must be especially understood by us that all engagements on my part would be dissolved, the moment you get drunk. No man is safe

# MORELLA

The narrator of the story marries a woman named Morella whose erudition is 'profound.' This scholarly woman studies the German philosophers Fichte and Schelling who dealt with the 'doctrines of Identity' and 'the notion of that identity *which at death is or is not lost forever.*' Morella spends all her time in bed reading and teaching her husband but she begins to deteriorate physically. He longs for her to die but she clings to life for months.

One day, she calls her husband to her bedside and informs him that it is 'a day of all days, either to live or die … I am dying—yet shall I live.' She dies during the birth of their child, saying, 'I am dying. But within me is a pledge of that affection … which thou didst feel for me, Morella. And when my spirit departs shall the child live.'

As his daughter grows older, the narrator remarks upon her uncanny resemblance to her mother. Still, however, he does not give the child a name. When he takes her to be baptized, her mother's soul is brought back into her and when the priest asks her name, the narrator answers, 'Morella'. The daughter shouts out, 'I am here!' and dies. When the narrator carries her body to the family vault, he discovers that there is no trace of the remains of his wife.

*… with my own hands I bore her to the tomb; and I laughed with a long and bitter laugh as I found no traces of the first in the channel where I laid the second.*

*The earth grew dark, and its figures passed by me, like flitting shadows, and among them all I beheld only—Morella.*
Illustration by Harry Clarke, 1919.

The Great Moon Hoax lithograph
of the 'ruby amphitheater' for *The
New York Sun*, August 28, 1835.

# THE GREAT MOON HOAX

On August 25, 1835, a story appeared in the *New York Sun* newspaper trumpeting the discovery of life on the moon by Sir John Herschel, one of the pre-eminent astronomers of the time, using a huge telescope 'of an entirely new principle.' It was the first of six such pieces, allegedly reprinted from the Scottish paper, the *Edinburgh Courant*, describing fantastic animals such as bison, goats, unicorns, bipedal beavers that had no tails and bat-like winged humanoids – '*Vespertilio-homo*' – who were reported to build temples on the moon. The author was reported to be an associate of Herschel, the fictional Dr. Andrew Grant.

The hoax was not discovered until several weeks afterwards, but the newspaper never retracted its claims. Meanwhile, the circulation of the *Sun* increased dramatically during the hoax and did not decline afterwards, helping to make it a hugely successful newspaper. Herschel, initially amused by the escapade, later became irritated by questions from people who believed it to be true.

Poe's 'Hans Pfaall' was published several months before the 'Great Moon Hoax', but it was all too obvious from its satirical and comic tone that it was a hoax. However, he believed his original idea was stolen and used to greater effect by the supposed writer of the 'Great Moon Hoax', Richard Adams Locke. 'I am convinced that the idea was stolen from myself', he claimed, an early manifestation of his obsession with plagiarism that would continue throughout his career.

who drinks before breakfast! No man can do so, and attend to business properly.'

Soon, Poe was back in Richmond and reinstated at the *Messenger*. Having persuaded the Clemms to reject Neilson Poe's offer, his crisis was over and he brought Maria and Virginia to Richmond where they lodged in a boarding house.

More good news arrived in December when White promoted him to editor. Poe wrote to Kennedy in January 1836. 'My health is better than for years past, my mind is fully occupied, my pecuniary difficulties have vanished, I have a fair prospect of future success—in a word, all is right.'

## MARITALLY COUPLED COUSINS

Virginia was just thirteen when Poe married her in May 1836. To modern eyes this is shocking and, of course, it would be entirely illegal nowadays. However, such marriages were legal at that time. All that was required for marriage under the age of twenty-one in the state of Virginia was the approval of the girl's parents and two witnesses.

It was legal in every state of the Union to marry a cousin prior to the Civil War but by the 1880s, cousin marriage was being prohibited in a number of states. Maria gave her approval but Poe's wedding certificate notes only one witness. It has been suggested that this might explain the fact that Virginia's age on the certificate is listed as twenty-one. Perhaps one of the witnesses failed to turn up and rather than cancel the wedding, it was decided just to amend her age.

Poe did hint that it was many years before the marriage was consummated and Virginia never fell pregnant. 'Poe was very proud and very fond of her,' one friend recalled, 'and used to delight in the round, childlike face and plump little figure, which he contrasted with himself, so thin and half-melancholy-looking, and she in turn idolized him.'

Another comment suggested that 'although he loved her with an undivided heart he could

not think of her [in the beginning] as his wife, as any other than his sister, and indeed he did not for two years assume the position of husband, still occupying his own chamber by himself.' He paid for tutors to teach her harp and piano and tried himself to educate her.

## SPEAKING HIS MIND

Meanwhile, he was churning out huge amounts of copy for the *Messenger*. He wrote ninety-four articles between December 1835 and August 1836 on a bewildering range of subjects including daguerreotypes, mesmerism, galvanism, exploration, hidden treasure, murder, premature burial and apocalyptic prophecies.

His book reviews were often very harsh, unusual in one who was himself ultra-sensitive to criticism. He modeled his cutting style on the severe reviewers to be found in British quarterlies – John Wilson (1785 – 1854) in *Blackwood's*, William Gifford (1756 – 1826) in the *London Quarterly*, Francis Jeffrey (1773 – 1850) in the *Edinburgh Review* and John Croker (1780 – 1857) in the *Quarterly Review* who was accused of killing Keats with his scathing review of 'Endymion'.

Poe thought of himself as not belonging to any literary circle and he did indeed have few friends in the world of books – therefore, to his mind, there was nothing to prevent him from expressing his opinions freely. At the same time, he was keen to break through parochialism and improve the standard of writing.

He wrote: 'As for American Letters, plain-speaking about them is, simply, the one thing needed. They are in a condition of absolute quagmire.' Undoubtedly, though, there was an element of bitterness and even jealousy in his more cutting review work. He saw writers of mediocre talent succeed while he struggled for money, recognition and respect. He was keen to create a reputation for himself and, of course, to increase the circulation of the *Messenger*.

## THE PROBLEM WITH POE

Other members of the press were less impressed, however. The *Richmond Courier* warned him: 'The criticisms are pithy and often highly judicious, but the editor must remember that it is almost as injurious to obtain a character for regular cutting and slashing as for indiscriminate laudation.'

The New York monthly magazine *Knickerbocker* was also unhappy with his approach: 'His criticisms, so called, are generally a tissue of coarse personal abuse or personal adulation.' And his reviews often worked against his best interests as he made many enemies in the small world of writing and publishing. For instance, he slammed a novel, *Norman Leslie*, by Theodore Fay (1807 – 1898), editor of the weekly newspaper, *New York Mirror*, calling it '... the most inestimable piece of balderdash with which the common sense of the good people of America was ever so openly or so villainously insulted.' Fay was an important and influential man and by insulting him, Poe upset a good many more of Fay's equally influential friends and associates.

## STRUCK BY THE MUSE

Poe's friend, Lambert Wilmer (1805 – 1863), was astonished at the amount of work Poe got through and the fact that he seemed to work every hour of the day. In fact, he tended to write in the morning and sometimes continue through to late in the day. Then, to relax, he would perhaps read and recite poetry, go for a long walk in the countryside or work in his garden.

He wrote on half-sheets of notepaper that he pasted together at the ends to make them into one continuous piece. He would then roll this up tightly and as he read it, he let the finished sections unravel onto the floor. He was often struck by the muse when out walking and this would lead to a frenetic spurt of writing.

# THE BEAUCHAMP-SHARP TRAGEDY

In 1821, Kentucky Attorney General Solomon P. Sharp allegedly fathered an illegitimate child with Anna Cooke, the daughter of a planter. The baby was stillborn but Sharp denied anyway that he was the father. Jereboam O. Beauchamp later fell in love with Cooke who told him that she would only marry him if he killed Sharp to avenge her honor. He agreed and in June 1824 the two were married.

In the early morning of November 7, 1825, Beauchamp rode to Sharp's house in Frankfort, Kentucky and knocked on the door. When Sharp opened the door, he fell to his knees, realizing the purpose of Beauchamp's visit. Beauchamp plunged a dagger into his heart, killing the Attorney General instantly, and fled the scene before the alarm was raised. A reward was offered for the arrest of the suspects and on November 9, Beauchamp was arrested at his home as he and Anna prepared to flee to Missouri.

The trial began on May 8, 1826 with Beauchamp pleading not guilty but despite the absence of physical evidence and a murder weapon, the jury took only an hour to find Jereboam Beauchamp guilty of murder. He was sentenced to be hanged. Anna and Beauchamp tried everything to have the verdict overturned and then the couple failed to kill themselves with doses of laudanum. They also tried to stab themselves to death but only Anna succeeded. Beauchamp was seriously wounded but the authorities decided to hang him before he bled to death. Supported on the gallows by two men, he was hanged on July 7.

Many regarded the murder as an honor killing while there was speculation that Sharp's political opponents had instigated the crime. Apart from Edgar Allan Poe's *Politian*, there have been a number of literary works dealing with the incident, including Robert Penn Warren's *World Enough and Time*.

EXECUTION OF BEAUCHAMP FOR THE MURDER OF COL. SHARP.

The execution of Jereboam O. Beauchamp, 1826.

# THE NARRATIVE OF ARTHUR GORDON PYM OF NANTUCKET

The first chapter tells how the young Arthur Gordon Pym, born on the island of Nantucket, gets drunk with his friend, Augustus Barnard, and takes to the seas with him on his sailing boat, the *Ariel*. The two are caught in a violent storm and are rescued by a whaling ship, the *Penguin*. They decide not to inform their parents of their adventure.

In the next section of the book, Pym stows away with his dog Tiger aboard the whaling vessel, the *Grampus*, captained by Augustus's father, and on which Augustus is sailing. Augustus provides Pym and the dog with food and water as they hide until the ship is too far from shore to turn round. Pym becomes delirious in his cramped conditions and loses contact with Augustus who has suddenly stopped bringing him supplies. He discovers a letter written in blood and attached to Tiger that warns him to remain hidden, that his life depends on it.

When Augustus finally appears, he explains that there has been a mutiny on board. The mutineers have murdered some of the crew while other crew-members, including Augustus's father, have been cast adrift in a small boat. Augustus is allowed to remain on board due to his friendship with a mutineer named Dirk Peters, who now regrets his part in the mutiny.

Peters, Pym and Augustus hatch a plot to regain control of the vessel. It involves Pym, dressed in the clothes of a murdered sailor, appearing as a ghost. In the ensuing confusion, they will seize control. The plan works and all the mutineers are killed or thrown overboard, apart from Richard Parker whom they need to sail the *Grampus*.

They encounter a dreadful storm and only survive by lashing themselves to the hull. The storm abated, they have no provisions and look likely to die. They see a Dutch ship approach, but there is a terrible stench and they realize the men they see on deck are actually corpses. They catch sight of one figure:

*On his back, from which a portion of the shirt had been torn, leaving it bare, there sat a huge sea-gull, busily gorging itself with the horrible flesh, its bill and talons deep buried, and its white plumage spattered all over with blood. As the brig moved farther round so as to bring us close in view, the bird, with much apparent difficulty, drew out its crimsoned head, and, after eyeing us for a moment as if stupefied, arose lazily from the body upon which it had been feasting, and, flying directly above our deck, hovered there a while with a portion of clotted and liver-like substance in its beak. The horrid morsel dropped at length with a sullen splash immediately at the feet of Parker.*

Starving, they are forced to draw lots to find out which of them is to be killed for food. Parker loses and gives the other two a chance of survival, but Augustus dies from wounds he has received. Pym and Peters are eventually rescued by the *Jane Guy*, a ship out of Liverpool.

The next section takes the *Jane Guy* around the Cape of Good Hope and southward to the unexplored regions of Antarctica. Close to the South Pole, they find a mysterious island called Tsalal, inhabited by a tribe of friendly natives led by Too-Wit. They begin trading but on the night before the *Jane Guy* is due to sail away, the natives attack and everyone apart from Peters and Pym is slaughtered. The ship is burned.

The final section of the book follows Peters and Pym as they try to escape. They steal a small boat from the natives, taking one of them prisoner, and drift further south. As the sea turns a milky color and becomes warmer, they are caught in a rain of ashes and then encounter a huge bank of fog that splits open to allow them entry. A huge, white, shrouded figure appears before them.

*And now we rushed into the embraces of the cataract, where a chasm threw itself open to receive us. But there arose in our pathway a shrouded human figure, very far larger in its proportions than any dweller among men. And the hue of the skin of the figure was of the perfect whiteness of the snow.*

This is followed by an appendix in which it is noted that the last chapters of Pym's narrative have been lost.

*There arose in our pathway a shrouded human figure.* Illustration for *The Narrative of Arthur Gordon Pym of Nantucket* by Yan' Dargent, 1862.

In December 1835 and January 1836, the *Messenger* published installments of Poe's unfinished play, *Politian*, a fictionalized version of a real-life event known as the 'Kentucky Tragedy' or the 'Beauchamp-Sharp Tragedy', the 1825 murder of the Attorney General of Kentucky, Solomon P. Sharp (1787 – 1825) by the lawyer, Jereboam O. Beauchamp (1802 – 1826).

## LOVING THE EXTRAVAGANT

*Politian* was far from a success with the magazine's readers, leading the *Messenger* to bring the installments to a hurried close. The *Lynchburg Virginian's* review was fairly typical: 'Scenes from *Politian*, like the prose productions from the same pen (Mr Poe) evince great powers, wasted on trifles. Why, (to adopt the catechetical style of his own criticism,) why does Mr Poe throw away his strength on shafts and columns, instead of building a temple to his fame? Can he not execute as well as design?'

Meanwhile, Kennedy had remained in contact with Poe and continued to encourage his development with useful advice after *Politian* appeared in the magazine: 'You are strong enough now to be criticized,' he wrote to the younger writer, 'Your fault is your love of the extravagant. Pray beware of it. You find a hundred intense writers for one natural one.'

In May 1836, *Tales of the Folio Club* was once again rejected, this time by the New York publishers Harper & Brothers. They were concerned about the number of the stories in the collection that had already been published in magazines as well as what they described as a lack of unity between them. '… readers in this country have a decided and strong preference for works (especially fiction) in which a single and connected story occupies the whole volume.'

He had made the *Southern Literary Messenger* a success, raising its circulation from 500 copies to 3,500 and had earned a profit of $10,000 for White, although Poe, of course, had received little of that. He was spiraling once again into depression and that meant only one thing – he was drinking again. White, who was himself having personal problems had had enough. He fired Poe for the final time in December 1836.

## INTRODUCING ARTHUR GORDON PYM

Poe moved to Manhattan with Maria and Virginia, eventually ending up in Carmine Street, close to Washington Square. Responding to the advice from Harper & Brothers, he started writing a novel, *The Narrative of Arthur Gordon Pym of Nantucket*. But other work was hard to find.

The financial crisis known as the Panic of 1837 led to an economic depression and no one was hiring. They survived on his infrequent magazine contributions and on money that they brought in by taking lodgers. They lived on bread and molasses for long periods but at least Poe was staying sober. One lodger later recalled:

> For eight months, or more, 'one house contained us, as one table fed.' During that time I saw much of [Poe], and had an opportunity of conversing with him often, and I must say I never saw him the least affected with liquor, nor even descend to any known vice, while he was one of the most courteous, gentlemanly and intelligent companions … He had a wife of matchless beauty and loveliness, her eye could match that of any houri, and her face defy the genius of a Canova to imitate; a temper and disposition of surprising sweetness; besides, she seemed as much devoted to him and his every interest as a young mother is to her first born … Poe had a remarkably pleasing and prepossessing countenance, what the ladies would call decidedly handsome.

Harper & Brothers initially planned to publish *Arthur Gordon Pym*, Poe's only novel, in May 1837, but the financial crash forced them to delay publication until July 1838. The book was eventually published in two volumes and bore the extraordinarily unwieldy sub-title:

*Comprising the Details of Mutiny and Atrocious Butchery on Board the American Brig Grampus, on Her Way to the South Seas, in the Month of June, 1827. With an Account of the Recapture of the Vessel by the Survivors; Their Shipwreck and Subsequent Horrible Sufferings from Famine; Their Deliverance by Means of the British Schooner Jane Guy; the Brief Cruise of this Latter Vessel in the Atlantic Ocean; Her Capture, and the Massacre of Her Crew Among a Group of Islands in the Eighty-Fourth Parallel of Southern Latitude; Together with the Incredible Adventures and Discoveries Still Farther South to Which That Distressing Calamity Gave Rise.*

The idea for the novel came from a newspaper story. In February 1836, the *Norfolk Beacon* published an account of the sinking of a ship named *Ariel* in a storm at sea.

Described by one critic as 'one of the most elusive major texts of American literature,' this ingenious story is astonishing and ridiculous in equal measure. A spiritual allegory that is also something of a travelogue, an out-and-out adventure saga, a hoax and a coming-of-age story, it is clumsy as well as gripping. There are dreadful continuity errors but at the same time the plot is carefully wrought. Poe himself was dissatisfied with the work, calling it 'a very silly book.'

## A DESIRE FOR ANNIHILATION

Reviewers agreed. William Burton (1804–60) – a future employer of Poe – described it in his publication, *Burton's Gentleman's Magazine*, as 'a rapid succession of improbabilities.' He continued: 'A more impudent attempt at humbugging the public has never been exercised ... Arthur Gordon Pym puts forth a series of travels outraging possibility, and coolly requires his insulted readers to believe his account ... We regret to find Mr Poe's name in connexion with such a mass of ignorance and effrontery.'

Another critic shared the disappointment of many readers at the abrupt ending to the novel. 'There are too many atrocities, too many strange horrors, and finally, there is no conclusion to it; it breaks off suddenly in a mysterious way, which is not only destitute of all *vraisemblance*, but is purely perplexing and vexatious. We cannot, therefore, but consider the author unfortunate in his plan.'

Many readers did, indeed, feel cheated by the abrupt ending of *Arthur Gordon Pym*. Some have suggested that Pym dies at the end and his tale is being told posthumously. Or does he die as he re-tells the story just at the moment he encounters the mysterious white-skinned figure? It deals with one of Poe's recurring themes, that of man's unconscious desire for annihilation or destruction.

Unfortunately, even with the publication of the book in Britain, it did not make Poe any money and failed to sell enough copies to warrant a second printing in the United States. By this time, Poe, Virginia and Maria were back in Philadelphia and he was trying to find work as a civil service clerk.

Unsuccessful in that endeavor, he trained in lithography but still there was no let-up in the family's unrelenting poverty, one visitor describing them as 'literally suffering for want of food.' He was doing some poorly paid journalism but we do not really know what he was writing. However, he was about to enter a golden era of writing as his maturity approached.

# THE BEAUTIFUL ILLUSTRATIONS THAT MADE POE'S STORIES TERRIFYING

## TALES OF MYSTERY AND IMAGINATION
### ILLUSTRATED BY HARRY CLARKE

When Edgar Allan Poe's collection of short stories, *Tales of Mystery and Imagination*, was reprinted in 1919, a copy of the 'deluxe' edition, published by George G. Harrap & Co, cost 5 guineas. The book was a very high quality production with hand-made paper and gold lettering on a leather binding, and twenty-four full-page illustrations by Irish artist, Harry Clarke (1889 – 1931).

Clarke's beautiful, spooky illustrations, such as this one for 'Ms. Found in a Bottle', brought Edgar Allan Poe's characters to life in terrifying detail. The Poe/Clarke combination proved so popular, that Harrap released a revised, expanded edition in 1923, with eight extra color illustrations by Clarke.

# PART 2

# THE GROTESQUE AND ARABESQUE

... as I stepped up to it in extremity of terror,
mine own image, but with features
all pale and dabbled in blood,
advanced to meet me ...

Edgar Allan Poe *from* 'William Wilson'

# CHAPTER 4

# A SUDDEN TURN TO EVIL

In 1838, Poe wrote what he felt was his best story to-date – 'Ligeia'. It appeared in the September edition of *The American Museum* magazine edited by two friends of Poe, Dr. Nathan C. Brooks (1809 – 98) and Dr. Joseph E. Snodgrass (1813 – 80) who paid him $10 for the story. Later, George Bernard Shaw (1856 – 1950) would describe it as 'not merely one of the wonders of literature: it is unparalleled and unapproached.'

There is brilliant writing in 'Ligeia' especially in the vivid descriptions of the rooms that are the settings for the story. Once again, he returns to his eternal theme of the states of life and death and the power to overcome death. Mainly, however, there is a unity of purpose to the story, possibly the first time that Poe has achieved this without using satire or a sly nod to the reader.

## THE CONCHOLOGIST'S FIRST BOOK

Sadly, however, he still had to try to make a living and one of his efforts around this time was perhaps not his proudest moment. His friend, Thomas Wyatt, had written *The Conchologist's First Book; or, A System of Testaceous Malacology, Arranged expressly for the use of schools* for Harper & Brothers who were reluctant to publish a cheap $1.50 edition. Wyatt was determined to re-publish it himself, but in order not to irritate his publisher, wanted to put another name on the cover.

As Wyatt later put it, he wanted to publish it 'with the name of some irresponsible person whom it would be idle to sue for damages, and Poe was selected for the scape-goat.' He offered Poe fifty dollars to allow him to put his name on the cover and Poe also did some editing work on the book. The fifty dollars was, of course, very handy at the time, but there was a price to pay. *Arthur Gordon Pym* had been published by Harper & Brothers and they were not going to be happy to see his name being used in such a way.

Five years later, when he sought a publisher for his stories, Harpers were still angry with him. He was told by a friend, 'They have *complaints* against you, grounded on certain movements of yours, when they acted as your publishers some years ago; and appear very little inclined at present to enter upon the matter which you have so much at heart.' Ironically, *The Conchologist's First Book* was the only one of Poe's books to go into a second edition during his lifetime.

## BURTON'S GENTLEMAN'S MAGAZINE

Suddenly, there was some good news for Poe who had earned a mere $143 in the last two and a half years. In May 1839, he contacted William Burton, owner of *Burton's Gentleman's Magazine* to ask if there might be an editorial position at his office.

*Burton's Gentleman's Magazine* was large and beautifully printed but Burton, who was also an actor, was on tour a lot and needed someone to stand in for him. Poe's success with the *Southern Literary Messenger* made him the ideal candidate for the job. Unfortunately, he was offered a lower salary than he had been anticipating. Burton wrote to Poe pleading poverty:

# WILLIAM EVANS BURTON

William Burton – often known by the nickname 'Billy' – was born in London in 1804, the son of a printer. Left in charge of the family printing business following the death of his father, he decided to launch a monthly magazine. It failed, but through it, Burton met many actors and moving in those circles led to him taking to the stage himself. By 1825, he was a member of a provincial company that toured England. Burton's forte was low comedy and he was very good, although he longed to be a tragic actor.

He first appeared in London at the Pavilion Theater in 1831 and in 1832 was at the Haymarket Theater playing Marall to the great Shakespearian actor Edmund Kean's Sir Giles Overreach in Massinger's popular drama *A New Way to Pay Old Debts*. Burton wrote a play, *Ellen Wareham*, that at one time played in five different London theaters at the same time.

He married, but when the marriage failed in 1834, he emigrated to the United States, appearing in Philadelphia in *The Poor Gentleman*. The critic Lewis Gaylord Clark described him as 'a vagrant from England, who has left a wife and offspring behind him there, and plays the bigamist … with another wife, and his whore besides; one who cannot write a paragraph in English to save his life.' He established a highly successful career as an actor-manager in New York, Philadelphia and Baltimore, the theater he leased in New York being re-named Burton's Theater.

Between 1839 and 1840, he employed Edgar Allan Poe as editor of a publication he established, *Burton's Gentleman's Magazine*. In 1840, he sold the magazine and used the money to renovate his theater. He died on February 10, 1860 in New York City, aged fifty-six.

# LIGEIA

The narrator describes the impossible beauty and extensive learning of the woman with whom he has fallen in love and then married – Ligeia, the 'airy and spirit-lifting vision more wildly divine than the phantasies which hovered vision about the slumbering souls of the daughters of Delos'. She is German and he thinks he met her 'in some large, old decaying city near the Rhine', but cannot remember her surname or any of her family history, only her beauty.

Ligeia becomes ill and eventually dies but just before her death, she utters a line from the English philosopher Joseph Glanvill (1636 – 80), 'Man doth not yield himself to the angels, nor unto death utterly, save only through the weakness of his feeble will.'

The narrator is grief-stricken and after a few months buys an abbey 'in one of the wildest and least frequented portions of fair England'. Eventually, he marries Lady Rowena Trevanion, of Tremaine, although the marriage is loveless. Two months later, Rowena falls ill and while under the influence of opium the narrator feels a presence in the bedroom as he cares for her. He sees three or four large drops of a ruby fluid fall into Lady Rowena's goblet. Her condition gets worse and a few days later she dies.

Keeping vigil by Lady Rowena's body, the narrator hears a sound and notices color return to her cheeks but it fades and she dies again. This recurs throughout the night until, as dawn breaks, the body once more revives, stands up and, covered in its shroud, walks into the middle of the room. The tale ends with a horrific discovery:

*Shrinking from my touch, she let fall from her head, unloosened, the ghastly cerements which had confined it, and there streamed forth, into the rushing atmosphere of the chamber, huge masses of long and disheveled hair; it was blacker than the raven wings of the midnight! And now slowly opened the eyes of the figure which stood before me. 'Here then, at least,' I shrieked aloud, 'can I never—can I never be mistaken—these are the full, and the black, and the wild eyes—of my lost love—of the lady—of the LADY LIGEIA.*

*And now slowly opened the eyes of the figure which stood before me.* Illustration for 'Ligeia' by Harry Clarke, 1919.

*I wish to form some such engagement as that which you have proposed, and know of no one more likely to suit my views than yourself. The expenses of the Magazine are already woefully heavy; more so than my circulation warrants ... Competition is high—new claimants are daily rising ... My contributors cost me something handsome, and the losses upon credit, exchange, etc., are becoming frequent and serious. I mention this list of difficulties as some slight reason why I do not close with your offer, which is indubitably liberal, without any delay.*

*Shall we say ten dollars per week for the remaining portion of this year? Should we remain together, which I see no reason to negative, your proposition shall be in force for 1840. A month's notice to be given on either side previous to a separation.*

*Two hours per day, except occasionally, will, I believe, be sufficient for all required.*

Two hours a day for such a job was, of course, arrant nonsense. Poe's job involved proofreading, writing filler copy, revising and preparing manuscripts for the press and being responsible for the printing of the magazine. Burton had a high opinion of himself and treated Poe as little more than an employee, permitting him to do little editing of the magazine.

Moreover, he did not like Poe's biting criticism of often famous and revered authors such as James Fenimore Cooper (1789 – 1851), author of *The Last of the Mohicans*. To Burton's dismay, Poe described his recent publications as 'a flashy succession of ill-conceived and miserably executed literary productions, each more silly than its predecessor.'

## HIS IS A HIGH DESTINY

Poe found the magazine altogether too light for his more literary taste and the treatment meted out to him by Burton and his paltry salary led to an argument before the end of his first month of employment. Burton wrote to him: 'I cannot permit the magazine to be made a vehicle for that sort of severity which you think "so successful with the mob" ... You must, my dear sir, get rid of your avowed ill-feelings towards your brother authors.'

Poe, however, had gained respect elsewhere. The *St. Louis Bulletin* wrote glowingly about his time at the helm of the *Messenger*.

*The first impetus to the favor of literary men ... was given by the glowing pen of Edgar A. Poe, now assistant editor of Burton's Gentleman's Magazine; and although he has left it, [it] has well maintained its claims to respectability. There are few writers in this country ... who can compete successfully, in many respects, with Poe. With an acuteness of observation, a vigorous and effective style, and an independence that defies control, he unites a fervid fancy and a most beautiful enthusiasm. His is a high destiny.*

## BURYING THE INSUFFERABLE SECRET

Poe was now reaching the peak of his powers and in the same month – September 1839 – two of his greatest stories were published. 'William Wilson' appeared in a local publisher's gift annual and 'The Fall of the House of Usher' was published in the *Gentleman's Monthly*.

'The Fall of the House of Usher' has a Gothic setting, and, like 'Ligeia', the tale is of an indeterminate date. There is a main character who is oversensitive and once again there is the notion of life after death. The difference is probably that whereas the narrator of 'Ligeia' was never a character with whom the reader could sympathize, Roderick Usher is one we relate to – a man faced with an extraordinary situation and a peculiar madness. It was the beginning of a tradition of such narrators and the same can be found in many works of fiction down through the years from *Moby Dick* to *The Great Gatsby*.

'The Fall of the House of Usher' contains all the quintessential elements of a story by Edgar Allan Poe – a gloomy, doom-laden landscape; a crumbling mansion that almost seems to be alive; an atmosphere of sorrow and regret; an emaciated, dying woman; arcane books; wild weather; premature burial and return from the grave.

The House of Usher is brought down by physical elements but also by the deep psychological problems of this family that has lived there for generations. There is an 'oppressive secret' within the family that Roderick Usher is not at liberty to divulge.

Of course, the story implies that incest may have taken place between brother and sister but it is left deliberately vague. The premature burial by Usher of his sister is an attempt to bury that secret but it fails and brings the whole edifice, physical and metaphorical, crashing to the ground.

## AN OUTCAST AMONG OUTCASTS

'William Wilson' is set in the outskirts of London where Poe spent his formative years. The 'misty-looking village of England' mentioned in the story is Stoke Newington where John Bransby's school was located and, indeed, the teacher in the story is given Bransby's name.

'William Wilson' is Poe's deepest exploration of the doppelgänger, or ghostly double. The narrator's rival is without doubt his alter-ego or conscience, made manifest in another body and haunting him. It is a carefully written story with few adjectives and very little imagery. He eschewed the poetic approach to creating a mood or effect and instead produced a tale based on rationality and logic.

Although it had already appeared in the gift catalogue, 'William Wilson' was also published in the October 1839 issue of *Burton's Gentleman's Magazine*. It would be the first of Poe's stories to be translated into another language when, in 1844, it was printed in the Paris newspaper *La Quotidienne*.

Poe sent the story to American author, Washington Irving (1783 – 1859), in search of some endorsement. Irving responded: 'It is managed in a highly picturesque Style and the Singular and Mysterious interest is well sustained throughout.' Irving also wrote to him in connection with 'The Fall of the House of Usher': '[I] should think that a collection of tales, equally well written, could not fail of being favorably received.'

Ultimately, however, Poe faced the same prejudice against short story collections when he approached the Philadelphia publisher, Lea & Blanchard. They would publish a collection, they said, entitled *Tales of the Grotesque and Arabesque*. But the print run would be 1,750 – soon reduced to 500 – and the only payment Poe would receive would be 200 sample copies.

## TERROR OF THE SOUL

Published in two volumes that arrived in bookshops at the end of 1839, *Tales of the Grotesque and Arabesque* contained the heavily revised twenty-five stories that Poe had written thus far, but was of fairly uneven standard. The 'grotesque' part of the book incorporated tales that were comic or had a satirical slant while the 'arabesque' tales were more serious and imaginative.

Poe dedicated the book to Colonel William Drayton (1776 – 1846), a prominent Congressman, banker and writer, who may have earned his dedication by contributing to the cost of the book's printing. The brief Preface found Poe railing against his tales being viewed as *Germanic* – 'terror is not of Germany, but of the soul.'

Reviews were generally favorable, although there was the odd negative one. The *Boston Notion* was very disappointed with Poe's tales, complaining that they 'fall below the average of newspaper trash ... They consist of a wild, unmeaning, pointless, aimless set of stories, outraging all manner of probability, and without anything of elevated fancy or fine humor to redeem them ... The congregation of nonsense is merely caricature run mad.'

The *New York Mirror*, by contrast, said that the stories demonstrated 'the development of great intellectual capacity, with a power for vivid description, an opulence of imagination, a fecundity of invention, and a command over the elegances of diction which have seldom been displayed, even by writers who have acquired the greatest distinction in the republic of letters.'

The *Philadelphia Saturday Courier* also saw much to like in the tales: 'They are generally wildly imaginative in plot; fanciful in description, oftentimes to the full boundaries of the grotesque; but throughout indicating the polished writer, possessed of rare and varied learning. Some of them will bear good comparison with the productions of Coleridge.'

Nonetheless, sales were poor and when eighteen months later, Poe suggested a second edition with the addition of eight new stories, one of which was 'The Murders in the Rue Morgue', the publishers declined his offer, even when he offered to forfeit the royalties from the book. They were still trying to clear stock of the first edition from their inventory.

## A REMARKABLE JOURNEY IN A BULLETPROOF BOAT

Meanwhile work continued at *Burton's Gentleman's Magazine* and in January 1840, Poe published the first of six installments of the serial novel *The Journal of Julius Rodman: Being an Account of the First Passage Across the Rocky Mountains of North America Ever Achieved by Civilized Man*.

Some believed *Julius Rodman* to be factual, a genuine historical document and, bizarrely, a paragraph from it was included in an official report on the Oregon Territory that was put together for the United States Senate in 1840.

'It is proper to notice here,' the report stated, 'an account of an expedition across the American continent, made between 1791 and 1794, by a party of citizens of the United States, under the direction of Julius Rodman, whose journal has been recently discovered in Virginia, and is now in course of publication in a periodical magazine at Philadelphia.' In the long run, however, it was a fairly ridiculous story.

## PUNS, PUZZLES AND CIPHEROLOGY

Poe was at this time taking on hack jobs of all kinds, including work for *Alexander's Weekly Messenger* that described itself as 'the largest and cheapest family newspaper in the world.' He told readers stories of his cat, made up terrible puns for them and indulged the recent passion for puzzles and ciphers by asking readers to see if they could defeat him with a secret encoded message.

'We pledge ourselves to read it forthwith however unusual or arbitrary may be the characters involved,' he wrote. He would decipher almost a hundred such puzzles over the next six months. In the end, he was overwhelmed by the numbers of ciphers arriving on his desk and had to plead with readers to stop.

He was also making plans for his own magazine, made all the more urgent by rumors that Burton was going to sell *Gentleman's Monthly*. It was going to be called *Penn Magazine*, a monthly that he claimed would be free of 'any tincture of the buffoonery, scurrility, or profanity' of European magazines. He also apologized for his critical excesses and promised that his magazine would resemble *The Knickerbocker* and the *North American*, two highly reputable periodicals published in New York and Boston respectively.

# WASHINGTON IRVING

Washington Irving was born in New York in 1783. He studied law, but began to gain a name for the letters he wrote to the New York *Morning Chronicle*. For health reasons, he was sent to Europe where he traveled from 1804 to 1806, and where he began to perfect the social and conversational skills that would make him one of the world's most popular guests.

Admitted to the Bar in 1806, a year later he launched the literary magazine *Salmagundi* in which under pseudonyms, he lampooned New York society and politics. In 1809, he published the bestselling satirical work, *A History of New York from the Beginning of the World to the End of the Dutch Dynasty* under the name 'Diedrich Knickerbocker'.

In the War of 1812, he served as an officer in the New York State Militia, but, at the war's conclusion, he left for Europe in an attempt to salvage the family business that, like many, had been devastated by the war and the trade ban. He remained in Europe for the next seventeen years and, with *The Last of the Mohicans* author, James Fenimore Cooper, was one of the earliest American writers to gain fame there.

In England, he composed the short story 'Rip Van Winkle' and in 1819 published *The Sketch Book of Geoffrey Crayon, Gent*, a collection of short prose pieces that included 'Rip Van Winkle' and another enduring short story, 'The Legend of Sleepy Hollow'. While in Europe, he also published books such as *A History of the Life and Voyages of Christopher Columbus* and *Chronicle of the Conquest of Granada*.

On his return to the United States, he responded to criticism by other writers, such as James Fenimore Cooper, that he had written only about Europe, by producing *A Tour on the Prairies* and *The Adventures of Captain Bonneville*. From 1842 to 1846, he was U.S. Ambassador to Spain. He died on November 28, 1859.

# THE JOURNAL OF JULIUS RODMAN

The story is told as if it is a true account of the remarkable journey of English merchant Julius Rodman leading an expedition up the Missouri River and into the north-west of the country. It has been drawn, the story asserts, from the pages of a diary that has been submitted by Rodman's heir, James E. Rodman. It follows 'the unparalleled vicissitudes and adventures experienced by a handful of men in a country which, until then, had never been explored by "civilized man."'

Rodman undertakes the journey because of his health. He is a hypochondriac and is traveling 'to seek, in the bosom of the wilderness, that peace which his peculiar disposition would not suffer him to enjoy among men.' Accompanying him on this perilous expedition are Pierre Junôt and his slave Toby, Alexander Wormley, a Virginian named Andrew Thornton and the Greely brothers – John, Robert, Meredith, Frank and Poindexter. It is a party that is described as 'mere travelers for pleasure' who had no commercial or financial objectives in the expedition.

They set off in canoes and a thirty-foot long bulletproof boat and the diary describes in great detail what they see *en route* and the weather they experience. There are illnesses, boats are capsized, antelopes stampede and they fight Sioux Indians. Rodman dislikes the Native Americans intensely, describing them as 'an ugly, ill-made race' and he seizes any opportunity to fire his gun at them: 'The effect of the discharge was very severe, and answered all our purposes to the full. Six of the Indians were killed, and perhaps three times as many badly wounded.'

In the last chapter, the group is attacked by two grizzly bears. Greely is mauled by one of them and Rodman and another try to stop the attack, shooting the animal, but failing to stop it. They are attacked themselves and cornered on a cliff-edge. Greely manages to save them by shooting the bear dead.

*We were completely at the mercy of the Sioux. Some of the chiefs had spears, with fanciful flags attached, and were really gallant-looking men.* From Chapter 4, *Journal of Julius Rodman*, April 1840.

## VENTING THE VITRIOL

It was too much for Burton, whom Poe considered a crook anyway, especially as the *Gentleman's Monthly* brought in a profit of three to four thousand dollars every year and yet Burton only paid him a measly five hundred. Burton fired Poe, knowing that *Penn Magazine* would be a serious rival to his own. After his dismissal, Poe wrote a vitriolic letter to his former boss in which he vented his pent-up anger and frustration:

*You first 'enforc'd', as you say, a deduction of salary* [to pay Poe's debts]; *giving me to understand thereby that you thought of parting company.—You next spoke disrespectfully of me behind my back—this as an habitual thing—to those whom you supposed your friends, and who punctually retailed me, as a matter of course, every ill-natured word which you uttered. Lastly you advertised your magazine for sale without saying a word to me about it ...*

*Your attempts to bully me excite in my mind scarcely any other sentiment than mirth ... if by accident you have taken it into your head that I am to be insulted with impunity, I can only assume you are an ass.*

Things became very nasty between the two men, with Poe accusing Burton of initiating a fraudulent competition in the magazine and Burton labeling Poe a drunk. In fact, *Burton's Gentleman's Monthly* was sold in October 1840, six months after Poe had left, six months during which he could have been earning instead of making stuttering attempts to get *Penn* off the ground. Of course, the split between the two meant that *Julius Rodman* remained uncompleted.

Unfortunately for Edgar Allan Poe, in February 1841, just as he was preparing the first issue of his own magazine for the printer, there was a run on the banks bringing financial chaos. It brought the end to any hopes he had of publishing his magazine. There was some good news around this time, however. George Graham (1813 – 94), who had bought Burton's magazine from him for $3,500, decided to rename it *Graham's Magazine* and invited Poe back as editor.

## STALKED BY URBAN LONELINESS

The only story that Poe produced for the remainder of that turbulent year was very different to *Julius Rodman*. 'The Man of the Crowd' appeared in the December 1840 issues of both *Atkinson's Casket* and the *Gentleman's Monthly*. It works as a transitional tale between Poe's Gothic-style stories of the late 1830s and his ratiocinative tales of the early years of the following decade, possessing elements of each style. It is a story that is stalked by urban loneliness and the notion of the anonymity of the face in the crowd.

It is never really clear why the narrator of 'The Man of the Crowd' becomes so fixated by the old man that he so obsessively follows, but we can divine that he is actually a side of the narrator's own personality.

German philosopher and cultural critic Walter Benjamin (1892 – 1940) wrote that '[The Man of the Crowd] is something like an X-ray of a detective story. It does away with all the drapery that a crime represents. Only the armature remains: the pursuer, the crowd, and an unknown man who manages to walk through London in such a way that he always remains in the middle of the crowd.' Writer and English Professor William Brevda says that 'Poe splits the human psyche into pursuer and pursued, self and other, ego and id, 'detective' and criminal, past and future ...'

# THE FALL OF THE HOUSE OF USHER

An unnamed narrator approaches a gloomy-looking house on horseback. The dark and mysterious house belongs to Roderick Usher, a friend of the rider who is seized by a feeling of 'insufferable gloom' as he gazes on it.

*I looked upon the scene before me—upon the mere house, and the simple landscape features of the domain—upon the bleak walls—upon the vacant eye-like windows—upon a few rank sedges—and upon a few white trunks of decayed trees—with an utter depression of soul which I can compare to no earthly sensation more properly than to the after-dream of the reveler upon opium—the bitter lapse into everyday life—the hideous dropping off of the veil. There was an iciness, a sinking, a sickening of the heart—an unredeemed dreariness of thought which no goading of the imagination could torture into aught of the sublime.*

The house itself seems solid enough, but there is a crack running from the roof to the ground at the front of the building. The rider has come at the request of his friend who has told him he is unwell both physically and emotionally. The narrator explains that of the Usher family, only one member has survived in each generation. Therefore it has a direct line of descent that has no outside branches.

He finds Roderick paler and less energetic than he used to be and Roderick explains that he is plagued by nerves and that his senses are unbearably heightened. It occurs to the narrator that Roderick is afraid of the house. Making matters worse is the illness of Roderick's sister, Madeline who suffers from a mysterious ailment. At one point, the narrator catches a fleeting glimpse of her passing slowly through the apartment. For a few days, the narrator sits with Roderick trying to help him, listening to him play guitar and reading him stories.

When Madeline eventually dies, Roderick fears that the physicians will attempt to exhume her body so they can carry out medical research on her. Therefore, he decides to give her a temporary resting place in the tombs below the house. Helping Roderick to place her in the tomb, the narrator notices her rosy cheeks and also for the first time realizes that she and Roderick are twins.

His sister's death makes Roderick's condition even worse and one night he knocks on the narrator's door in an agitated state. Going to the window, he points out a bright-looking gas that seems to be surrounding the house but the narrator tells him it is nothing out of the ordinary. The narrator suggests that he reads to him in order to calm him down but as he reads, he hears noises that mimic those in the story. He tries to ignore them at first, but they get louder.

Roderick by this time is slumped in his chair and muttering incoherently. He says that he has been hearing such noises for days. He believes that they have buried Madeline alive and that she is trying to escape the tomb. Suddenly, the door is blown open by the wind and to their horror they see Madeline standing there. 'There was blood upon her white robes, and the evidence of some bitter struggle upon every portion of her emaciated frame.'

Madeline attacks her brother as she dies, and as he falls to the ground, he also dies, of fear. '[Madeline] in her violent and now final death-agonies, bore him to the floor a corpse, and a victim to the terrors he had anticipated.'

The narrator flees and as he does so, the House of Usher breaks apart along the line of the crack and crumbles to the ground.

Illustration for 'The Fall of the House of Usher' by Harry Clarke, 1923.

# WILLIAM WILSON

The narrator, an 'outcast among outcasts', tells the reader that he would prefer to keep his real name secret and asks us to recognize him as 'William Wilson'. He says that the telling of his tale will help to explain his sudden turn to evil.

He tells of his childhood and his time at school in a large Elizabethan house, where he met another boy with exactly the same name and birth date as him. Furthermore, the other boy looks like him. He feels he is better than his fellow students apart from this boy, and the boy becomes a competitor for the affection of his schoolmates and in the activities of the school.

He notes how the rival even imitates his way of speaking – although he never speaks louder than a whisper – and they have similar builds and even dress alike. Some of the other students think they are brothers, but the narrator rejects the idea of any connection. At the same time, he remains on speaking terms with the other boy and cannot hate him.

Soon, however, they fall out and there is a scuffle between them. Something about it throws the narrator back to memories of his earliest infancy and he feels that he had been acquainted with the other boy even then. 'I cannot better describe the sensation which oppressed me than by saying that I could with difficulty shake off the belief of my having been acquainted with the being who stood before me, at some epoch very long ago—some point of the past even infinitely remote.'

Not long after, the narrator goes into the other William Wilson's room to play a practical joke on him. However, in that room he sees a different William Wilson and is terrified.

*Was it, in truth, within the bounds of human possibility, that what I now saw was the result, merely, of the habitual practise of this sarcastic imitation? Awe-stricken, and with a creeping shudder, I extinguished the lamp, passed silently from the chamber, and left, at once, the halls of that old academy, never to enter them again.*

The narrator becomes a student at Eton, but in trying to forget his past he abuses alcohol and indulges in debauched behavior. One night, in the midst of a party, a mysterious visitor is announced and the narrator discovers a young man the same size as him and dressed similarly. In the dim light, however, he is unable to make out the man's face. The visitor grabs the narrator's arm and whispers 'William Wilson' before vanishing.

Moving on to Oxford University, the narrator starts gambling, fleecing less able students of their money. He meets a young man named Glendinning who seems an ideal target for his devious card tricks. He allows Glendinning to win at first but soon the young man is heavily indebted to the narrator. Glendinning utters 'an ejaculation evincing utter despair … [it] gave me to understand that I had effected his total ruin.' Suddenly, however, a figure rushes into the room and denounces the narrator as a fraud before just as quickly leaving. The narrator is disgraced and is forced to leave the country.

He travels to Rome but at a masked ball in the palace of the Duke di Broglio, he hears a whisper in his ear – 'William Wilson'. He turns to find a man dressed in exactly the same costume as him. He takes him into a side room where he draws a sword and stabs his rival. Suddenly, the room changes and a mirror appears where his rival had fallen.

*… as I stepped up to it in extremity of terror, mine own image, but with features all pale and dabbled in blood, advanced to meet me with a feeble and tottering gait. Thus it appeared, I say, but was not. It was my antagonist—it was Wilson, who then stood before me in the agonies of his dissolution. His mask and cloak lay, where he had thrown them, upon the floor. Not a thread in all his raiment—not a line in all the marked and singular lineaments of his face which was not, even in the most absolute identity, mine own!*

*It was Wilson; but he spoke no longer in a whisper, and I could have fancied that I myself was speaking while he said:*

*'You have conquered, and I yield. Yet, henceforward art thou also dead—dead to the World, to Heaven and to Hope! In me didst thou exist—and, in my death, see by this image, which is thine own, how utterly thou hast murdered thyself.'*

The masquerade in the palazzo of the
Neapolitan Duke di Broglio. Byam Shaw's
illustration for 'William Wilson', 1909.

# THE MAN OF THE CROWD

The unnamed narrator who is recovering from an illness, sits in a cafe for most of one afternoon, reading a newspaper and watching the world go by. He analyzes the different types of people who pass, such as the 'tribe of clerks', split into two distinct divisions. There are 'the junior clerks of flash houses—young gentlemen with tight coats, bright boots, well-oiled hair, and supercilious lips' and 'the upper clerks of staunch firms, or of the "steady old fellows" … These were known by their coats and pantaloons of black or brown, made to sit comfortably, with white cravats and waistcoats, broad solid-looking shoes, and thick hose or gaiters. They had all slightly bald heads, from which the right ears, long used to pen-holding, had an odd habit of standing off on end.'

As the day turns into early evening, he suddenly spies 'a countenance (that of a decrepit old man, some sixty-five or seventy years of age)—a countenance which at once arrested and absorbed my whole attention, on account of the absolute idiosyncrasy of its expression.' He has an urge to keep the raggedly dressed man in view and goes out into the street to start following him. He is led through street after street, through markets and past shops, but stopping nowhere. They enter a poorer part of the city, but still the old man keeps walking, as he does through the night and into the next day. They end up back in the street where the pursuit had started and at last, 'wearied unto death,' the narrator stands in front of him. But it seems as if the old man does not even see him. He merely walks off, leaving the narrator to say:

> This old man … is the type and the genius of deep crime. He refuses to be alone. He is the man of the crowd. It will be in vain to follow, for I shall learn no more of him, nor of his deeds. The worst heart of the world is a grosser book than the 'Hortulus Animae,' and perhaps it is but one of the great mercies of God that 'er lasst sich nicht lesen.'

The last few words in German translate as 'it does not permit itself to be read' as we know from the first paragraph of the story where the narrator uses it in connection with a 'certain German book.'

*It was the most noisome quarter of London.* Harry Clarke's 1923 illustration for 'The Man of the Crowd'.

# CHAPTER 5

# MURDER, MYSTERY AND MADNESS

With one remarkable story – 'The Murders in the Rue Morgue' – Edgar Allan Poe invented a new genre of fiction: the detective story. The most influential short story of the entire nineteenth century, it emerged, to some extent, from his long-standing interest in mind games, puzzles and the secret codes known as cryptographs.

In 'The Murders in the Rue Morgue', he introduces a character, C. Auguste Dupin, who is adroit at puzzle-solving, the first fictional detective. He shares many features of future characters of other writers, especially Sherlock Holmes from the pen of Arthur Conan Doyle (1859 – 1930). For example, he has a friend who serves as narrator and the final conclusion is revealed prior to the explanation of it by the detective. Dupin would appear in another two of Poe's stories – 'The Purloined Letter' and 'The Mystery of Marie Rogêt'.

## THESE TALES OF RATIOCINATION

The most immediate influence on Poe's story was the world's first real-life private detective, Eugène François Vidocq (1775 – 1857), although the rising popularity of true-crime reporting in the 1830s also influenced his work. Two true crime books in particular would have been in Poe's mind – *The Murder of Maria Marten*, written by James Curtis in 1827 and the 1836 coverage in the *New York Herald* of the murder of the prostitute Helen Jewett by James Gordon Bennett (1795 – 1872).

'The Murders in the Rue Morgue' was widely praised for its inventiveness. The Pennsylvania *Enquirer* said that 'it proves Mr Poe to be a man of genius ... with an inventive power and skill, of which we know no parallel.' Poe seems to have been keen to play down to some extent his new type of story, as can be seen from a letter he wrote to the poet Philip Pendleton Cooke: 'These tales of ratiocination owe most of their popularity to being something in a new key. I do not mean to say that they are not ingenious – but people think them more ingenious than they are – on account of their method and *air* of method. In the "Murders in the Rue Morgue", for instance, where is the ingenuity in unraveling a web which you yourself ... have woven for the express purpose of unraveling?'

It is true that there is what could be called an element of 'bad faith' in Poe's ratiocinative tales. The reader could never guess the twist in 'Rue Morgue', for instance; there is not the slightest possibility of working out who the killer is. This goes against the normal convention. However, it is the machinations of Dupin's mind that appeal, and there is a frisson of delight and admiration for his cleverness when he reveals the murderer and the method.

## METHOD IN THE MADNESS

Poe followed up 'The Murders in the Rue Morgue' with 'The Mystery of Marie Rogêt'. Again the sharp inquisitive mind of C. Auguste Dupin is let loose on a mystery that is baffling the police, and the plot is once more set in Paris. The story is based on a real-life crime, the murder of Mary Cecilia Rogers, a sales girl in a Manhattan shop. She had disappeared on July 25, 1841, and her body was found floating in the Hudson River three days later in Hoboken, New Jersey.

# EUGÈNE FRANÇOIS VIDOCQ

Eugène François Vidocq was born into a wealthy family in 1775 in Arras, northern France. As a teenager, he spent much of his time in the fighting halls of Arras where he gained a reputation as a fencer, earning the nickname 'Le Vautrin' (Wild Boar) and funding his lifestyle by stealing, often from his parents. He was aiming to emigrate to the Americas but after all his money was stolen, was forced to join a group of traveling entertainers.

Eventually, he returned to Arras where he was forgiven by his parents.

He enlisted in the French army for several years before returning to Arras where he gained a reputation as a womanizer and fought many duels as a consequence of his seductions. He re-enlisted in the army but did not remain there long before wandering around Belgium and France having further, often amorous, adventures.

During a spell in prison in Paris, Vidocq became embroiled in a controversy concerning a forged pardon for another prisoner. He always denied any involvement but was sentenced to a further eight years hard labor, escaping several times but always being arrested. Finally, in 1809, having been recaptured for the umpteenth time he offered his services as a prison informant. This led to his release and he continued to work as a secret agent for the Paris police.

At the end of 1811, he organized a plainclothes unit, the Brigade de la Sûreté that was formally recognized the following year with him as leader. A majority of its members were ex-criminals like himself. When the Sûreté was dissolved in 1832, following his resignation, he founded Le Bureau des Renseignements (Office of Information), effectively the world's first private detective agency.

Vidocq died in 1857 at the age of eighty-one leaving behind a ghost-written autobiography, *Memoirs*, from which Poe borrowed the name Dupin. Unpublished passages from Vidocq's memoirs were serialized in *Burton's Gentleman's Monthly* in 1828.

# THE MURDERS IN THE RUE MORGUE

*The mental features discoursed of as the analytical, are, in themselves, but little susceptible of analysis. We appreciate them only in their effects. We know of them, among other things, that they are always to their possessor, when inordinately possessed, a source of the liveliest enjoyment. As the strong man exults in his physical ability, delighting in such exercises as call his muscles into action, so glories the analyst in that moral activity which disentangles. He derives pleasure from even the most trivial occupations bringing his talent into play. He is fond of enigmas, of conundrums, of hieroglyphics; exhibiting in his solutions of each a degree of acumen which appears to the ordinary apprehension preternatural. His results, brought about by the very soul and essence of method, have, in truth, the whole air of intuition.*

The story concerns the double murder of Madame L'Espanaye and her daughter in an apartment building in the fictional street of Rue Morgue in Paris. The newspapers describe how the mother's throat has been so badly cut that her head was barely attached to her body when she was found and, bizarrely, after the daughter was strangled she was stuffed into a chimney in the apartment. The murders have occurred in a room that is locked from the inside. When witnesses are interviewed, they each say they heard the murderer speaking a different language.

Auguste Dupin and his associate, the narrator of the story, have cut themselves off from everything and only go out at night.

*Had the routine of our life at this place been known to the world, we should have been regarded as madmen—although, perhaps, as madmen of a harmless nature. Our seclusion was perfect. We admitted no visitors. Indeed the locality of our retirement had been carefully kept a secret from my own former associates; and it had been many years since Dupin had ceased to know or be known in Paris. We existed within ourselves alone.*

They read about the murders in the newspapers and learn that a man named Adolphe Le Bon has been arrested. He is a bank courier who had escorted Madame L'Espanaye home that afternoon with a large sum of money. Dupin is intrigued by the case and offers his services to the Prefect of the Police.

Dupin weighs up the fact that none of the witnesses can agree on what language the murderer was speaking – one thinks it Russian, another French, another English and another Italian – and decides that in all likelihood it was not a human voice they heard. Furthermore, at the scene of the murders he discovers hair in one of the murdered women's hands that is not human. Dupin works out from this and from the extraordinary climbing abilities of the perpetrator that he must be an ourang-outang.

He places an advertisement in the newspaper asking if anyone has lost such a creature that is answered by a sailor, as Dupin had expected. The sailor visits Dupin and offers a reward for the ourang-outang's return. Under questioning, he admits that he owns an ourang-outang that he found in Borneo. It had escaped with his shaving razor and as he chased it, it had climbed into the apartment in the Rue Morgue occupied by the two women.

The animal attempted to shave Madame L'Espayane, in imitation of his master, but he accidentally slit the woman's throat as he did so. It became angry and strangled the daughter, after which it attempted to hide the body in the chimney. Seeing all this, the sailor had panicked and ran away while the ourang-outang made good his escape through the window and down the wall of the building via a lightning rod and in through the window of the apartment below.

The Prefect of Police is irritated that Dupin has solved the crime, 'and was fain to indulge in a sarcasm or two, about the propriety of every person minding his own business.' But Dupin is untouched by it and finds the policeman's sarcasm not worthy of a response.

Engraving of 'The Murders in the Rue Morgue',
1870 by Daniel Vierge (1851 – 1904). Vierge was
a Spanish-born French illustrator who, with the
photo-engraver Charles Gillot, revolutionized
the reproduction of illustrations at a time when
photographic reproduction in print was not
technically feasible until the late nineteenth century.

The newspapers reported on the case for weeks, theorizing that she had been killed by a gang of ruffians. Poe, however, posited that she had actually been strangled by her lover, a sailor. In fact, a naval officer later admitted that she had died on the operating table during an illegal abortion and her body had been tied up and thrown into the river.

Poe moved the murder to Paris but used the original details. He wrote in 1842: '... under the pretence of showing how Dupin ... unraveled the mystery of Marie's assassination, I, in fact, enter into a very rigorous analysis of the real tragedy in New York.'

'The Mystery of Marie Rogêt' takes place a couple of years after Dupin has uncovered the perpetrator of 'The Murders in the Rue Morgue' and it bears the subtitle 'A Sequel to The Murders in the Rue Morgue'. The two stories, in all honesty, have little in common apart from Dupin and the Parisian setting and, in fact, the later story is not nearly as good as the first. In 'Marie Rogêt', Dupin spends his time analyzing the evidence of the case, debunking the various theories of the journalists frenziedly reporting it. He does propose a method in which the murder could have been committed but fails to name the woman's killer. The story's conclusion is unsatisfying and frustrating for readers looking for a solution. Rather, it is a story about ratiocination, and not about the unraveling of a mystery.

## ENCOUNTERING CHARLES DICKENS

During his two years at *Graham's*, Poe wrote reviews of works by a number of important writers, including Bolingbroke, Goldsmith, Cooper, Marryat, Macaulay, Bulwer-Lytton, Longfellow, Tennyson and Lowell. As ever, he delighted readers by sparing no one, whether famous or not. One review, of a work by James McHenry (1785 – 1845), author of *The Antediluvians*, noted wittily that 'should he be arraigned for writing poetry, no sane jury would ever convict him.'

He also had the good fortune to come into contact with the great English author, Charles Dickens (1812 – 70), a number of whose books he had already reviewed favorably. When he correctly predicted early on in the serialization of Dickens' *Barnaby Rudge* that 'Barnaby, the idiot, is the murderer's own son,' he claimed to have received a letter from Dickens who suggested that in order to have predicted it, he must have been involved in dealings with the devil.

When Dickens arrived in Philadelphia in March 1842 on his hugely successful American lecture tour, Poe sent him a copy of *Tales of the Grotesque and Arabesque* and a couple of his reviews of *Barnaby Rudge*. He also asked if he could have an interview to which Dickens responded: 'I shall be very glad to see you, whenever you will do me the favor to call ... I have glanced over the books you have been so kind as to send me; and more particularly at the papers to which you called my attention. I have the greater pleasure in expressing my desire to see you, on their account.'

They met at the United States Hotel where Poe was able to conduct two long interviews. Best of all, Dickens promised Poe that he would try to find a publisher for him in England. He was as good as his word, but could not find any takers, writing to Poe in November: 'I should have forwarded you the accompanying letter from Mr Moxon before now, but that I have delayed doing so in the hope that some other channel for the publication of your book on this side of the water would present itself to me. I am, however, unable to report any success. I have mentioned it to publishers with whom I have influence, but they have, one and all, declined the venture.'

After Poe's death, Dickens helped Maria Clemm by purchasing copies of her nephew's work.

# CHARLES DICKENS

Charles Dickens is recognized as one of the greatest writers in the English language, the creator of some of the world's best-known fictional characters. During his lifetime, his fifteen novels, five novellas, hundreds of short stories and non-fiction articles were extraordinarily popular and are read and enjoyed to this day.

Dickens was born in Portsmouth, England, in 1812, son of a clerk in the Navy Pay Office. In 1815, his father was posted back to London where they lived in Fitzrovia before moving to Sheerness and then Chatham, Kent. His father spent some time in debtors' prison and Dickens began to build up the indignation at the conditions in which working class people had to live that featured in so much of his work. Aged fifteen, he worked in a law office but also worked in his spare time as a freelance reporter.

He submitted his first story to *Monthly Magazine* in 1833 and reported on election campaigns for the *Morning Chronicle* newspaper. His first collection of articles, *Sketches by Boz*, was published in 1836 and its success was followed by a serialization of *The Pickwick Papers,* the final installment of which sold 40,000 copies. Next, he wrote *Oliver Twist* which was published in 1838. That same year he married Catherine Thomson Hogarth, daughter of a newspaper editor. Meanwhile, Dickens' success as a novelist continued with *Nicholas Nickleby*, *The Old Curiosity Shop* and his first historical novel, *Barnaby Rudge: A Tale of the Riots of Eighty.* All were published in monthly installments before being issued in book form.

In 1842, Dickens made his first visit to the United States and Canada. He spent a month in New York, lecturing on International Copyright, a particular irritant of his since his works had been subject to piracy in America. He proved to be immensely popular and during this trip met and befriended Edgar Allan Poe.

Returning to England, he wrote *A Christmas Carol* which helped to promote a renewed enthusiasm for Christmas in England. He followed this with *Dombey and Son*, written between 1846 and 1848 and *David Copperfield*, written between 1849 and 1850.

At the age of forty-five he fell in love with an 18 year-old actress, Ellen Ternan and separated from his wife. During the next decade he undertook a series of immensely popular reading tours that were highly remunerative. Other major works, such as *A Tale of Two Cities* (1859) and *Great Expectations* (1861) continued his unparalleled success.

He returned to the United States in 1867, but was taken ill during a series of farewell readings in England, Scotland and Ireland, and the tour was canceled. This allowed him time to work on his unfinished last novel *The Mystery of Edwin Drood*.

He returned to the stage for a last series of readings, delivering his final performance at a Royal Academy banquet in the presence of the Prince and Princess of Wales on May 2, 1870. He died of a stroke on June 9, 1870, aged fifty-eight.

Charles Dickens (1812 – 1870).

## MEETING NATHANIEL HAWTHORNE

Poe also met the American writer, Nathaniel Hawthorne (1804 – 64) around this time, a writer he liked even more than Dickens. Hawthorne was yet to be famous but Poe wrote glowingly of his short-story collection, *Twice-Told Tales*: '... these effusions of Mr Hawthorne are the product of a truly imaginative intellect, restrained, and in some measure repressed, by fastidiousness of taste, by constitutional melancholy, and by indolence ... Of Mr Hawthorne's tales we would say, emphatically, that they belong to the highest region of Art ... We look upon him as one of the few men of indisputable genius to whom our country has yet given birth.' He also threw in a customary allegation of plagiarism, accusing Hawthorne of having stolen the idea for his story 'How's Masque' from his own 'William Wilson'. Unfortunately Hawthorne's story had been written before Poe's!

Hawthorne wrote to Poe praising his reviews but also encouraging him to get on with his own creative efforts:

*I have read your occasional notices of my productions with great interest—not so much because your judgment was, upon the whole, favorable, as because it seemed to be given in earnest. I care for nothing but the truth; and shall always much more readily accept a harsh truth, in regard to my writings, than a sugared falsehood.*

*I confess, however, that I admire you rather as a writer of tales than as a critic upon them. I might often—and often do—dissent from your opinions in the latter capacity, but could never fail to recognize your force and originality, in the former.*

In his Hawthorne review, Poe made some influential and important points about how he thought poetry and short stories should be written:

*A rhymed poem should not exceed in length what might be perused in an hour. Within this limit alone can the highest order of true poetry exist ... In almost all classes of composition, the unity of effect or impression is a point of the greatest importance ... Unity cannot be thoroughly preserved in productions whose perusal cannot be completed at one sitting ... Thus a long poem is a paradox ...*

The same could be said, according to Poe, of short stories:

*Having conceived, with deliberate care, a certain unique or single effect to be wrought out, [the author] then invents such incidents—he then combines such events as they may best aid him in establishing his preconceived effect ... In the whole composition there should be no word written, of which the tendency, direct or indirect, is not to the one pre-established design.*

## THE DARK SHADOW OF TUBERCULOSIS

Suddenly, however, Virginia was ill. One evening early in 1842, as she sang at their piano in the parlor, she had a coughing fit that brought up bright red blood. It was undoubtedly the beginnings of tuberculosis. Poe wrote about the incident in a poignant letter to a friend not long after:

*My dear little wife has been dangerously ill. About a fortnight since, in singing, she ruptured a blood vessel, and it was only yesterday that the physicians gave me any hope of her recovery. You might imagine the agony I have suffered, for you know how devotedly I love her.*

The illness put added strain on the Poe finances. It must be remembered that he was the first American writer to support himself entirely from the proceeds of his pen. All the others had jobs – Ralph Waldo Emerson (1803 – 82) was a clergyman, James Russell Lowell (1819 – 91) and Henry Wadsworth

# NATHANIEL HAWTHORNE

Nathaniel Hawthorne was born in Salem, Massachusetts in 1804. His father died four years later, leaving Hawthorne and his mother in poverty. When he was fourteen, his increasingly reclusive mother moved them to an isolated farm in the woods of Raymond, Maine.

He attended Bowdoin College in Maine, at the same time as the poet, Henry Wadsworth Longfellow and his unsuccessful first novel, *Fanshawe*, was published anonymously in 1828. Returning to Salem, he shut himself away for twelve years, writing stories and poetry.

He contributed stories to a number of periodicals that were collected as *Twice-Told Tales* ('twice-told' because they had already been published in magazines). Still unsuccessful as a writer, in 1839 he accepted a job at Boston Custom House. Now married, in 1841 he sought a home for himself and his wife at an idyllic, semi-socialist community at Brook Farm near Boston, the experience providing inspiration for his 1852 novel, *The Blithedale Romance*.

He continued to write, publishing a series of stories for children from New England history – *Grandfather's Chair*, *Famous Old People* and *Liberty Tree* and while living in Concord, Massachusetts in 1842, he published *Biographical Stories* for children. Sketches and studies written for the *Democratic Review* were published as *Mosses from an Old Manse* in 1846. Around this time, he was forced to accept a job at the Custom House again.

In 1850, Hawthorne's *The Scarlet Letter*, the best known of all his works, was published and he followed that with a prolific run of books – *The House of the Seven Gables* (1851), *Wonder Book* (1852), *The Snow Image* (1852) and *The Blithedale Romance*.

As a result of his friendship with President Franklin Pierce, Hawthorne served as American Consul in Liverpool in England between 1853 and 1857. He died, aged fifty-nine, in 1864.

Longfellow (1807 – 82) taught in universities, Cooper inherited a fortune from his father, and Hawthorne worked for Boston Customs House. Poe's straitened circumstances led to his wild drinking sprees and a smoldering anger that sometimes came through in his stories.

## MONEY FOR NOTHING

One of the problems contributing to Poe's continual absence of funds, was the lack of an International Copyright law. Why would an American publisher pay Edgar Allan Poe to publish his work when it could publish an established writer such as Charles Dickens for free. As we have seen, Dickens was also incensed by the piracy of his work and campaigned for International Copyright.

In Poe's essay, 'Some Secrets from the Magazine Prison-House', he wrote angrily: 'The want of an International Copyright Law, by rendering it nearly impossible to obtain anything from the booksellers in the way of remuneration for literary labor, has had the effect of forcing many of our very best writers into the service of the Magazines and Reviews.'

# TUBERCULOSIS IN THE NINETEENTH CENTURY

Tuberculosis was a dark shadow that hung over the life of Edgar Allan Poe and over the life of everyone in the nineteenth century. Also known as 'consumption', or the 'White Plague', at the time it was the cause of more deaths in the industrialized world than any other disease. By the latter part of the century, seventy to ninety per cent of the urban populations of Europe and North America were infected with the TB bacillus. And the prognosis was not good – around eighty per cent of those who developed active tuberculosis died of it and about forty per cent of working-class deaths were from tuberculosis.

The perception of TB in the nineteenth century was somewhat bizarre. It was seen as a 'romantic disease' that somehow bestowed upon the victim heightened sensitivity. It took a long time to die and, therefore, was thought of as providing a 'good death', allowing sufferers time to settle their affairs.

It began to signify spiritual purity and temporal wealth, a view that persuaded many young upper-class women to aspire to pale skin in order to achieve the consumptive look. The poet, Lord Byron, popularized the notion of TB as the disease of artists when he wrote, 'I should like to die from consumption.'

Scientists, doctors and politicians blamed the poor and their tenements for the spread of tuberculosis. They were berated for ignoring public health campaigns intended to halt the spread of the disease, such as the prohibition of spitting in public, strict guidelines for looking after children and quarantines.

Eventually, the identification by Robert Koch of the tuberculosis bacillus in 1882 convinced medical practitioners that it was contagious. Deaths from the illness declined throughout Europe and in the United States in the late nineteenth century.

Robert Koch (1843 – 1910).

Magazines were notoriously bad and, unfortunately, notoriously late payers. How true it all was and if proof were needed of the dire straits in which writers found themselves, Maria Clemm would collect all the rejected manuscripts and books that Poe received and sell them to help make ends meet. After his death, she said, 'I attended to his literary business, for he, poor fellow, knew nothing about money transactions. How should he, brought up in luxury and extravagance?'

His next story perhaps reflected his wife's illness. 'The Masque of the Red Death: A Fantasy' deals with a dangerous plague. Often viewed as an allegory about the inevitability of death, it has also been given many other readings. It first appeared in the May 1842 issue of *Graham's Magazine*.

## POE'S TOMAHAWK

By spring of 1842, Poe was tired of the drudgery of his work at *Graham's* – a lot for very little pay. His friend Thomas Holley Chivers (1809 – 58), a doctor and a poet who would furiously defend Poe's name after his death, wrote to him:

> [Graham] ought to give you ten thousand dollars a year for supervising it. It is richly worth it. I believe it was through your editorial ability that it was first established. If so, he is greatly indebted to you. It is not my opinion that you ever have been, or ever will be, paid for your intellectual labors. You need never expect it, until you establish a Magazine of your own ...
>
> There is, in the perspicuous flow of your pure English, a subtle delicacy of expression which always pleases me—except when you tomahawk people.

Poe was undoubtedly bitter at having to tailor his intellect to the audiences of first *Burton's* and then *Graham's*. 'I have not only labored solely for the benefit of others (receiving for myself a miserable pittance) but have been forced to model my thoughts at the will

of men whose imbecility was evident to all but themselves.' He was earning a pittance, $800 a year compared to the $25,000 profit Graham was making from the magazine.

In April 1842, having taken some time off due to illness, Poe returned to the office to discover that the other editor, Charles Peterson (1818 – 87), had assumed his duties. He immediately resigned and his great rival Rufus Griswold (1815 – 57) succeeded him as editor. Griswold joined at a salary of $1,000 a year, more than Poe's pay by $200. Poe said:

> ... my reason for resigning was disgust with the namby-pamby character of the Magazine—a character which it was impossible to eradicate. I allude to the contemptible pictures, fashion-plates, music and love tales. The salary, moreover, did not pay me for the labor I was forced to bestow. With Graham who is really a very gentlemanly, although exceedingly weak man, I had no misunderstanding.

## INSISTING UPON THE JULEPS

One bone of contention between Poe and Graham was Poe's putative magazine, *Penn*. When Poe had joined his magazine, Graham had promised that he would provide money for *Penn* within a year. Of course, as *Graham's* became increasingly successful under Poe's stewardship, its proprietor became increasingly reluctant to finance a rival magazine.

He was also reluctant to lose his very successful editor and, indeed, in September 1842, Graham offered Poe his old position back, but he declined. He was not averse to trashing Griswold's control of the magazine: '... the brilliant career of *Graham's Magazine* under Mr Poe's care, and its subsequent trashy literary character since his retirement,' alluding to Griswold's tenure.

Poe hit the bottle once again, on one occasion disappearing for several days before being found outside Jersey City 'wandering

# THE MASQUE OF THE RED DEATH

The setting for the story is the castle-like abbey of Prince Prospero. A plague has come to his land and wiped out half the population.

*No pestilence had ever been so fatal, or so hideous. Blood was its Avatar and its seal—the redness and the horror of blood. There were sharp pains, and sudden dizziness, and then profuse bleeding at the pores, with dissolution. The scarlet stains upon the body and especially upon the face of the victim, were the pest ban which shut him out from the aid and from the sympathy of his fellow-men. And the whole seizure, progress and termination of the disease, were the incidents of half an hour.*

The Prince summons a thousand of his courtesans to the seclusion of his castle and locks the gates to keep the plague outside. Inside is everything they will need for the Prince 'had provided all the appliances of pleasure. There were buffoons, there were improvisatori, there were ballet-dancers, there were musicians, there was Beauty, there was wine. All these and security were within. Without was the "Red Death".'

In the sixth months of their voluntary incarceration, the Prince stages a magnificent masked ball, held in seven rooms. Each room is decorated in a specific color – blue, purple, green, orange, white and violet. The seventh room is painted and decorated in black and is illuminated by a scarlet light thrown onto it by scarlet window-panes.

In this room is a large ebony clock that chimes the hour. Whenever it chimes, the orchestra stops playing and everyone stops dancing. As soon as the chimes end, everyone resumes. As the clock chimes midnight, a figure enters the room:

*… the figure in question had out-Heroded Herod, and gone beyond the bounds of even the prince's indefinite decorum … The figure was tall and gaunt, and shrouded from head to foot in the habiliments of the grave. The mask which concealed the visage was made so nearly to resemble the countenance of a stiffened corpse that the closest scrutiny must have had difficulty in detecting the cheat. And yet all this might have been endured, if not approved, by the mad revelers around. But the mummer had gone so far as to assume the type of the Red Death. His vesture was dabbled in blood—and his broad brow, with all the features of the face, was besprinkled with the scarlet horror.*

Horrified and deeply insulted, Prospero demands to know who the person is who has dressed thus, adding that he wants to hang him. But the guests, too frightened to approach the figure, allow him to pass through the six rooms unhindered. Prospero draws his dagger and pursues him until he has cornered him in the seventh room.

The figure turns to face the prince. 'There was a sharp cry—and the dagger dropped gleaming upon the sable carpet, upon which, instantly afterwards, fell prostrate in death the Prince Prospero.' The guests now leap onto the figure and drag his mask from his face and his robe from his body, only to discover that the figure really is the Red Death 'who had come like a thief in the night.' One by one they catch the disease and fall dead to the floor.

*And the flames of the tripods expired. And Darkness and Decay and the Red Death held illimitable dominion over all.*

*The dagger dropped gleaming upon the sable carpet.* Illustration for 'The Masque of the Red Death' by Harry Clarke, 1919.

around like a crazy man.' A month later, he got hopelessly drunk during a business trip to New York and had to send apologies to all he had encountered. 'Would you be kind enough to put the best possible interpretation upon my behavior while in N—York? You must have conceived a queer idea of me—but the simple truth is that Wallace [Kentucky poet William Ross Wallace (1819 – 81)] would insist upon the juleps, and I knew not what I was either doing or saying.'

Meanwhile, Virginia's illness was waxing and waning and it was causing Poe untold distress. 'Her life was despaired of,' he poignantly wrote later, 'I took leave of her forever & underwent all the agonies of her death. She recovered partially and again I hoped. Then again—again—again & even once again at varying intervals ... I became insane, with long intervals of horrible sanity. During these fits of consciousness I drank, God only knows how often or how much.'

*Graham's Lady's and Gentleman's Magazine*, May, 1841.

CHAPTER 6

# THE SOUND OF HUMAN TERROR

In the midst of all his problems and with poverty grinding away at his soul, Poe produced a corker of a story. Published in the 1842 version of *The Gift: A Christmas and New Year's Present for 1843*, 'The Pit and the Pendulum' was a predicament story to end all predicament stories. The narrator is about to be punished for an unknown crime and is offered a horrible choice of death – he can plunge to death in a bottomless pit of unknown horrors filled with ravenous rats, or he can wait and be sliced up by the razor-sharp pendulum.

As in many Poe stories, we do not know the narrator's name, but we do know the time and place of the events. It takes place in Toledo, Spain, during the Spanish Inquisition. Although, at the end of the story, Poe ignores the fact that the Spanish Inquisition was centuries before the French captured Toledo.

Regardless of Poe's mangled history, as a study of unrelieved torture and horror, the story is hugely effective, building suspense through sensations of fear and an atmosphere of unremitting doom.

## UPON THE VULTURE EYE

Around this time, he also wrote another of his best-loved stories, 'The Tell-Tale Heart', a tense, first-person study in terror, narrated by a person presumed to be a man, although it is never made clear. He is clearly insane but believes himself not to be.

Poe submitted 'The Tell-Tale Heart' to the *Boston Miscellany* whose editor rejected it but added that he might accept a story 'if Mr Poe would condescend to furnish more quiet articles.' Of course, the rejection might have been revenge for Poe's slating of the editor's work the previous year, describing it as 'insufferably tedious and dull.'

The story finally appeared in the first issue of James Russell Lowell's new magazine, *The Pioneer*. Unfortunately, *The Pioneer* went bankrupt immediately after publication when Lowell became ill and Poe did not get paid. He wrote to Lowell explaining that, in the circumstances he would not chase payment: 'As for the few dollars you owe me ... I may be poor, but must be very much poorer, indeed, when I even think of demanding them.'

## A WOEBEGONE POE

Money still at the forefront of his mind, Poe now turned to the possibility of a government desk job. His friend and fellow writer, Frederick W. Thomas (1806 – 66), had written to him the previous year asking him if he would be interested in working at the Customs House in Washington. Thomas was a friend of the son of President Tyler and had some influence.

The job itself sounded like a walk in the park. 'You stroll into your office a little after nine in the morning leisurely,' wrote Thomas, 'and you stroll from it a little after two in the afternoon homeward to dinner, and return no more that day.'

The wages were $1,500 a year and Poe jumped at the chance, leaving Philadelphia on March 8, 1843 for an interview in Washington. The trip was a disaster. Thomas was unwell and, anyway, there were twelve hundred applications for the job. Soon, as he waited for news of an interview, nervous and bored in a strange city, Poe began to drink.

83

# THE PIT AND THE PENDULUM

The story is set during the Spanish Inquisition when the narrator is brought to trial and sentenced to death. He faints when his sentence is pronounced, awaking to find himself in total darkness, he knows not where. He is baffled because the normal mode of execution is *auto-da-fe* – burning at the stake – or hanging. He stands up, fearing he has been locked up in a tomb, and takes a few steps.

Believing himself to be in one of Toledo's notorious dungeons, he decides to explore the place. He tears off a piece of his clothing and attaches it to the wall so that he can measure the extent of his prison by walking around its perimeter, counting his steps until he returns to the piece of cloth. But he stumbles and falls to the ground where he drifts off to sleep.

When he awakens, he finds beside him water and bread that he devours hungrily before exploring the prison that he estimates to be about a hundred paces around. Crossing the room, which is still enveloped in darkness, he trips on the hem of his robe and as he lies on the ground, realizes that his head is dangling over a hole. There is a deep, circular pit in the center of the dungeon with water at the bottom as he discovers when he drops a stone into it. Falling asleep again, he wakes to find more bread and water. He drinks but immediately falls asleep, realizing that the water must be drugged.

When he awakens, the prison is dimly lit and he sees that he has overestimated its size. He is tied to a wooden board by a long strap that goes round his body. There is a plate of meat beside him, but no water. Looking up, he notices the figure of Time painted on the ceiling and instead of holding the customary scythe, he is holding a pendulum contraption that is swinging back and forth.

*There was something, however, in the appearance of this machine which caused me to regard it more attentively. While I gazed directly upward at it (for its position was immediately over my own) I fancied that I saw it in motion. In an instant afterward the fancy was confirmed. Its sweep was brief, and of course slow. I watched it for some minutes, somewhat in fear, but more in wonder.*

He is distracted by rats that are now swarming around his food but when he looks upwards again he sees that the swinging pendulum is descending towards him and its trajectory will bring its sharp edge directly over his heart. He has an idea, and rubs some of the meat from his plate onto the leather strap that is restraining him.

The rats are attracted by the food and, climbing on top of the narrator, begin to eat the meat, at the same time gnawing their way through the strap. He returns his attention to the pendulum and just as it swings directly above his heart he frees his hands and stops its swing. He stands up and the pendulum starts to rise again towards the ceiling. The Inquisitors, he realizes, have in all likelihood been watching his every move.

Next, the walls of the prison heat up and begin to move inwards, forcing him towards the pit in the middle of the dungeon. When he has barely any space to stand on, the walls cool down although it may still be too late as he begins to faint and fall towards the pit. Suddenly, he is saved.

*An outstretched arm caught my own as I fell, fainting, into the abyss. It was that of General Lasalle. The French army had entered Toledo. The Inquisition was in the hands of its enemies.*

*Down—steadily down it crept. To the right—to the left—far and wide—with the shriek of a damned spirit.* Illustration for 'The Pit and the Pendulum' by Harry Clarke, 1919.

# THE TELL-TALE HEART

The narrator has suffered from a nervous condition of some kind that, he claims, has sharpened his senses, so that he can hear 'all things in the heaven and the earth.' But, he insists, he is not mad. 'Observe,' he says, 'how healthily—how calmly I can tell you the whole story.'

He shares a house with an old man who has 'the eye of a vulture—a pale blue eye, with a film over it.' This eye drives the narrator to distraction and although he says he loves the old man and that he has never done him any wrong, he resolves to kill him, thus freeing himself of the eye forever.

The week before he carries out his plan, he had been extremely nice to the old man but every night, he quietly opened his door a little and put his head through the opening. He also slipped a lantern into the opening and undid it just enough for a tiny sliver of light to fall upon the 'vulture eye.'

On the eighth night, he does as before, but he accidentally makes a noise that stirs the old man who sits up in bed, shouting 'Who's there?' For a whole hour they remain like that, the narrator with his head and the lantern through the open door and the old man sitting up in bed, listening.

The old man is terrified and utters a noise, 'the sound of human terror.' The narrator opens the lamp a little and the 'single ray of light shot from out and fell full upon the vulture eye' which was wide open, 'all dull blue, with a horrible veil over it' that chills the narrator's bones. He hears a sound, the beating of the old man's heart, 'a low, dull, quick sound, such as a watch makes when inside a piece of cotton.'

As the old man's terror increases and his heart beats faster and louder, the narrator becomes angry and afraid that a neighbor will hear the sound. He bursts into the room and smothers him with the heavy bed. He then dismembers the corpse and places the body parts below the floorboards of the old man's bedroom.

There is a knock at the door and he opens it to find two policemen. A neighbor has reported hearing a noise as if someone is in distress. The narrator invites them in and lets them search the house.

He then pulls chairs into the old man's room and sits them down just above the spot where the body is concealed. The narrator begins to hear a noise. '… after a while, I felt myself getting weak and wished them gone. My head hurt, and I had a ringing in my ears; but still they sat and talked. The ringing became more severe. I talked more freely to do away with the feeling. But it continued until, at length, I found that the noise was not within my ears.'

He becomes increasingly agitated, but the police officers remain pleasant and smile at him. Suddenly, he can take no more.

*'Villains!' I cried, 'Pretend no more! I admit the deed! Tear up the floorboards! Here, here! It is the beating of the hideous heart!'*

*The old man's hour had come! With a loud yell, I threw open the lantern and leaped into the room.* Illustration of 'The Tell-Tale Heart' by Harry Clarke, 1923.

# JAMES RUSSELL LOWELL

The American Romantic poet, James Russell Lowell was born in 1819, son of a wealthy Boston Unitarian minister. He graduated from Harvard in 1838, having been a rebellious and difficult student. In 1843, he launched *The Pioneer*, with contributions from Nathaniel Hawthorne, poet John Whittier, and Edgar Allan Poe.

Lowell's earliest published poems appeared in the *Southern Literary Messenger* and he wrote a series on 'Anti-Slavery in the United States' for the *London Daily News*. In 1845, he published *Conversations on Some of the Old Poets* and in 1848 the satire *A Fable for Critics* was published anonymously. In it he lampooned, in a good-natured way, his fellow poets and critics.

Poe was referred to as part genius and 'two-fifths sheer fudge,' to which he took great exception. His review of the book in the *Messenger* was not flattering, describing it as 'loose—ill-conceived and feebly executed, as well in detail as in general … we confess some surprise at his putting forth so unpolished a performance.'

In 1846, at the outbreak of America's war with Mexico, Lowell penned a satirical poem in the Yankee dialect. From that, in 1848, came the *Biglow Papers*, one of the biggest books of the year, selling 1,500 copies in the first week alone. Sadly, he made no profit from the book, having had to pay the cost of printing himself. Denouncing both the Mexican War and war in general, the book featured three main characters, each of whom represented different aspects of American life and spoke in authentic American dialects.

After losing his mother, wife, daughter and son within a short space of time, Lowell suffered from depression, leading his friend, the poet Longfellow, to describe him as 'lonely and desolate.'

But he took the position of Professor of Modern Languages and Literature at Harvard in 1855 and from 1857, he edited the *Atlantic Monthly*.

The second series of *Biglow Papers* appeared during the American Civil War in which he was a fervent abolitionist. In 1877, he was appointed U.S. Ambassador to Spain and in 1880 was transferred to Great Britain where he remained until 1885. He died on August 12, 1891, aged seventy-two.

He is reported to have been walking around behaving eccentrically and insulting anyone he came into contact with, including the man trying to get him the job, Frederick Thomas. His friend Jesse Dow (1809 – 50), realizing that something had to be done, wrote to a publisher friend of Poe in Philadelphia: 'I think it advisable for you to come and safely see him home. Mrs Poe is in a bad state of health, and I charge you, as you have a soul to be saved, not to say a word to her about him until he arrives with you.' Maria Clemm was waiting at Philadelphia station to collect him on his woebegone return.

Poe was again forced to write groveling letters of apology to those he had offended: 'Don't say a word about the cloak turned inside out, or other peccadilloes of that nature ... Forgive my petulance and don't believe I think all I said.' Interestingly, Thomas indicated that, as others had noticed, it did not take much to get Edgar Poe drunk:

> I have seen a great deal of Poe, and it was his excessive, and at times marked sensibility which forced him into his 'frolics', rather than any mere appetite for drink, but if he took but one glass of weak wine or beer or cider the Rubicon of the cup was passed with him, and it almost always ended in excess and sickness.

However, his old friend, Lambert Wilmer, was perhaps a little more realistic when he said, 'It gives me inexpressible pain to notice the vagaries to which he has lately become subject. Poor fellow!—he is not a teetotaller by any means and I fear he is going headlong to destruction, moral, physical, and intellectual.'

## VIGOROUS, PUNGENT AND ORIGINAL

Poe focused again on publishing his own magazine, the name now changed to *Stylus*. He told his friend James Russell Lowell, 'How dreadful is the present state of our Literature! We want two things, certainly:— an International Copyright Law, and a well-founded Monthly Journal, of sufficient ability, circulation, and character, to control and give tone to, our Letters.'

Early in 1843, he created a partnership with Thomas Clarke who was the publisher of the Philadelphia *Saturday Museum*, to publish his magazine. In February, he even issued a prospectus for *Stylus* announcing that it would be:

> ... more varied and more unique [sic];—more vigorous, more pungent, more original, more individual, and more independent. It will discuss not only the Belles-Lettres, but, very thoroughly, the Fine Arts, with the Drama; and, more in brief, will give each month, a Retrospect of our Political History ...
>
> It shall, in fact, be the chief purpose of the Stylus, to become known as a journal wherein may be found, at all times, upon all subjects within its legitimate reach, a sincere and a fearless opinion.

## PLANS IN TATTERS

In February, Clarke used his magazine to publish a biographical essay on Poe, written by the Philadelphia poet, Henry Hirst (1813 – 74), and intended to increase Poe's profile in the lead-up to the launch of *Stylus*. Based on material Poe himself had supplied, the piece perpetuated the myth of him having spent time in Greece and St. Petersburg, stories that were believed for the next hundred years.

There were extracts from his poetry and comments from others in praise of his work. There was also a description of him aged thirty-four, as he now was. '... he is somewhat slender, about five feet eight inches in height, and well proportioned; his complexion is rather fair; his eyes are gray and restless, exhibiting a marked nervousness; while the mouth indicates great decision of character; his forehead is extremely broad ... His hair is nearly black and partially curling.'

By May, his plans for *Stylus* were in tatters. His drinking had begun to concern Clarke but more importantly, *Saturday Museum*, was beginning to struggle, leading him to withdraw his offer of financial support. Poe moved the family into a smaller house where he was fortunate enough to have an understanding landlord who did not pressure him unduly when, as often was the case, the rent was overdue.

The five-story cottage in North Seventh Street, in the Spring Garden District, had a garden down one side and a porch to the rear. They rented out the front room to a lodger and themselves lived in the middle room. A neighbor described Poe at the time as always having a serious expression on his face and looking careworn. She added, '... he, his wife, and Mrs Clemm kept to themselves. They had the reputation of being very reserved— we thought because of their poverty and his great want of success.'

## THE GOLD BUG SENSATION

Then in June 1843, at one of his lowest points, Poe entered another newspaper short-story competition. The *Dollar Newspaper* was a 'weekly family journal' and not really Poe's style but in the issue of June 14, it announced that the winner of their short story competition was:

> THE GOLD BUG ... *written by Edgar Allan Poe, Esq., of this city—and a capital story the committee pronounce it to be.*

'The Gold Bug' utilizes Poe's skill with cipher-solving, focusing on the decryption of a very tough puzzle. It also involves pirates and a reference to Captain Kidd who had been in the news the year before when a woman claiming to be his sister attempted to make a legal claim on his treasure. The only problem had been that Captain Kidd had been hanged in 1701 and she would probably have had to be well over 140 years old to be his sister.

'The Gold Bug' became a sensation, the *Dollar Newspaper* reporting *'A GREAT RUSH FOR THE PRIZE STORY!'* and running to second and third printings. Suddenly Edgar A. Poe was hot. *Graham's* magazine swiftly issued a pamphlet, 'The Prose Romances of Edgar A. Poe, Volume 1' and at Philadelphia's American Theater a stage version of the story was hastily put together and staged. A Baltimore store sold 'Gold Bug' lottery tickets. In May 1844, Poe estimated that around 300,000 copies of the story had been circulated but, of course, none of the proceeds came to Poe. All he got was the hundred dollars prize money.

## THE DEMONS OF DAMNATION

In August of 1843, Poe wrote 'The Black Cat', featuring a narrator who is fond of black cats. Interestingly, he is in the grip of the 'Fiend of Intemperance' which badly affects his life. Like 'The Tell-Tale Heart', it is a story of the psychology of guilt in which a murderer commits a crime, thinks he has got away with it but is revealed by his own actions.

More than any of Poe's stories, 'The Black Cat' illustrates the ability of the human mind to watch its own destruction while being powerless to halt it. The narrator of 'The Black Cat' is fully aware of his mental deterioration, and during the story, he recognizes the changes within him. He tries to prevent it happening, but ultimately, he finds himself unable to reverse his spiral into madness.

In virtually all of Poe's tales, we know nothing about the narrator's background and, like 'The Tell-Tale Heart,' the narrator begins this story by asserting that he is not mad – 'Yet, mad am I not—.' At the same time, he wants to tell the world a sane version of the events that 'have terrified—have tortured— have destroyed me.' During the process of proving his sanity, we clearly see the actions of a madman.

```
53‡‡†305))6*;4826)4‡.)4‡);806*;48†8
agoodglassinthebishopshostelinthede

¶60))85;1‡(;:‡*8†83(88)5*†;46(;88*96
vilsseatfortyonedegreesandthirteenmi

*?;8)*‡(;485);5*†2:*‡(;4956*2(5*—4)8
nutesnortheastandbynorthmainbranchse

¶8*;4069285);)6†8)4‡‡;1(‡9;48081;8:8‡
venthlimbeastsideshootfromthelefteyeo

1;48†85;4)485†528806*81(‡9;48;(88;4
fthedeathsheadabeelinefromthetreeth

(‡?34;48)4‡;161;:188;‡?;
roughtheshotfiftyfeetout
```

> The Gold Bug's decoded cryptogram was solved by
> a simple substitution cipher using letter frequencies.
> Though he did not invent 'secret writing' or cryptography,
> Poe certainly popularized it during his time.

## THE LYCEUM MOVEMENT

July 1843 saw Poe trying something else to bring in a regular income. He registered to study law in the office of Henry Hirst who had written the biography of him in the *Saturday Museum*. But his studies did not last long and soon he was back trying to earn a living from writing.

Then he thought of lecturing which was very popular in America at the time. Initiatives such as the Lyceum movement became important in adult education at a time when university education was still the privilege of the few. The Lyceum movement sought to improve the social, intellectual and moral fabric of society with lectures, dramatic performances, classroom-style instruction and debates. At the very least, they might keep people out of bars and taverns.

There was a circuit of halls across the United States where lecturers, entertainers and readers could perform. Charles Dickens had taken advantage of this hunger for learning, but Poe described it as 'the present absurd rage for lecturing.'

Nonetheless, he signed up to deliver a lecture in Philadelphia on 'Poetry in America', to take place on November 21, 1843.

## THE FEARLESS AND FAVORLESS TOUR

He was advertised as the *'Author of the Gold Bug, &c.'* but people also wanted to hear the man whose reviews were fearless and favorless. The hall was full to overflowing and the hundreds outside who were refused admission were unable to hear him destroy, in his 'tomahawk' style, Rufus Griswold's recently published anthology, *The Poets and Poetry of America*.

Poe earned $100 for the evening. One newspaper said that 'the Lecture was received with the most enthusiastic demonstrations of applause, and it was agreed by all, that it was second to none, if not superior to all lectures ever delivered at the Wirt Institute.'

It was a lecture that Poe would return to in Wilmington the following week and in New York in February 1844. By spring of 1844, he had delivered the lecture in a number of nearby cities and would have to go further afield if he wanted to continue in this type of work. But that was risky – given his track record when away from home …

# THE GOLD BUG

The narrator is a friend to William Legrand, a descendent of an old New Orleans Huguenot family who, having lost his fortune, now lives in a shack on Sullivan's Island nine miles from Charleston, South Carolina.

Legrand lives a simple life, with only a Newfoundland dog and a servant – a former slave named Jupiter – for company. He spends much of his time fishing, exploring the island and collecting shells and entomological specimens.

On a cold day in October, the narrator pays Legrand a visit, having not seen him for some time. Legrand tells him about a bizarre bug he has found. It is brilliant gold in color with three black spots and long antennae. He has loaned the bug to a soldier from Fort Moultrie and is, therefore, unable to show it to the narrator but he draws a picture of it on a piece of paper.

As the narrator takes the paper, his hand is knocked by Legrand's dog, causing it to move closer to the fire. He now sees the outline of a skull on the paper instead of the insect. Visibly upset, Legrand holds a candle up to the paper to examine it more closely before locking it in a drawer in his desk.

A month later, Jupiter arrives at the narrator's house with a note from Legrand, begging him to come to his shack as soon as he can. The note's tone makes the narrator uneasy and he worries that perhaps Legrand is unwell. Jupiter confirms that his master is acting strangely, suggesting that he has been bitten by the gold bug and it has affected his behavior. He has been talking about gold in his sleep.

They go to Sullivan's Island where Legrand greets them excitedly, telling the narrator that the beetle will soon make him rich. He shows him the insect in a glass case but the narrator insists that Legrand is ill and promises to stay with him for a few days until he is recovered. Legrand, however, insists that the only cure would be for the narrator to accompany him on an expedition. The narrator agrees on condition that when they return he must let him take care of him.

They set out, carrying a scythe and shovels and with Legrand carrying the beetle, swinging from a piece of cord he has attached to it. They board a small boat to the mainland and walk for several hours before arriving at a remote spot. Legrand stops at a large tree and asks Jupiter to climb it, taking the beetle with him.

Jupiter protests but eventually climbs the tree. On a dead limb high up, he finds a skull nailed to it. Unsurprised, Legrand orders his servant to drop the beetle through the skull's left eye and let it dangle. Legrand then measures out fifty feet beyond where the beetle has dropped and asks the narrator and Jupiter to start digging. They dig for two hours but find nothing.

As they prepare to leave, they realize that Jupiter does not know his right from his left and has dropped the beetle through the wrong eye-socket. They return and try again. This time, as they dig, they uncover two skeletons under which is a wooden chest. Inside the chest is a hoard of treasure. Legrand delightedly mocks the narrator for believing him to be insane.

Legrand now launches into a lengthy explanation of how he knew exactly where the treasure could be located. He explains that he had found the piece of paper – in reality a thin parchment – close to where he had found the beetle. When he had further heated the piece of paper he discovered on it a series of symbols and numbers. He deciphered it, finding the message 'A good glass in the bishop's hostel in the devil's seat—forty-one degrees and thirteen minutes—north-east and by north—main branch seventh limb east side—shoot from the left eye of the death's-head—a bee-line from the tree through the shot fifty feet out.'

He had asked around if anyone had heard of a 'Bishop's Hotel or Hostel and an old woman had led him to a large rock known as Bessop's Castle.' He had found a ledge that was the 'devil's seat', went home to get a telescope and spotted the skull in the tree when gazing at an angle of forty-one degrees. The rest was fairly straightforward.

Thus, the narrator becomes a wealthy man and Legrand's fortune and position in society are restored.

*Main branch seventh limb east side—shoot from the left eye of the death's-head.* Illustration by Herpin for 'The Gold-Bug', 1895.

# THE BLACK CAT

The narrator explains that he is not mad and is not dreaming and that, as he is to die tomorrow, he wishes to unburden his soul. He wants to place before the world a series of incidents – 'mere household events' – that have terrified him recently.

He was, he says, a docile, gentle child which led to him being mocked by his friends. Fond of animals, he was indulged by his parents who bought a variety of pets for him. His love of animals never left him and, if anything, grew as he got older.

He married young and, fortunately, his wife also liked animals. They had a variety of pets, including a cat named Pluto, 'a remarkably large and beautiful animal, entirely black and sagacious to an astonishing degree.' His wife reminded him, jokingly, that cats are sometimes thought to be witches in disguise.

Pluto followed the narrator everywhere. However, as time passed, the narrator became increasingly addicted to alcohol, the 'Fiend of Intemperance', and his character began to change. He was insensitive to others, was moody and irritable. He even became violent towards his wife. He still looked after Pluto, however, even though he treated his other animals badly. Eventually, even Pluto became a victim of his bad temper.

One night, the narrator returned home drunk and believing the cat to be avoiding him, became very angry. He seized the animal and with a pen-knife, gouged out one of its eyes. The next morning he felt great remorse for what he had done. The cat recovered but would run away whenever the narrator approached. This angered him and one day he grabbed it, slipped a noose around its neck and hung it from the branch of a tree. He carried out this deed with the 'bitterest remorse', knowing that his soul was now damned.

That night the narrator awoke to find his house on fire and he, his wife and servant only just managed to escape with their lives. When he visited the ruins of the building the following morning, he found a crowd standing around one of the few walls to remain standing.

*About this wall a dense crowd were collected, and many persons seemed to be examining a particular portion of it with very minute and eager attention. The words 'strange!' 'singular!' and other similar expressions, excited my curiosity. I approached and saw, as if graven in bas relief upon the white surface, the figure of a gigantic cat. The impression was given with an accuracy truly marvelous. There was a rope about the animal's neck.*

The narrator was both amazed and terrified but reasoned that the cat had been cut down by the crowd during the fire the previous night and thrown into his chamber to wake him. The falling walls had compressed the cat's body into the plaster which had only recently been applied, 'the lime of which, with the flames, and the *ammonia* from the carcass, had then accomplished the portraiture as I saw it.'

He decided to find another cat to take Pluto's place and one night in a bar he spied a black cat with a splotch of white on its chest. It followed him home and became a part of the household. The narrator, however, soon took a dislike to the creature and began to avoid its presence. He discovered later that, like Pluto, it had only one eye.

The more he avoided it, the more it seemed to want to follow him around. He began to feel dread around it as the cat provided a constant reminder of his dastardly deed. He began to have bad dreams and decided to kill this cat, too. As he was about to smash its skull with a blow of an axe, his wife stopped him.

Then, instead of killing the cat, he turned on her and brought the axe down upon her head, killing her. To hide her body, he decided to brick it up in a cellar wall after which he looked for the cat but it had disappeared. That night he had his first peaceful night since the cat had entered their lives.

Four days after the murder, the police arrived to search his premises for his missing wife but finding nothing, were about to leave. He arrogantly boasted to them about how well his house has been constructed and rapped on the wall behind which lay the body of his wife.

*But may God shield and deliver me from the fangs of the Arch-Fiend! No sooner had the reverberation of my blows sunk into silence, than I was answered by a voice from within the tomb!—by a cry, at first muffled and broken, like the sobbing of a child, and then quickly swelling into one long, loud, and continuous scream, utterly anomalous and inhuman—a howl—a wailing shriek, half of horror and half of triumph, such as might have arisen only out of hell, conjointly from the throats of the damned in their agony and of the demons that exult in the damnation.*

The police immediately began to tear down the wall, uncovering the already rotting corpse of his wife and 'Upon its head, with red extended mouth and solitary eye of fire, sat the hideous beast whose craft had seduced me into murder, and whose informing voice had consigned me to the hangman. I had walled the monster up within the tomb!'

It was the cat.

## 'The Black Cat'
### by Aubrey Beardsley
### (1872 – 1898)

This illustration from 1894 was for one of Poe's darkest tales, evoking many black cat superstitions. Poe owned a black cat himself, and explained his feelings, 'The writer of this article is the owner of one of the most remarkable black cats in the world—and this is saying much; for it will be remembered that black cats are all of them witches.'

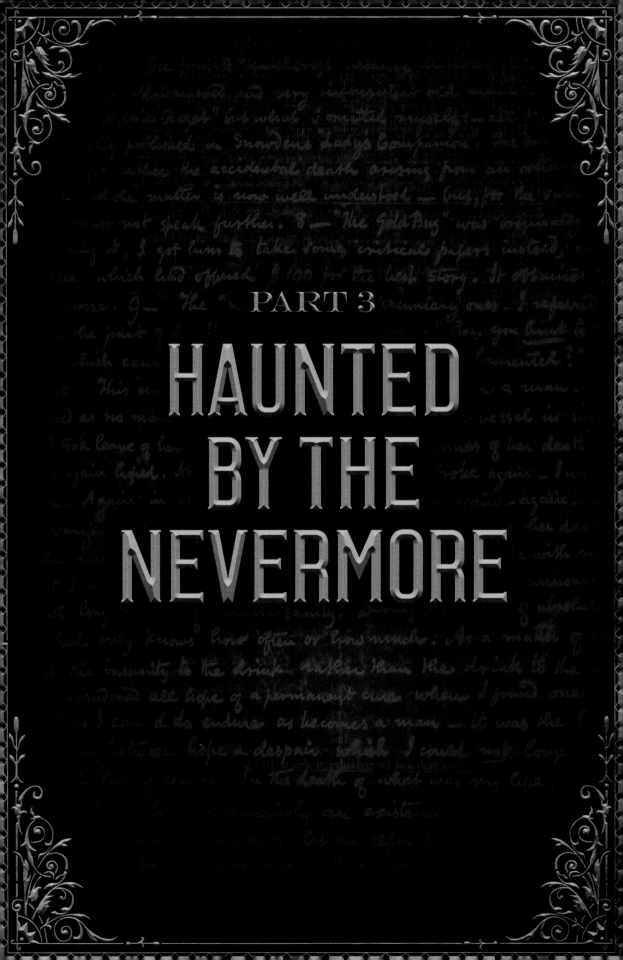

# PART 3

# HAUNTED BY THE NEVERMORE

And his eyes have all the seeming
of a demon's that is dreaming,
And the lamp-light o'er him streaming
throws his shadow on the floor;
And my soul from out that shadow
that lies floating on the floor
Shall be lifted—nevermore!

Edgar Allan Poe *from* 'The Raven'

# CHAPTER 7

# THE SOLEMN SLUMBERS OF THE DEAD

As the center of the publishing and newspaper world, it seemed only natural for Poe to be in New York. In April 1844, therefore, Poe moved with Virginia to the city in which he would spend the rest of his life. Having found accommodation at 130 Greenwich Street, in southern Manhattan, he wrote to Maria to let her know they were well. He remarked on not having eaten for a while when they arrived at their lodgings.

*Last night, we had the nicest tea you ever drank, strong & hot—wheat bread & rye bread—cheese—tea cakes (elegant) a great dish (2 dishes) of elegant ham, and 2 of cold veal, piled up like a mountain and large slices—3 dishes of cakes, and every thing in the greatest profusion. No fear of starving here. The landlady seemed as if she couldn't press us enough, and we were at home directly ... [This morning] I ate the first hearty breakfast I have eaten since I left our little home. Sis [Virginia] is delighted and we are both in excellent spirits. She has coughed hardly any and had no night sweat. She is now mending my pants which I tore against a nail.*

Maria soon joined them and they lived in a series of different lodgings, struggling to pay the rent and finding ever-cheaper places to stay. Poe was a popular lecturer and supported them in that way, as well as with pieces of journalism and by borrowing from friends, as usual.

## BEING A MECHANICAL PARAGRAPHIST

He had been writing odd pieces for the New York *Evening Mirror* for about eighteen months when the editor, Nathaniel Parker Willis (1806 – 1867) offered him a job as assistant editor and 'mechanical paragraphist.' The pay would be $750 a year and in return he had to 'sit at a desk, in a corner of the editorial room, ready to be called upon for any of the miscellaneous work of the moment—announcing news, condensing statements, answering correspondents, noticing amusements—everything but the writing of a "leader", or constructing any article upon which his peculiar idiosyncrasy of mind could be impressed.'

It was not the type of job that Poe saw himself doing. After all, he had been editor of several magazines, but the desperate state of his finances made it an offer he couldn't refuse. In November, he began to publish in the *Evening Mirror* what he called 'Marginalia' – notes and thoughts that came out of his deep and extensive reading. He would continue to publish these in various periodicals until he died.

## PURLOINING A PLACE IN HISTORY

In spring 1844, Poe produced 'The Purloined Letter', the third of his detective stories featuring the extraordinary ratiocinative powers of Monsieur C. Auguste Dupin. Just before its publication in *The Gift for 1845*,

# NATHANIEL PARKER WILLIS

The popular and well-liked author, poet and editor, Nathaniel Parker Willis was born into a family of publishers in Portland, Maine in 1806. His father and grandfather, each of whom was also named Nathaniel Willis, both owned newspapers, his grandfather proprietor of several in Massachusetts and Virginia, his father founding *Youth's Companion*, a newspaper for children. Willis would become the highest paid newspaper editor of his day.

He attended Yale University where he began to write and publish poetry and after graduating, worked overseas as a correspondent for the *New York Mirror*. He was criticized by some for reporting private conversations. This created a great deal of trouble for him, leading on one occasion to a bloodless duel with the writer and editor, Captain Frederick Marryat, author of *Mr Midshipman Easy* and *The Children of the New Forest*. Moving back to New York in 1837, he began to establish a reputation as a writer, bringing in $100 per article and earning up to $10,000 a year.

In 1844, along with George Pope Morris, he reorganized the weekly newspaper, the *New York Mirror*, re-naming it the *Evening Mirror* and making it a daily. In 1846, Willis left the *Evening Mirror* to launch the *National Press*, eight months later renamed the *Home Journal*. It would be re-named again as *Town & Country* in 1901 and is still being published to this day.

He championed many writers of the day, including the women poets Frances Sargent Osgood, Anne Lynch Botta, Grace Greenwood and Julia Ward Howe. Many important works received good reviews in the pages of the magazine including Henry David Thoreau's *Walden* and Nathaniel Hawthorne's *The Blithedale Romance*.

Willis died after a long illness on his sixty-first birthday, January 20, 1867. His pallbearers included Henry Wadsworth Longfellow, James Russell Lowell and Oliver Wendell Holmes.

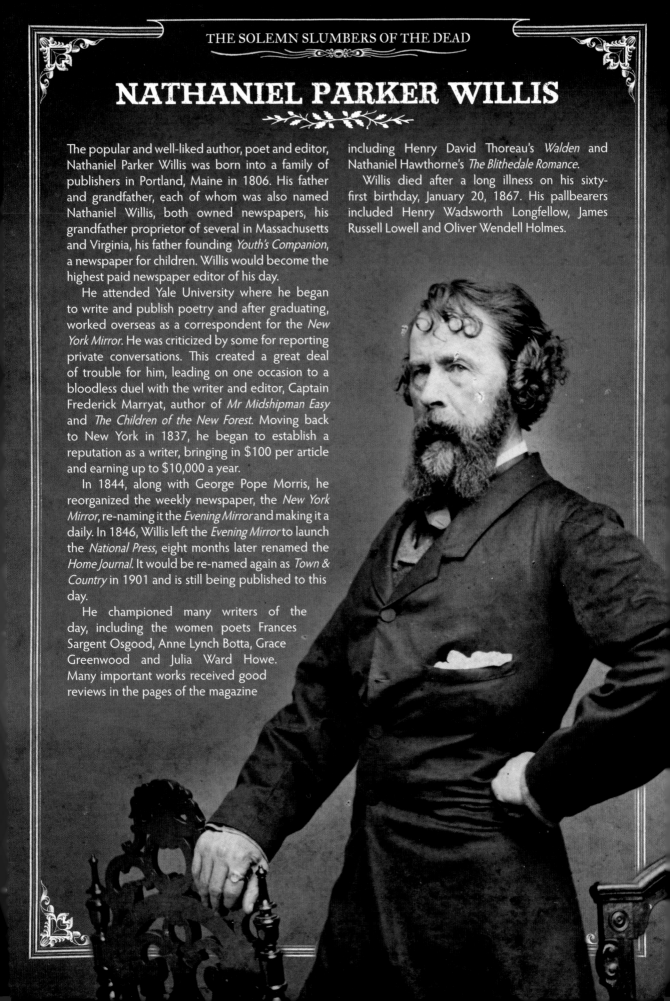

# THE PURLOINED LETTER

The narrator is discussing with the Parisian amateur detective C. Auguste Dupin some of his most famous cases when they are interrupted by G—, the Prefect of Police. G— wishes to discuss a case with the famous detective.

A letter has been stolen from the bedroom of an unnamed young woman in the royal apartments by the important government Minister D—. The letter contains information that could harm the reputation of a powerful person.

The young woman was reading the letter when the person whom it concerned came into the room. She quickly put it down, but the sinister and unscrupulous Minister D— also walked in and noticing what the letter contained, stole it. He now has considerable power over the young lady.

Dupin asks whether the Minister's residence has been searched as in order for the letter to be useful it would have to be readily available. G— assures him that a search has been made but no trace has been found. A search of the Minister himself failed to reveal the missive.

There is a very generous reward on offer and the Prefect says that he is willing to put a great deal of effort into finding the letter. Dupin asks him to describe it again and suggests that the police conduct another search.

A month later there is another visit from the Prefect who admits that the letter has still not been found, even with an increased reward of 50,000 francs. Dupin instructs him to write a cheque on the spot. The Prefect does so, and when he hands it to Dupin, Dupin, in return, hands over the letter. Astonished, G— rushes off to restore the letter to its rightful owner while Dupin explains to the narrator how he has come by it.

He explains that the police are competent enough but only within their own limited capabilities. The Prefect, he muses, takes Minister D— for a fool simply because he is a poet. D— was clever enough to realize that the police would think he had devised an elaborate hiding place for the letter, but instead, he had hidden it in plain sight.

Dupin describes a visit he made to the Minister at his hotel. He wore a pair of green spectacles that he said were because of his weak eyes but the true purpose of the glasses was to hide his eyes as he searched for the letter. He found it half-torn, in a cheap card rack, hanging from a dirty ribbon.

Engaging D— in conversation, he examined the letter a little more closely, finding that it differed from the one the Prefect had described. It was written in a different hand and was sealed with D—'s monogram and not the coat of arms of the family concerned. Furthermore, it looked as if it had been rolled one way and then another.

Dupin worked out that D— had written a new address on the reverse of the stolen letter, re-folded it the opposite way and then sealed it with his own seal. So that he might have an excuse to return the following day, Dupin left a gold snuff box behind as if accidentally.

When he returned, he struck up the same conversation they had enjoyed the previous day but they were suddenly interrupted by the sound of a pistol shot and screams from the street outside. Dupin had organized for this incident to take place as a diversionary tactic.

When D— went to find out what was going on, Dupin took D—'s letter, replacing it with a duplicate version so that D— would not suspect what had occurred. He adds that he is hopeful that D— will try to use the letter and in this way, hopefully, his political career will be brought to a dramatic close.

> *In this matter, I act as a partisan of the lady concerned. For eighteen months the Minister has had her in his power. She has now him in hers; since, being unaware that the letter is not in his possession, he will proceed with his exactions as if it was. Thus will he inevitably commit himself, at once, to his political destruction. His downfall, too, will not be more precipitate than awkward … He is the monstrum horrendum, an unprincipled man of genius.*

It transpires that D— had once done an 'evil turn' to Dupin in Vienna and Dupin had warned him then that he would not forget. In order for D— to know who has been responsible for stealing the letter from him, he has written a cryptic message on the blank sheet he has left behind:

*Un dessein si funeste, S'il n'est digne d'Atrée, est digne de Thyeste.*
(If such a sinister design isn't worthy of Atreus, it is worthy of Thyestes.)

Illustration for 'The Purloined Letter' by Frederic Lix, 1862.

Poe wrote to James Russell Lowell that he thought 'The Purloined Letter' to be 'perhaps the best of my tales of ratiocination' and the editor of *The Gift* described it as 'one of the aptest illustrations which could well be conceived of that curious play of two minds in one person.'

Where there was brutal violence in 'The Murders in the Rue Morgue', there is a great deal more subtlety in the plot of 'The Purloined Letter'. And it has little action, most of it taking place in a room where Dupin and the narrator are seated. Its plotting is tighter than 'Marie Rogêt', the story building to an ending that ties up all the loose ends.

In terms of characterization, Poe has learned from 'The Gold Bug' and the characters are more rounded – for instance, G— the 'by-the-book' police officer and the narrator now with some decent dialogue and a part to play. There is even a developing rapport between Dupin and his friend that would be repeated in countless detective partnerships down through the years.

The detective story had well and truly arrived with all its conventions in place and the strange feeling of satisfaction derived by the reader at the end when the mystery has been unraveled. He did not know it at the time, but Edgar Allan Poe need never have picked up his pen again and his place in literary history would still be assured.

## THE GREAT BALLOON HOAX

A sensational headline appeared on the front cover of the New York newspaper, the *Sun*, on April 13, 1844:

### ASTOUNDING NEWS!
#### BY EXPRESS, VIA NORFOLK!

THE
### ATLANTIC CROSSED
IN
### THREE DAYS!
### SIGNAL TRIUMPH
OF
### MR MONCK MASON'S
### *FLYING*
# MACHINE!!!

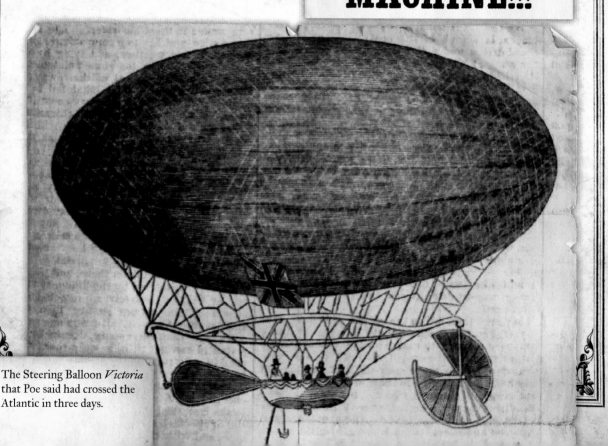

The Steering Balloon *Victoria* that Poe said had crossed the Atlantic in three days.

*Eight Englishmen, including the aforementioned, aeronaut, Monck Mason, and the popular writer, Harrison Ainsworth, were reported to have crossed the Atlantic in a giant airship named the Victoria. 'The Great Problem is at length solved! The air, as well as the earth and the ocean, has been subdued by science, and will become a common and convenient highway for mankind.'*

It was, of course, a hoax, perpetrated by Edgar Poe just a week after his arrival in New York. It took the city by storm, Poe reporting that 'the whole square surrounding the *Sun* building was literally besieged, blocked up— ingress and egress being alike impossible, for a period soon after sunrise until about two o'clock P.M. ... I never witnessed more intense excitement to get possession of a newspaper. As soon as the first few copies made their way into the streets, they were bought up, at almost any price, from the news-boys, who made a profitable speculation.' The excitement did not last long, however, people having been duped once too often by the *Sun*. Paid only his regular fee by the newspaper, Poe once again failed to profit from a good idea.

With this hoax, Poe was once again reflecting on the gullibility of people as well as the hunger for progress that prevailed at the time. It concerned him, as he wrote in a letter to Thomas Chivers: 'I disagree with you in what you say of man's advance towards perfection. Man is now only more active, not wiser, nor more happy, than he was 6,000 years ago.'

## THE GRAVES OF ALL MANKIND

In 1844, Poe also wrote 'The Premature Burial', based on the common nineteenth century fear of being buried alive. It arose partly from the great plagues and diseases of previous times when amongst the masses of people being taken for burial were sometimes found people who were still alive. Being buried alive was not a new theme for Poe, of

course. He had already used it in 'Berenice' and 'The Fall of the House of Usher' and it would come into another of his stories, 'The Cask of Amontillado', written two years after 'The Premature Burial'.

## WRITING 'THE RAVEN'

Meanwhile, Poe continued writing reviews but poetry was still what he loved most. One poet he greatly admired was Elizabeth Barrett (1806 – 61) who later married Robert Browning (1812 – 89). She joined the pantheon of Poe's favorite poets, the other places occupied by Coleridge, Keats, Byron, Moore and Tennyson.

Using the meter of Elizabeth Barrett's poem 'Lady Geraldine's Courtship', he composed some of his most famous lines – the opening phrases of his phenomenally successful poem, 'The Raven'.

*Once upon a midnight dreary, while I pondered, weak and weary,*

*Over many a quaint and curious volume of forgotten lore—*

*While I nodded, nearly napping, suddenly there came a tapping,*

*As of some one gently rapping, rapping at my chamber door.*

*'Tis some visitor,' I muttered, 'tapping at my chamber door—*

*Only this and nothing more.'*

Praised for its musicality, stylized language and eerie supernatural atmosphere, the poem tells of the visit by a mysterious talking raven – standing for intuitive truth – to a student who is bemoaning the loss of his love, Lenore. The raven, seated on a bust of Pallas – representing intellectual wisdom – only exacerbates the sadness of the student by repeating the word 'Nevermore'.

It follows the man's slow descent into madness as he asks the raven a series of questions that are answered negatively. He realizes that after death there will be no reunion with his lost love.

> 'Prophet!' said I, 'thing of evil!—prophet still, if bird or devil!—
>
> Whether Tempter sent, or whether tempest tossed thee here ashore,
>
> Desolate yet all undaunted, on this desert land enchanted—
>
> On this home by Horror haunted—tell me truly, I implore—
>
> Is there—is there balm in Gilead?—tell me—tell me, I implore!'
>
> Quoth the Raven 'Nevermore.'

Inspired in part by the talking raven in Charles Dickens' novel, *Barnaby Rudge*, the poem possesses what Poe described as 'a unity of effect,' a pattern that is easily followed and beautifully delineated by him. It builds through repetition to the ultimate and utter despair of the student.

> And the Raven, never flitting, still is sitting, still is sitting
>
> On the pallid bust of Pallas just above my chamber door;
>
> And his eyes have all the seeming of a demon's that is dreaming,
>
> And the lamp-light o'er him streaming throws his shadow on the floor;
>
> And my soul from out that shadow that lies floating on the floor
>
> Shall be lifted—nevermore!

## SITTING LOOSELY ON HIS CLASSICS

Poe wrote 'The Raven' with the intention of pleasing both the literary elite and the ordinary public and was well aware that he had, indeed, created something special.

When he finished it, he sent a draft to the English poet, Richard Horne (1802 – 84) whose epic poem 'Orion' Poe had admired. He asked him what he thought of 'The Raven' but also requested that Horne pass the poem to Elizabeth Barrett.

Barrett replied to Horne that she found Poe's poem very strange and also took the opportunity to somewhat snootily point out an error in Poe's review of her work. 'There is certainly a power—but ['The Raven'] does not appear to me the natural expression of a sane intellect in whatever mood ... Mr Poe, who attributes the *Oedipus Coloneus* to Aeschylus [it should have been Sophocles] (*vide* review on me), sits somewhat loosely, probably, on his classics.'

## HAUNTED BY THE NEVERMORE

A little later, however, Barrett realized that she had perhaps been a bit churlish, given that he had provided a glowing review of her book and wrote again to Horne: 'Will you tell him—what is quite the truth—that in my own opinion he has dealt with me most generously, and that I thank him for his candor as for a part of his kindness. Will you tell him also that he has given my father pleasure; which is giving it to *me* more than twice. Also, the review is very ably written, and the reviewer had so obviously and thoroughly *read* my poems as to be a wonder among my critics.'

Poe would pay tribute to Elizabeth Barrett by dedicating to her his book *The Raven and Other Poems*, published in November 1845.

In April 1846, after the publication of 'The Raven', Barrett wrote again, thanking Poe for the dedication and describing the impact that the poem had made in England.

> Receiving a book from you seems to authorize or at least encourage me to try to express what I have long felt before—my sense of the high honor you have done me in your country and mine, of the dedication of your poems ...

*Take thy beak from out my heart, and take thy form from off my door! Quoth the raven— 'Nevermore.'* Illustration for the poem 'The Raven', written in 1844.

*Your 'Raven' has produced a sensation, a 'fit of horror,' here in England. Some of my friends are taken by the fear of it and some by the music. I hear of persons haunted by the 'Nevermore,' and one acquaintance of mine who has the misfortune of possessing a 'bust of Pallas' never can bear to look at it in the twilight. I think you would like to be told our great poet, Mr Browning ... was struck much by the rhythm of that poem.*

## THE GREATEST POEM EVER WRITTEN

Poe wrote about the composition of his most famous poem in the essay 'The Philosophy of Composition', written in 1846, in which he cites length, 'unity of effect and a logical method as the indicators of good writing. It appears evident, then, that there is a distinct limit, as regards length, to all works of literary art – the limit of a single sitting – and that, although in certain classes of prose composition, such as *Robinson Crusoe* (demanding no unity), this limit may be advantageously overpassed, it can never properly be overpassed in a poem.'

He was evidently very happy with 'The Raven', as is demonstrated by a reported conversation on a New York street with William Ross Wallace:

*'Wallace,' said Poe, 'I have just written the greatest poem that ever was written.'*

*'Have you?' said Wallace. 'That is a fine achievement.'*

*'Would you like to hear it?' said Poe.*

*'Most certainly,' said Wallace.*

*Thereupon Poe began to read the soon-to-be-famous verse in his best way—which ... was always an impressive and captivating way. When he had finished it he turned to Wallace for his approval of them—when Wallace said:*

*'Poe—they are fine; uncommonly fine.'*

*'Fine?' said Poe, contemptuously. 'Is that all you can say for this poem? I tell you it is the greatest poem that was ever written.'*

It may have been something of an exaggeration to describe 'The Raven' as 'the greatest poem ever written,' but it certainly caused a stir.

## A MASTERLY VERSIFICATION

Poe had originally taken it to George Graham and although he turned down the chance to publish it, he gave him $15 anyway, out of charity. It was sold to *The American Review* for $9 and was due for publication in its February 1845 issue, under the name 'Quarles', a reference to the English poet Francis Quarles who wrote in the sixteenth and seventeenth centuries.

Its first publication with Poe's name on it was on January 29, 1845, in Nathaniel Parker Willis's *Evening Mirror*. Willis introduced it by saying: 'We are permitted to copy (in advance of publication) from the 2d number of *The American Review*, the following remarkable poem by EDGAR POE ... [It is] unsurpassed in English poetry for subtle conception, masterly ingenuity of versification, and consistent, sustaining of imaginative lift ... It will stick to the memory of everybody who reads it.'

## CASTING THE ENCHANTMENT

The morning after publication in the *Mirror*, Edgar Allan Poe woke up to find himself famous. In fact, 'The Raven' became the most popular poem that any American had ever written and it would be published in periodicals across the country, including the *New York Tribune*, the *Broadway Journal*, the *Southern Literary Messenger*, the *Literary Emporium*, the *Saturday Courier* and the *Richmond Examiner*. There were imitations of it and parodies and the word 'Nevermore' was on everyone's lips.

# ELIZABETH BARRETT BROWNING

The English poet, Elizabeth Barrett Browning, was born in 1806 at Coxhoe Hall in Durham, England, the oldest of twelve children. The Barrett family who were part Creole, had lived in Jamaica for two hundred years and she was the first of the family born in England in all that time. In Jamaica, they owned sugar plantations, but Elizabeth's father, Edward Barrett Moulton Barrett, had decided to bring up his family in England, although he retained his interests in the Caribbean.

Educated at home, Elizabeth was a precocious child, having by the age of ten read John Milton's 'Paradise Lost', several Shakespeare plays and a number of other important works of English literature. By twelve, she had penned her first epic poem but two years later developed the lung complaint that would blight the remainder of her life. She was treated with opiates such as laudanum and morphine and would be dependent upon them until she died.

Despite her problems, she taught herself Hebrew so that she could read the Old Testament and became fascinated by Classical Greece. She was also a passionate Christian. In 1826, she published anonymously her collection of poetry, *An Essay on Mind and Other Poems* which reflected her love for the work of Byron and interest in Greek politics.

In 1828, her mother died by which time the abolition of slavery and mismanagement of the Jamaican plantations had seriously reduced the Barrett family income. In 1832, the estate was sold at auction and the family moved to Sidmouth in Devon, England before settling at Gloucester Place in London. In 1833, while in Sidmouth, Elizabeth published her translation of Aeschylus's *Prometheus Unbound*.

She was bitterly opposed to slavery and was dismayed when her father began sending her siblings to Jamaica to help with the family business there. Still under his tyrannical rule in London, she published *The Seraphim and Other Poems* in 1838, but around this time contracted tuberculosis and was forced to spend a year by the sea at Torquay, during which her brother Edward drowned in a sailing accident. She was devastated and became an invalid and a recluse, spending the next five years in her bedroom at her father's house in Wimpole Street in London.

In 1844, she issued the collection entitled simply *Poems* that gained the attention of the hugely successful poet, Robert Browning. In the next twenty months, the couple exchanged 574 letters but their relationship was opposed by Elizabeth's father. They eloped, therefore, in 1846, settling in the Italian city of Florence where the climate was good for her health. In 1850, her *Sonnets from the Portuguese*, dedicated to her husband, and written in secret before the couple eloped, was published. These beautiful love poems are recognized as her best work.

Her later work stressed social and political themes and she published a verse novel, *Aurora Leigh*, in 1857. She died in Florence on June 29, 1861, aged fifty-five.

Elizabeth Barrett Browning (1806 – 1861).

Suddenly, Poe was in demand, lionized at literary soirées and salons at which, dressed in his customary black garb, he would be invited to give a reading of his poem. He would even adjust the light of the room, turning down the lamps in order to create an atmosphere favorable to his delivery.

'Then,' as one witness recalled, 'standing in the center of the apartment he would recite those wonderful lines in the most melodious of voices ... So marvelous was his power as a reader that the auditors would be afraid to draw breath lest the enchanted spell be broken.'

## THE BIRD BEAT THE BUG HOLLOW

Poe was in his element, enjoying mixing in polite society and charming those he met. The poet, Anne Lynch Botta (1815 – 91), reflected on the well-behaved, refined side of his personality, such a contrast to his wild, self-destructive streak.

> *Poe always had the bearing and manners of a gentleman—interesting in conversation, but not monopolizing; polite and engaging, and never, when I saw him, abstracted or dreamy. He was always elegant in his toilet, quiet and unaffected, unpretentious in his manner.*

'The Raven' had succeeded beyond his wildest imaginings in making Poe famous and he claimed to Frederick Thomas that his sole purpose in writing it was to become well known: ' "The Raven" has had a great run—but I wrote it for the express purpose of running—just as I did the "Gold Bug", you know. The bird beat the bug, though, all hollow.'

## THE POWER OF ORIGINALITY

The plaudits flooded in – if the cash did not. *Graham's* ran a biographical essay on Poe written by James Russell Lowell in February 1845. Although noting how unpleasant Poe's harsher reviews could be, Lowell estimated Poe to have significantly contributed to American literature and stated that his name would live on.

> *Mr Poe is at once the most discriminating, philosophical, and fearless critic upon imaginative works who has written in America ... [but he] sometimes seems to mistake his phial of prussic-acid for his inkstand ...*
>
> *Mr Poe has two of the prime qualities of genius, a faculty of rigorous yet minute analysis, and a wonderful fecundity of imagination ...*
>
> *As a critic, Mr Poe was aesthetically deficient. Unerring in his analysis of dictions, meters, and plots, he seemed wanting in the faculty of perceiving the profounder ethics of art. His criticisms are, however, distinguished for scientific precision and coherence of logic. They have the exactness and, at the same time, the coldness of mathematical demonstrations. Yet they stand in strikingly refreshing contrast with the vague generalisms and sharp personalities of the day. If deficient in warmth, they are also without the heat of partisanship ... They are especially valuable at illustrating the great truth, too generally overlooked, that analytic power is a subordinate quality of the critic ...*
>
> *On the whole, it may be considered certain that Mr Poe has attained an individual eminence in our literature, which he will keep. He has given proof of power and originality.*

## NO CONSCIENCE OR CHARACTER

Poe and Lowell met for the only time in New York in late May and each seems to have been disappointed in the other. Then, as ever, attacking a friend who has helped him, Poe launched an assault on the upper-class poet in the August issue of the *Broadway Journal*, accusing him of plagiarizing Wordsworth.

Lowell remarked disappointedly to an acquaintance, 'I have made Poe my enemy by doing him a service ... Poe, I am afraid, is wholly lacking in that element of manhood which, for want of a better name, we call character.' Following Poe's death, he bitterly noted, 'Had he possessed conscience in any proportion to his brain, our literature could hardly have had a greater loss.'

In fact, Poe had made an enemy of a man he should not have. Lowell took him to task in his satirical poem *A Fable for Critics*, especially for things that Poe had been saying about Lowell's friend, the poet Longfellow.

> There comes Poe, with his raven, like Barnaby Rudge,
>
> Three-fifths of him genius and two-fifths sheer fudge;
>
> Who talks like a book of iambs and pentameters
>
> In a way to make people of common sense damn meters;
>
> Who has written some things quite the best of their kind,
>
> But the heart somehow seems all squeezed out by the mind;
>
> Who—But hey-day! What's this? Messieurs Matthews and Poe,
>
> You mustn't fling mud-balls at Longfellow so!

## POE THE MONOMANIAC

Inwardly, Poe resented Longfellow's success. He had a chair at Harvard and was married to a wealthy woman. Having once described him as 'unquestionably the best poet in America,' Poe now began to revise his opinion, even going so far as to call him 'a determined imitator and a dexterous adapter of the ideas of other people.'

He accused him of plagiarizing Tennyson's 'Death of the Old Year' in his poem 'Midnight Mass For the Dying Year': 'We have no idea of commenting, at any length, upon this plagiarism, which is too palpable to be mistaken, and which belongs to the most barbarous class of literary piracy, that class in which, while the words of the wronged author are avoided, his most intangible, and therefore his least defensible and least reclaimable property, is appropriated.'

Poe – not averse to a bit of borrowing himself, of course – engaged in a correspondence in his magazine columns throughout the year with someone calling himself 'Outis' who was outraged by his claims about Longfellow. The publisher Charles Briggs (1804 – 77) said around this time that 'Poe is a monomaniac on the subject of plagiarism' and noted that his war with Longfellow – who maintained an admirably dignified silence throughout – annoyed a good few people.

When Poe died in 1849, Longfellow was magnanimous, putting his more radical critical comments down to a deep sense of injustice regarding his own work:

> What a melancholy death is that of Mr Poe—a man so richly endowed with genius! I never knew him personally, but have always entertained a high appreciation of his powers as a prose-writer and a poet. His prose is remarkably vigorous, direct and yet affluent; and his verse has a particular charm of melody, an atmosphere of true poetry about it, which is very winning. The harshness of his criticisms, I have never attributed to anything but the irritation of a sensitive nature, chafed by some indefinite sense of wrong.

A generous and decent man, Longfellow helped Maria Clemm after Poe's death by purchasing five copies of an edition of Poe's works from her.

# THE PREMATURE BURIAL

The narrator begins by saying that there are certain topics that are fascinating but too horrific for 'legitimate fiction.' He cites the Lisbon Earthquake, the Passage of the Beresina, the Plague of London, the Massacre of St. Bartholomew and the Black Hole of Calcutta.

False accounts, he adds that try to emulate such horrors are a disgrace. Being buried alive is the most 'terrific of these extremes.' He provides a number of examples of people who have been buried alive and explains that he believes that people are buried alive all the time. He begins to relate his own experience.

The narrator suffers from a strange condition called catalepsy in which his muscles become rigid and his body can appear lifeless for weeks or months on end. His heartbeat becomes hardly noticeable and as time passes, these episodes appear to be lasting longer.

He is terrified that, if found in such a condition, he would be presumed dead and buried. Therefore, he tries to avoid falling asleep in case he should fall into one of these trances and when he does sleep, he has a nightmare.

*Methought I was immersed in a cataleptic trance of more than usual duration and profundity. Suddenly there came an icy hand upon my forehead, and an impatient, gibbering voice whispered the word 'Arise!' within my ear.*

The narrator sits up and the voice tells him that it was mortal but 'now is fiend.' It invites him to come with it to 'unfold to thee the graves.' The narrator believes the voice to belong to Death and next day he sees that Death has:

*… caused to be thrown open the graves of all mankind, and from each issued the faint phosphoric radiance of decay, so that I could see into the innermost recesses, and there view the shrouded bodies in their sad and solemn slumbers with the worm. But alas! the real sleepers were fewer, by many millions, than those who slumbered not at all; and there was a feeble struggling;*

*and there was a general sad unrest; and from out the depths of the countless pits there came a melancholy rustling from the garments of the buried. And of those who seemed tranquilly to repose, I saw that a vast number had changed, in a greater or less degree, the rigid and uneasy position in which they had originally been entombed.*

Death remarks how pitiful this sight is before the graves close again.

The narrator fears leaving his house in case he has an attack of his condition. In his family vault, he puts a spring-loaded lid on his coffin, he places food and water inside and ensures that there is adequate ventilation. He attaches a rope to a bell on top of the tomb so that he can raise the alarm if buried alive.

One day, he awakes in darkness believing his worst fears to have been realized. He cannot shout out because there is a heavy weight pressing on his chest. His mouth is bound and a wooden cover sits six inches above his face. He makes a great effort and cries out for help, receiving the answer 'Hillo! hillo, there!' and is picked up by some men. He has not been buried alive after all.

On a hunting trip near Richmond, Virginia he had been caught in a rainstorm and had taken shelter on a boat on the James River. He had clambered into a small berth beneath the deck and it was the deck that he sensed above his face. His mouth was not bound but was covered by a handkerchief he had wrapped around his head as he did not have a nightcap. The men picking him up are members of the boat's crew.

His life is suddenly changed. He realizes that it is ridiculous to live in fear and starts to go out without worrying what might become of him. His catalepsy disappears and he wonders if it might have been brought on by his paranoia. The human mind, he muses, can be very dark and one must turn from the internal world to that of the outside.

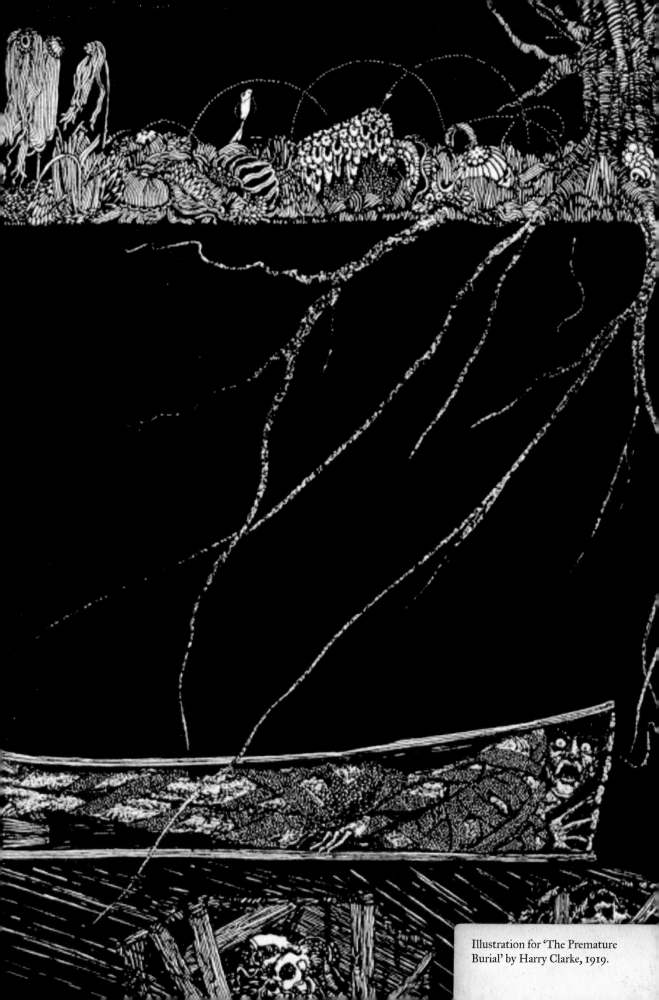

Illustration for 'The Premature
Burial' by Harry Clarke, 1919.

## THE PREMATURE BURIAL

Antoine Wiertz (1806 – 1865) was a Belgian artist whose work was influenced by Poe's stories. *L'Inhumation précipitée* (The Premature Burial) depicts a cholera victim awakening after being placed in a coffin.

A fear of being buried alive was deeply rooted in the culture of the nineteenth century. In Poe's time, it was a real problem as hundreds of cases were reported in which doctors mistakenly pronounced people dead. Coffins occasionally were equipped with emergency devices to allow the 'corpse' to call for help, should he or she turn out to be still alive. Belief in vampires has sometimes been attributed to premature burial, and in Britain, the London Association for the Prevention of Premature Burial campaigned for burial reforms to ensure that those buried were certainly dead. Edgar Allan Poe took advantage of the public's (and his own) fascination with being buried alive and it was a major feature in many of his stories.

## THE NAME OF THE GAME IS FAME

Regarding Lowell, however, Poe would not let it lie, of course, responding with a blast at him and his Abolitionist politics:

> *The Fable is essentially 'loose'—ill-conceived and feebly executed, as well in detail as in general ... a book at once so ambitious and so feeble—so malevolent in design and so harmless in execution—a work so roughly and clumsily yet so weakly constructed ...*
>
> *Mr Lowell is one of the most rabid Abolition fanatics; and no Southerner who does not wish to be insulted, and at the same time revolted by a bigotry the most obstinately blind and deaf, should ever touch a volume by this author.*

When all was said and done, however, Poe made a paltry nine dollars from 'The Raven' but his prospects certainly improved with the fame that had been his reward for writing it.

## EDITING THE BROADWAY JOURNAL

The *Broadway Journal*, owned by Charles Briggs, announced that Poe would be joining its masthead as an equal partner and would be contributing a page a week to the publication. He was taken on in the role of assistant-editor and was to be paid a third of the profits of the magazine at the end of each month.

The *Broadway Journal* had more serious intellectual intent than any of the magazines with which Poe had thus far been associated. Unfortunately, that also meant a lower circulation and less profit. He wrote many reviews in his time there, but was still in the habit of 'tomahawking' a writer every now and then – 'feeble puffing is not my forte,' he said, 'It will do these fellows good to hear the truth, and stimulate them to worthier efforts.'

Poe capitalized on his fame by lecturing and it always gave him another chance to take a tilt at Longfellow. On April 17, however, with the weather raging outside, he arrived on stage to an audience of only about a dozen people. An office boy from the *Broadway Journal* reported that the following morning, when Poe turned up for work, he had to be helped into the office, reeking of wine—

## The Daly Daguerreotype

This daguerreotype image is, unquestionably, among the finest likenesses of Poe known to exist. The picture was taken between 1844 and 1847, while Poe was living in New York, and was discovered in 1900, in the art collection of prominent New York playwright and theatrical producer, Augustin Daly (1838 – 1899).

---

# CHAPTER 8

# UNFOLDING THE WONDERFUL

Poe had stayed away from alcohol for a year and his performance at the *Mirror* was described by Nathaniel Parker Willis as 'punctual and industriously reliable.' Now, he was back on the bottle and drinking heavily.

He was drunk when he had his infamous meeting with James Russell Lowell, for instance. Claiming to be 'dreadfully unwell,' he canceled a lecture at New York University scheduled for July 1. On one occasion, he was found staggering drunkenly outside a bar on Nassau Street, while a patron of the bar yelled out that he was 'the Shakespeare of America.'

With Poe's literary star on the rise, there was a flurry of activity in an attempt to profit from it. Publisher Evert Duyckinck (1816 – 78) compiled a selection of Poe's stories to date and published them through Wiley & Putnam in a book entitled *Tales*. The book comprised of twelve stories, including each of his detective stories, printed in chronological order and taking up almost half of the book, as well as all his important stories, apart from 'The Tell-Tale Heart', 'The Masque of the Red Death', 'William Wilson' and 'Ligeia'. He also included less significant stories such as 'Lionizing'.

Poe was very unhappy about these omissions and felt that the cohesiveness of the book was diminished by their absence. But it was very good for his reputation. It was also a critical success, with journalist and woman's rights advocate Margaret Fuller praising it in the *New York Tribune*, for instance, although she wondered if he was too original and possibly ahead of his time.

## TREMBLING IN THEIR BEDS

Charles Dana (1819 – 97), reviewing it in the *Harbinger*, admitted that he disliked the stories but confessed to their power. He described them as 'clumsily contrived, unnatural, and every way in bad taste. There is still a kind of power in them; it is the power of disease.'

The London *Spectator* was delighted by the detective tales. 'To unfold the wonderful, to show that what seems miraculous is amenable to almost mathematical reasoning, is a real delight of Mr Poe … He exhibits great analytical skill in seizing upon the points of circumstantial evidence and connecting them together. He also has the faculty essential to the story-teller by "the winter's fire," who would send the hearers trembling to their beds.'

Poe's move to New York had been vindicated and he was now associating with some of America's best contemporary writers and poets – James Fenimore Cooper, Washington Irving, William Cullen Bryant (1794 – 1878) and William Gilmore Simms (1806 – 70).

## DEATH BY THE VISITATION OF GOD

In July 1845, a new Poe story, 'The Imp of the Perverse', was published in *Graham's*. It would later be included in the Boston gift book *May-Flower* for 1846. It is an odd tale, consisting of a long essay at the beginning with a murder thrown in at the end, as if to give the whole thing a point.

Just how personal is 'The Imp of the Perverse' to Edgar Poe? Some have suggested that it reflects his own 'imp' and is an attempt

# EVERT DUYCKINCK

Evert Duyckinck was born in New York in 1816 to a publisher father. Having studied law, he was admitted to the Bar in 1837. In 1840, he launched a literary magazine, *Arcturus*, with Cornelius Mathews (1817 – 1889) that ran for two years. The two men were described in the *New York Tribune* as the 'Castor and Pollux of Literature – the Gemini of the literary Zodiac.'

From 1844 to 1846, Duyckinck edited John L. O'Sullivan's highly regarded political magazine, *The United States Magazine and Democratic Review* which was also a literary magazine. It was among the first to publish the early work of Walt Whitman, James Russell Lowell and Henry David Thoreau.

In 1845, he helped Edgar Allan Poe to publish *Tales,* Poe describing him as 'distinguished for the bonhomie of his manner, his simplicity, and single-mindedness, his active beneficence, his hatred of wrong done even to any enemy, and especially for an almost Quixotic fidelity to his friends.'

In 1847, Duyckinck took over as editor of *The Literary World*, a weekly review of books written, until 1853, with his brother George. The two brothers were amongst the leading figures of the New York literary world in the 1840s and 1850s. But one associate noted that Duyckinck's literary tastes were far too highbrow for most readers: 'While Duyckinck was the most genial of companions, and the most impartial of critics, he was too much of a recluse, buried in his books, almost solitary in life, and entirely removed from the circle of worldly and fashionable life.'

Evert Duyckinck died, aged sixty-one, on August 13, 1878.

to justify some of his more irrational behavior. One biographer has it that the story is about the jealousy and sense of betrayal and injustice that resulted in the 'Longfellow War', his very public one-sided feud with Henry Wadsworth Longfellow. The 'war' was in progress as he was writing the story.

Unfortunately, it was not terribly well received, the *Nassau Monthly* at Princeton College describing it as 'humbug'. The reviewer wrote: 'He chases from the wilderness of phrenology into that of transcendentalism, then into that of metaphysics generally; then through many weary pages into the open field of inductive philosophy, where he at last corners the poor thing, and then most unmercifully pokes it to death with a long stick.'

## TRASHING BOSTON

Poe's own 'Imp of the Perverse' was soon in full flow. For a payment of fifty dollars he was invited to read a new poem at the opening of the Boston Lyceum lecture series at the Boston Odeon in October 1845. Unfortunately, Poe hated Boston. He had for many years been engaged in a spat with the work of the Boston Transcendentalists in his review columns, denouncing Ralph Waldo Emerson, their pre-eminent thinker: 'Emerson belongs to a class of gentlemen with whom we have no patience whatever—the mystics for mysticism's sake ... His present *rôle* seems to be the out-Carlyling of Carlyle.'

He dubbed the Transcendentalists 'Frog-pondians', naming them after the Frog Pond on Boston Common. 'They are getting worse and worse,' he told Frederick Thomas, 'and pretend not to be aware that there *are* any literary people out of Boston.' To compound his loathing of Boston and the Boston literary scene, of course, Longfellow, whom he had been trashing, was a Bostonian.

He had described the city scathingly as 'the chief habitation, in this country, of literary hucksters and phrase mongers.' To

make matters worse, he was unable to write anything of any value for the performance. The omens were not good, therefore, by the time Poe was ready to go on stage, especially as the previous speaker had bored the audience rigid for more than two hours.

Poe's opening speech – twenty minutes on American poetry – drove many to an early exit. He then launched into the recitation of what the author Thomas Wentworth Higginson (1823 – 1911), who was present that night, described as a 'rather perplexing poem' that left the audience 'thoroughly mystified.' In fact, in the absence of anything new, Poe had dug up his turgid 1829 work, 'Al Aaraaf'.

By the time he mollified the audience with a recitation of 'The Raven', few remained. The full horror of the evening is captured by the venomous Cornelia Walter (1813 – 98), editor of the *Boston Evening Transcript*:

*The poet immediately arose; but if he uttered poesy in the first instance, it was certainly of a most prosaic order. The audience listened in amazement to a singularly didactic exordium, and finally commenced the noisy expedient of removing from the hall, and this long before they had discovered the style of the measure, or whether it was rhythm or blank verse ... The audience had now thinned so rapidly and made so much commotion in their departure that we lost the beauties of the composition ... Another small poem succeeded. This was 'The Raven'—a composition probably better appreciated by its author than by his auditory.*

## PRECISELY NO POEM AT ALL

Poe further blotted his copybook at the generous supper to which his thoroughly disappointed hosts treated him afterwards. He boasted that he had perpetrated a terrific hoax on the people of Boston by reciting to them a poem he had composed when he had been only ten years old.

# THE IMP OF THE PERVERSE

As in 'The Premature Burial', the tale begins with a lengthy treatise by the narrator, this time on 'The Imp of the Perverse' that, he claims, causes people to commit acts that are against their own self-interest. 'If there be no friendly arm to check us, or if we fail in a sudden effort to prostrate ourselves backward from the abyss, we plunge, and are destroyed.' The narrator then begins to explain why he is in fetters, accused of murder, that it is because he is 'one of the many uncounted victims of the Imp of the Perverse.'

He had pondered for many weeks on the best way to commit the murder. Reading a French memoir, he learned of one method – a woman named Madame Pilau had almost died after exposure to a candle that had been accidentally poisoned. His intended victim, he knew, always read in bed and his apartment was small and badly ventilated. The narrator placed a poisoned candle in the bedroom and the victim was discovered dead the following morning, the Coroner's verdict being 'Death by the visitation of God.'

The narrator inherited his victim's estate and all went well for a number of years. There was no suspicion of foul play and he had disposed of all the evidence. As the years passed, however, his feeling of satisfaction at getting away with murder was replaced by 'a haunting and harassing thought' that he could not shake off. He tells how he dealt with it – 'I would perpetually catch myself pondering upon my security, and repeating, in a low undertone, the phrase, "I am safe".'

One day, walking along a street, he found himself muttering 'I am safe—I am safe—yes—if I be not fool enough to make open confession!' His heart went cold because he had a habit of being perverse. He walked faster, trying to dispel the feeling. He 'bounded like a madman through the crowded thoroughfares' and people, thinking he must have committed a crime, began to run after him. Someone struck him on the back and he could not help himself. Out poured his confession of the murder:

> … the long imprisoned secret burst forth from my soul. They say that I spoke with a distinct enunciation, but with marked emphasis and passionate hurry, as if in dread of interruption before concluding the brief, but pregnant sentences that consigned me to the hangman and to hell … But why shall I say more? Today I wear these chains, and am here! To-morrow I shall be fetterless—but where?

*I bounded like a madman through the crowded thoroughfares.* Illustration for 'The Imp of the Perverse' by Arthur Rackham, 1935.

# THE TRANSCENDENTALISTS

In response to the dry intellectualism that prevailed at Harvard University and the generally low level of spirituality of the times, a movement known as Transcendentalism emerged in the eastern part of the United States in the 1820s and 1830s. Transcendentalists believed in the inherent goodness of people and nature, holding that politics and organized religion were forces for evil and ultimately corrupted the purity of the individual. People were at their best, they insisted, when they were allowed to be truly self-reliant and independent and in that way a true, caring, responsible community could be created.

It developed partly out of Unitarianism which emphasized free conscience and the value of intellectual rationalism but Transcendentalists sought a more intense spiritual experience. They grounded their beliefs in principles that were not based on physical experience but that came from the spiritual essence of an individual.

The movement could be said to be a late flowering of the Romanticism that had earlier flourished in Britain and it was also influenced by the mystical spiritualism of the Swedish philosopher, Emanuel Swedenborg. Amongst its major figures, apart from Ralph Waldo Emerson, were Henry David Thoreau, Margaret Fuller, Louisa May Alcott, William Ellery Channing, Walt Whitman, Emily Dickinson and Theodore Parker.

The key moment for Transcendentalism was the 1836 publication of Emerson's essay 'Nature'. He said in a speech a year later, 'We will walk on our own feet; we will work with our own hands; we will speak our own minds … A nation of men will for the first time exist, because each believes himself inspired by the Divine Soul which inspires all men.'

A group of leading New England intellectuals founded the Transcendental Club in Cambridge, Massachusetts in 1836 and from 1840 their journal, *The Dial*, was published but by the late 1840s the movement was dying out.

Ralph Waldo Emerson (1803 – 1882), philosopher and leader of the Transcendentalists, giving a speech at the Concord School of Philosophy, USA.

Partly spurred on by Cornelia Walter's attacks on him, he further insulted Bostonians by giving his own boastful version of the incident in the *Broadway Journal* in November 1845.

*On arising, we were most cordially received. We occupied some fifteen minutes with an apology for not 'delivering,' as is usual in such cases a didactic poem: a didactic poem, in our opinion, being precisely no poem at all. After some farther words—still of an apology—for the 'indefiniteness' and 'general imbecility' of what we had to offer—all so unworthy of a Bostonian audience—we commenced, and, with many interruptions of applause, concluded ...*

*It could scarcely be supposed that we would put ourselves to the trouble of composing for the Bostonians anything in the shape of an original poem. We did not. We had a poem (of about 500 lines) lying by us—one quite as good as new ... That we gave them—it was the best we had—for the price—and it did answer remarkably well ...*

*We do not, ourselves, think the poem a remarkably good one: —it is not sufficiently transcendental. Still it did well enough for the Boston audience—who evinced characteristic discrimination in understanding, and especially applauding, all those knotty passages which we ourselves have not yet been able to understand ...*

*Were the question demanded of us—'What is the most exquisite of sublunary pleasures?' we should reply ... 'kicking up a bobbery' ...*

*If we cared a fig for their wrath we should not first have insulted them to their teeth, and then subjected to their tender mercies a volume of our Poems.*

Poe had at least been sober, however.

## DREAMY MOOD AND WANDERING FANCIES

Wiley & Putnam compiled a volume of Poe's poetry – *The Raven and Other Poems* – for publication on the back of the critical, if not financial success of *Tales*. In the Preface, Poe was self-deprecating in the extreme. 'I think nothing in this volume of much value to the public,' he wrote, 'or very credible to myself. Events not to be controlled have prevented me from making, at any time, any serious effort in what, under happier circumstances, would have been the field of my choice.'

The *Brook Farm Phalanx* said of it: 'Edgar Poe, acting the constabulary part of a spy in detecting plagiarisms in favorite authors, insulting a Boston audience, inditing coarse editorials against respectable editresses, and getting singed himself in the meanwhile, is nothing less than the hero of a grand mystic conflict of the elements.'

But many were highly appreciative of his poetry. Thomas Dunn English wrote that Poe's 'power to conceive and execute the [poetic] effect, betokens the highest genius' and described him as 'the first poet of his school.' Despite having received a tomahawk in the skull from Poe, the South Carolina novelist, William Gilmore Simms, called him 'a fantastic and a mystic—a man of dreamy mood and wandering fancies.' Meanwhile, Margaret Fuller (1810 – 50) wrote that his poems 'breathe a passionate sadness, relieved sometimes by touches very lovely and tender.'

## NOW—I AM DEAD

'The Facts in the Case of M. Valdemar' is a story of mesmerism, presented as if it was factual and many fell for Poe's hoax at the time. It was derived from a letter that he published in the *Broadway Journal* from a Dr. A. Sidney Doane who explained that he carried out an operation on a patient while the patient was 'in a *magnetic sleep*' and was published in the magazine's December 20, 1845 issue as well as in the December edition of *American Review: A Whig Journal*. It also appeared in England, initially as a pamphlet under the title 'Mesmerism in Articulo Mortis' and later as 'The Last Days of M. Valdemar'.

'M. Valdemar' is fairly gruesome in some of its descriptions, perhaps reflecting the fact that Poe had studied medical texts. The last words – 'a nearly liquid mass of loathsome— of detestable putridity' and other descriptions in the story undoubtedly made an impact on later writers such as H.P. Lovecraft from whose pen those words might have come.

Of course, Valdemar is suffering from tuberculosis and by this time Poe had plenty of experience of the illness, his wife having now been in the grip of the disease for four years.

## BROUGHT BACK TO LIFE

Amongst those believing that Poe's story was actually a real-life medical report was English magnetic healer, Robert Collyer (1823 – 1912), who was at the time visiting Boston. He wrote to Poe to tell him that he had performed a similar feat, reviving a man pronounced dead.

It transpired that the man who was revived was actually a drunk sailor who was 'brought back to life' with a hot bath. He did report the success of Poe's story in Boston, however. 'Your account of M. Valdemar's case has been universally copied in this city, and has caused a very great sensation.'

Another Englishman, Thomas South, made the story a case study in his 1846 book, *Early Magnetism in its Higher Relations to Humanity.* A Scottish *Journal* reader and believer in mesmerism, Archibald Ramsay, wrote to Poe asking him 'For the sake of ... Science and of truth' to confirm that it was not a hoax. Poe replied: '*Hoax* is precisely the word suited ... Some few persons believe it— but *I* do not—and don't you.'

Elizabeth Barrett Browning wrote to Poe, commending him on his talent for 'making horrible improbabilities seem near and familiar.' And poet Philip Pendleton Cooke (1816 – 50) told him the story was 'the most damnable, vraisemblable, horrible, hair-lifting, shocking, ingenious chapter of fiction that any brain ever conceived or hand traced. That gelatinous, viscous sound of man's voice! there never was such an idea before.'

Thomas Dunn English (1819 – 1902).

## TROUBLE AT THE BROADWAY JOURNAL

Charles Briggs, co-editor with Poe at the *Broadway Journal* was initially delighted with his new colleague. 'I like Poe exceedingly well,' he wrote to James Russell Lowell, 'Mr Griswold has told me shocking bad stories about him, which his whole demeanor contradicts.'

It was the drinking that finally ended his respect for Poe. Writing again to Lowell in late June 1845, he said, 'he has latterly got into his old habits and I fear will injure himself irretrievably.' Well aware that he was treading on thin ice, Poe pleaded with Evert Duyckinck to buy him out before Briggs fired him.

He talked about being unwell and worried that he would become seriously ill. He also reminded Duyckinck of Virginia's illness and added, 'I have resolved to give up the *B. Journal* and retire to the country for six months, or perhaps a year, as the sole means of recruiting my health and spirits. Is it not possible that yourself or [Cornelius] Mathews might give me a trifle for my interest in the paper?'

A month later, Briggs tried to gain complete control of the *Broadway Journal* by buying out the publisher John Bisco's share, but Bisco wanted more than Briggs was offering, forcing Briggs to withdraw from involvement with the magazine. Briggs complained to Lowell about Poe:

*I have never met a person so utterly deficient of high motive. He cannot conceive of anybody's doing anything, except for his own personal advantage ... It is too absurd for belief, but he really thinks that Longfellow owes his fame mainly to the ideas which he borrowed from Poe's writings in the Southern Literary Messenger ... The Bible, he says, is all rigmarole ... He knows that I am possessed of the secret of his real character and he no doubt hates me for it.*

## SOME KIND OF CONSPIRACY

Bisco and Poe carried on publishing but eventually, Bisco sold his share in the magazine to Poe for fifty dollars which, of course, Poe did not have. Bisco had to be content with an I.O.U. that was never paid. Nonetheless, Poe finally owned a magazine, becoming editor and proprietor of the *Broadway Journal* on October 24, 1845. It lasted just two months.

He tried to borrow money from friends to keep it going because, of course, he had none. In fact, his finances were going from bad to worse and in 1847 he would earn just $288; $166 in 1848; and $275 in 1849. He was trying to find only a hundred dollars to pay for the printing, the paper and the postage, but his pleas were rejected by Thomas Chivers, George Poe, John Pendleton Kennedy and Evert Duyckinck.

Neilson Poe, Griswold and the poet Fitz-Greene Halleck did send money – never repaid, of course. He spoke of some kind of conspiracy against him: 'There is a deliberate attempt now being made to involve me in ruin, by destroying the *Broadway Journal*. I could easily frustrate them, but for my total want of money ... I venture to appeal to you. The sum I need is $100.'

## DELAYING THE INEVITABLE

He managed to persuade Thomas Lane, a customs official and friend of Thomas Dunn English, to buy into the magazine in November but it was only delaying the inevitable. Meanwhile, Poe was under a great deal of stress.

He told Duyckinck around this time that he was 'dreadfully sick and depressed, but still myself. I seem to have just wakened from some horrible dream, in which all was confusion, and suffering ... I really believe that I have been mad—but indeed I have had abundant reason to be so ... My object in writing you this note is (once again) to beg your aid. Of course I need not say to you that my most urgent trouble is the want of ready money.'

# THE FACTS IN THE CASE OF M. VALDEMAR

The narrator has been studying mesmerism and realizes that no one has yet tried it on a dying person. How would it affect an individual at the point of death and could it possibly delay it? While trying to find a subject for his experimentation, he thinks of his friend, Ernest Valdemar, a well-known author.

The narrator has already managed to put him in a trance two or three times but has never quite managed to retain full control of him, perhaps because of the author's tuberculosis. Facing imminent death, Valdemar agrees to subject himself to the narrator's experiment and is, in fact, excited by the prospect.

When the narrator arrives at Valdemar's house to conduct the experiment, he finds that his patient is emaciated and suffering from a violent cough. His pulse is weak but he retains his wits and a little physical strength. He is attended by two doctors who inform the narrator that his lungs are seriously damaged and he has an aneurysm in his heart. They fully expect him to die at midnight the following day, a Sunday.

The narrator is reluctant initially to carry out his experiment, partly because there will be only two nurses present to witness it. He decides to postpone until the following evening by which time he has organized for a student to be present to take notes. Unable to wait any longer because Valdemar is at death's door, he begins his work at 8 p.m. on the Sunday evening.

Initially his treatment does not have the desired effect but when the two doctors arrive at 10 p.m., they are happy to allow him to continue as Valdemar is going to die anyway. At 10.55 p.m., Valdemar finally slips into a trance and the narrator continues his work. At midnight everyone is in agreement that the patient is in a perfect state of mesmerism and one of the doctors leaves. At 3 a.m. the narrator asks Valdemar if he is asleep. The sick man replies that he is and that he would like to die like this. When asked if he is in pain, he replies that he is not.

The doctor who had gone home is astonished when he returns in the morning to find the patient still alive and the physicians agree that he should be allowed to remain in this trance-like state until he finally dies which is expected to happen at any time.

When the narrator next asks Valdemar whether he is still sleeping, there is a sudden change in the patient's condition:

> The eyes rolled themselves slowly open, the pupils disappearing upwardly; the skin generally assumed a cadaverous hue, resembling not so much parchment as white paper; and the circular hectic spots which, hitherto, had been strongly defined in the center of each cheek, went out at once. I use this expression, because the suddenness of their departure put me in mind of nothing so much as the extinguishment of a candle by a puff of the breath. The upper lip, at the same time, writhed itself away from the teeth, which it had previously covered completely; while the lower jaw fell with an audible jerk, leaving the mouth widely extended, and disclosing in full view the swollen and blackened tongue. I presume that no member of the party then present had been unaccustomed to death-bed horrors; but so hideous beyond conception was the appearance of M. Valdemar at this moment, that there was a general shrinking back from the region of the bed.

Valdemar is pronounced dead but suddenly, his tongue starts to vibrate and they hear his voice:

> …the voice seemed to reach our ears—at least mine—from a vast distance, or from some deep cavern within the earth. In the second place, it impressed me (I fear, indeed, that it will be impossible to make myself comprehended) as gelatinous or glutinous matters impress the sense of touch.

He says 'Yes;—no;—I have been sleeping—and now—now—I am dead,' causing the student to faint and the nurses to flee, never to return. The narrator and the doctors try vainly for the next hour to revive Valdemar but his breathing has stopped. They are unable to draw blood and the narrator fails to get him to move an arm.

Meanwhile, Valdemar continues to try to answer their questions but is unable to articulate. New nurses are brought in to care for him while the narrator and the doctors rest, but in the afternoon, when they return, his condition remains the same. They believe that if they wake him up completely they will lose him.

For seven months he remains in this state, until the doctors and the narrator decide that they have no choice but to wake him. The narrator employs his mesmeric technique and one of Valdemar's eyes descends a little, emitting a foul-smelling liquid.

In between trance and being awake, Valdemar pleads with the narrator to either put him back to sleep or to wake him. The narrator decides to wake him but with dire results:

*As I rapidly made the mesmeric passes, amid ejaculations of 'dead! dead!' absolutely bursting from the tongue and not from the lips of the sufferer, his whole frame at once—within the space of a single minute, or even less, shrunk—crumbled—absolutely rotted away beneath my hands. Upon the bed, before that whole company, there lay a nearly liquid mass of loathsome—of detestable putridity.*

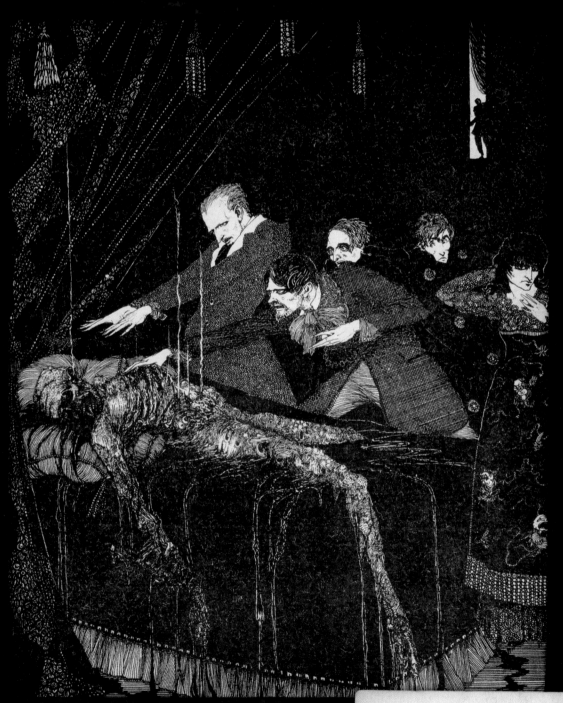

Illustration from 1919 by Harry Clarke for 'The Facts in the Case of M. Valdemar'.

## THE POOR BOY IS DERANGED

Virginia was by now very sick. One night in summer of 1845, Chivers had escorted a very drunk Edgar Poe home and at the house Maria Clemm was beside herself with worry about both Poe and his wife.

> *Oh! Dr. C! how I have prayed that my poor Eddy might not get in this way while you were here! But I knew, when he went away from here this morning, that he would not return in his right senses! Oh! I do believe that the poor boy is deranged! His wife is now at the point of death with Bronchitis, and cannot bear to see him! Oh! my poor*

> *Virginia! She cannot live long! She is wasting away, day by day—for the doctors can do her no good. But if they could, seeing this continually in poor Eddy, would kill her—for she dotes upon him! Oh! She is devoted to him! She fairly adores him! But would to God she had died before she had ever seen him! My poor child! He has been in bed here for a whole week with nothing in the world the matter with him—only lying here pretending to be sick, in order to avoid delivering the Poem promised, before one of the Literary Societies of the City: now he is in this deranged state again.*

## NO MARKET FOR HIS BRAIN

In December 1845, he went off on another drunken binge and left unfilled space in the *Broadway Journal* just as it was going to press. Thomas Lane tried his best to bring the writer under control but realizing it was pointless, decided to end publication. The magazine's final edition was published in January 1846.

The *Journal* would be Poe's last job. His former employer, George Graham, remarked that he now wandered 'from publisher to publisher, with his fine, print-like manuscript, scrupulously clean and neatly rolled,' but finding 'no market for his brain.' Graham noted how troubled Poe was by 'those morbid feelings which a life of poverty and disappointment is so apt to engender in the heart of a man—the sense of having been ill-used, misunderstood, and put aside by men of far less ability.'

Life would not get any better for Edgar Poe as he drifted through his final years, sailing from one personal calamity to another and writing less and less.

### Steel engraving by Frederick Halpin, 1859

Halpin's engraving for the frontispiece of *Poe's Poetical Works*, bears only a superficial resemblance to the poet, as one of Poe's neighbors at the time, Augustine O'Neil confirmed:

'I have seen Poe ... He was very neatly dressed in black ... rather small, slender, pale ... This boyish frontispiece gives but a faint idea of him as I saw him ... must have been at that time about thirty-six years old, but he looked to be forty.'

# CHAPTER 9

# ADRIFT ON A SEA OF SCANDAL

On Valentine's Day, 1846, Virginia Poe wrote her husband a poignant romantic acrostic:

> *Ever with thee I wish to roam—*
>
> *Dearest my life is thine.*
>
> *Give me a cottage for my home*
>
> *And a rich old cypress vine,*
>
> *Removed from the world with its sin and care*
>
> *And the tattling of many tongues.*
>
> *Love alone shall guide us when we are there—*
>
> *Love shall heal my weakened lungs;*
>
> *And Oh, the tranquil hours we'll spend,*
>
> *Never wishing that others may see!*
>
> *Perfect ease we'll enjoy, without thinking to lend*
>
> *Ourselves to the world and its glee—*
>
> *Ever peaceful and blissful we'll be.*

The only writing of Virginia's that has survived, this poem reminds us that her life was ebbing away as the condition of her 'weakened lungs' got worse. But, suddenly her husband now became embroiled in a strange scandal.

## ENAMORED AND EMOTIONAL

Elizabeth Ellet (1818 – 77) was a poet whose work Poe had critiqued. 'Some of [the poems] have merit. Some we think unworthy of the talents which their author has undoubtedly displayed.' Ellet became enamored with Poe and wrote some emotional letters to him that he showed to Virginia.

Meanwhile, he was also 'friendly' with another woman poet, Frances Sargent Osgood (1811 – 50) – known as Fanny. Ellet was extremely jealous of her, especially as Fanny was a much better writer than her. Poe even wrote several poems to Osgood, one of which was 'A Valentine'. It begins:

> *For her this rhyme is penned, whose luminous eyes,*
>
> *Brightly expressive as the twins of Lœda,*
>
> *Shall find her own sweet name, that, nestling lies*
>
> *Upon the page, enwrapped from every reader.*
>
> *Search narrowly the lines!—they hold a treasure*
>
> *Divine—a talisman—an amulet*
>
> *That must be worn at heart. Search well the measure—*
>
> *The words—the syllables! Do not forget*
>
> *The trivialest point, or you may lose your labor!*

Virginia had encouraged her husband in his friendship with Osgood and one day, Ellet visited the Poes and was outraged to hear Fanny Osgood and Virginia laughing uproariously at the contents of one of her letters to Poe.

In late January 1846, while visiting the Poe household again, Virginia, who was excited by the attention her husband was receiving, showed Ellet letters from Osgood to Poe that she considered to be indiscreet. Afterwards, Ellet advised Osgood that to protect her reputation she should ask for the letters to be returned to her. Accordingly, Osgood asked fellow writers and acquaintances of Poe, Margaret Fuller and Anne Lynch Botta, to approach Poe and request their return.

Poe was furious, suggesting that Ellet would do better to 'look after her *own* letters.' One of which was written in German and invited Poe to 'call for it at her residence that evening.' It is possible that Poe did not quite understand what was an obvious attempt at seduction.

Engraving of Elizabeth Ellet.

## FIGHTING DRUNK

Ellet asked her brother, Colonel William Lummis, to get back her correspondence. Lummis threatened to kill Poe if he failed to return the letters. Fearful for his life, Poe turned up at Thomas Dunn English's house, asking if he could borrow a pistol. English refused and expressed doubt that Poe had ever received any letters from Ellet. He suggested that Poe should withdraw comments he had made about her.

Furious, Poe punched English and a fight broke out between the two men. Poe came off worst, according to his erstwhile partner on the *Broadway Journal,* Thomas Lane: 'Poe was drunk and getting the worst of it, and was finally forced partly under the sofa, only his face being out. English was punching Poe's face, and at every blow a seal ring on his finger cut Poe.'

When Lane tried to separate the two men, the drunk Poe shouted out, 'Let him alone. I've got him just where I want him.' A few months later Poe gave his version of the fight, insisting that he was the winner. 'I gave E. a flogging which he will remember to the day of his death—and, luckily, in the presence of witnesses. He thinks to avenge himself by lies—but I shall be a match for him by means of simple truth.'

Poe took to his bed again after the fight and then offered an inadequate apology to Ellet, denying having said that she had been improper in her letters to him and that if he had said such a thing, it must have been because he had been temporarily insane. It was a statement he would regret because those who thought he was mad anyway publicized it abroad.

In the St. Louis *Reveille* there was a report, for instance, that stated: 'A rumor is in circulation in New York, to the effect that Mr Edgar Allan Poe, the poet and author, has been deranged, and his friends are about to place him under the charge of Dr. Brigham, of the Insane Retreat at Utica.'

ADRIFT ON A SEA OF SCANDAL

## A BIZARRE AND TAWDRY INCIDENT

In July 1846, Fanny Osgood's husband, the painter Samuel Osgood (1808 – 85), finally tired of Elizabeth Ellet's gossip-mongering. He instructed her to apologize formally to his wife or face a charge of libel. Ellet wrote immediately to Fanny, retracting her defamations and putting the blame for the scandal on Poe and Virginia. In 1848, after Virginia's death, Poe described Ellet to the poet Sarah Helen Whitman (1803 – 78) whom he was courting at the time, as:

> ... the most malignant and pertinacious of all fiends—a woman whose loathsome love I could do nothing but repel with scorn—[who] slanders me, in private society, without my knowledge and thus with impunity ... Her whole study, throughout life, has been the gratification of her malignity by such means as any other human being would rather die than adopt. You will be sure to receive anonymous letters so skilfully contrived as to deceive even the most sagacious. You will be called on, possibly, by persons whom you never heard of, but whom she has instigated to call & vilify me ... My poor Virginia was continually tortured (although not deceived) by her anonymous letters, and on her death-bed declared that Mrs E. had been her murderer.

It was a bizarre and tawdry incident and no one came out of it well. After Poe's death, Fanny Osgood described to Rufus Griswold the posse of poetic women who at the time had been pursuing Poe like groupies following a rock star.

> It is too cruel that I, the only one of these literary women who did not seek his acquaintance—for Mrs Ellet asked an introduction to him and followed him everywhere, Miss Lynch begged me to bring him there and called upon him at his lodgings, Mrs Whitman besieged him with valentines and letters long before he wrote or took any notice of her, and all others wrote poetry and letters to him,—it is too cruel that I should be singled out after his death as the only victim to suffer from the slanders of his mother.

Towards the end of her life, Fanny realized that the blame in the matter really lay at the door of Ellet and wrote to Griswold, warmly praising Edgar Allan Poe.

## FORDHAM AND THE 'MILLINER'S MAGAZINE'

The Poes were soon on the move again, re-locating to Turtle Bay in Manhattan, but in May they moved into a little cottage (now an Edgar Allan Poe museum) in what at the time was the rural village of Fordham, now swallowed up by the city and part of the Bronx. The two-story building, located at the top of Fordham Hill at 192nd Street and Kingsbridge Road, consisted on the ground floor of a sitting room, a small bedroom and a kitchen.

In the attic were Poe's study and a bedroom for Maria and he kept caged songbirds on the porch at the front. Nearby was the Jesuit St. John's College whose library the priests were happy to allow Poe to use. It was a simple existence and very peaceful. A visitor to the house recalled Poe writing with a cat wrapped around his shoulders.

From May 1846 until October 1848, in a series of essays in *Godey's Lady's Book*, Poe took revenge on many of the New York literati who had been so warm towards him after the success of 'The Raven' and who had then so rapidly dropped him because of the Elizabeth Ellet scandal.

Published in Philadelphia, *Godey's* was the United States' most widely circulated magazine in the period before the Civil War. When Poe was placing articles in it, the 'Queen of the Monthlies', as it was known, was selling 70,000 copies a month. Aimed at women, as the title suggests, it paid well but Poe disparaged it as 'a milliner's magazine.'

He wrote about many of his close

acquaintances – Margaret Fuller, Nathaniel Parker Willis, Evert Duyckinck, Fanny Osgood, Lewis Gaylord Clark (1808 – 73) and Thomas Dunn English, but was sometimes not quite as harsh as might have been feared. Now and then, however, he gave the proprietor, Louis Godey, what he was paying for and would let rip, providing the magazine with sensational copy and helping it to quickly disappear from the newsstands.

Members of his circle were afraid that they would be treated like Lewis Gaylord Clark whose magazine *Knickerbocker* was described by Poe in *Godey's* as 'tottering, month after month ... that dense region of unmitigated and unmitigable fog—that dreary realm of outer darkness, of utter and inconceivable dunderheadism ... in the august person of Lewis Gaylord Clark.' They cozied up to Poe and he loved it, writing, 'Yes, I am proud; I must be proud to see/Men not afraid of God, afraid of me.'

Of Nathaniel Parker Willis, Poe said, 'His face is somewhat too full, or rather heavy ... neither his nose nor his forehead can be defended' and of the travel writer, William Gillespie, he remarked that he 'walks irregularly, mutters to himself.'

## A VENOMOUS DESCRIPTION

Then, he tore into Charles Briggs, with whom he had worked at the *Broadway Journal*. 'The author of *Harry Franco* [Briggs had written a novel, *The Adventures of Harry Franco* in 1839] carries the simplicity of Smollett to insipidity, and his picturesque low life is made to degenerate into sheer vulgarity.'

He did not reserve his comments to literary work, having a go at Briggs's character and how he looked, saying that his 'personal appearance is not prepossessing' and that he was 'not a person to be disliked, though very apt to irritate and annoy.'

Briggs hit back in the New York *Evening Mirror*, dragging out the untrue story that Poe had been incarcerated in a mental hospital. This, plus Poe's flawed character and persistent poverty, Briggs claimed, made him totally unsuited to writing in this way about his fellow authors. He mocked Poe's appearance and even gave his height as six inches smaller than he actually was. It was a cruel and offensive description full of venom and disgust that had been building up for some time:

> *His face is pale and rather thin; eyes gray, watery and always dull; nose rather prominent, pointed and sharp; nostrils wide; hair thin and cropped short; mouth not very well chiselled, nor very sweet; his tongue shows itself unpleasantly when he speaks earnestly, and seems too large for his mouth ... chin narrow and pointed, which gives his head, upon the whole, a balloonist appearance ... his walk is quick and jerking, sometimes waving ... his hands are singularly small, resembling bird claws.*

## A WAR OF WORDS

Despite a letter of July 1846 from the novelist William Gilmore Simms advising Poe to avoid the scandal and rows in which he seemed to be increasingly involved – 'These broils do you no good—vex your temper, destroy your peace of mind, and hurt your reputation,' – Poe plowed on regardless. He had said in 1844: 'I have never yet been able to make up my mind whether I regard as the higher compliment, the approbation of a man of honor and talent, or the abuse of an ass or a blackguard.'

Thomas Dunn English was next, but this time it got out of hand, involving Poe in a lengthy libel suit. He had already fallen out with English when he had been insulting about his appearance during his drunken escapades in Washington in 1843 and English avenged himself by cruelly portraying Poe as a drunken literary critic in his novel of later that year, *The Doom of the Drinker*. He also accused him of plagiarism, guaranteed to rile Poe.

Of course, the two men had gone so far in their hostility as to engage in a fistfight during the Ellet affair. Now Poe took his revenge. On June 20, he wrote 'No spectacle can be more pitiable than that of a man without the commonest school education busying himself in attempting to instruct mankind on topics of polite literature. The absurdity in such cases does not lie merely in the ignorance displayed by the would-be instructor, but in the transparency of the shifts by which he endeavors to keep this ignorance concealed.' Poe denied that he even knew English.

Three days later, English fired a salvo back at Poe in the New York *Morning Telegraph* as well as again in the *Evening Mirror*.

*That he does not know me is not a matter of wonder. The severe treatment he received at my hands for brutal and dastardly conduct, rendered it necessary for him, if possible, to forget my existence ...*

*He said that though his friendship was of little service, his enmity might be dangerous. To this I rejoined that I shunned his friendship and despised his enmity ...*

*He told me that he had vilified a certain well known and esteemed authoress, of the South, then on a visit to New York; that he had accused her of having written letters to him which compromised her reputation; and that her brother (her husband being absent) had threatened his life unless he produced the letters he named ... He then begged the loan of a pistol to defend himself against attack ... He sent a letter to the brother of the lady he had so vilely slandered, denying all recollection of having made any charges of the kind alleged, and stating that, if he had made them, he was laboring under a fit of insanity to which he was periodically subject ...*

*His review of my style and manner is only amusing when contrasted with his former laudation, almost to sycophancy, of my works ... He professes to know every language and to be proficient in every art and science under the sun—when ... he is ignorant of all ...*

*He mistakes coarse abuse for polished invective, and vulgar insinuation for sly satire. He is not alone thoroughly unprincipled, base and depraved, but silly, vain and ignorant.*

## RASCALLY FISTICUFFS

A few weeks later, Poe's reply could be found in the Philadelphia weekly, *Spirit of the Times*. He claimed to have challenged English to a duel but the other man had failed to turn up. He also claimed to have been victorious in their fistfight, 'having bestowed on Mr E. the "fisticuffing" of which he speaks.' He said that he had to be 'dragged from his prostrate and rascally carcase by Professor Thomas Wyatt, who, perhaps, with good reason, had fears for the vagabond's life.'

He further described English as 'a black-guard of the lowest order' and a 'coward or a liar.' He lowered the tone of the argument even further when he remarked on 'the family resemblance between the whole visage of Mr English and that of the best-looking but most unprincipled of Mr Barnum's baboons ... Does he really conceive that there exists a deeper depth of either moral or physical degradation than that of the hog-puddles in which he has wallowed since his infancy ... among the dock-loafers and wharf-rats, his cronies?'

Moreover, Poe defended himself against accusations of his drunkenness, citing 'a terrible evil,' by which he meant Virginia's tuberculosis, and denied any accusations of fraud or forgery which had been laid at his door by English.

English responded three days later, on July 13, by once again denigrating Poe's character and challenging him to bring the case to court. 'It is not a week since he was intoxicated in the streets of New York ... Let him institute a suit, if he dare, and I pledge myself to make my charges good by the most ample and satisfactory evidence.'

## HEADING FOR A DRUNKARD'S GRAVE

English next satirized Poe as the critic, Marmaduke Hammerhead, in his novel *1844, or The Power of the S.F.*, serialized in the *Evening Mirror* in September and October. 'He never gets drunk more than five days out of the seven;' wrote English, and 'tells the truth sometimes by mistake.' He predicts 'the approaching wreck of his fine abilities' and a 'drunkard's grave' for Hammerhead.

The war with English was taking its toll on Poe. In very low spirits, ill and still, as always, grindingly poor, his friends had deserted him as the storm of invective had increased in ferocity. Eventually, on July 23, he confronted English head-on, filing a suit for libel, seeking damages of five thousand dollars. It was based on English's accusations of forgery and of taking money from him under false pretences.

English fled to Washington just before the case came to court on February 17, 1847 and his lawyers were unable to produce any witnesses who would back up their client's claims regarding Poe's character. Poe's team called three witnesses, one of whom swore that the allegation of forgery was untrue while the other two testified that Poe's only character failing was that he liked a drink. He was awarded $225.06 in damages and costs of $101.42. He immediately bought some luxuries for the house and a brand new black suit.

## A HAWK GRASPING A SNAKE

While his war with Thomas Dunn English was in full flow, Poe wrote the revenge fantasy, 'The Cask of Amontillado', the story of a man taking revenge on someone who has insulted him – very apt considering what he was embroiled in at the time. He returns to the topic of being buried alive and once again – as in 'The Black Cat' and 'The Tell-Tale Heart', the story is narrated in the first person by the murderer.

'The Cask of Amontillado' was published in *Godey's* November 1846 issue. It seems likely that Poe was inspired to write it by a story he had heard when he was in the army at Castle Island in Massachusetts. He saw a monument to a Lieutenant Robert Massie and was told that Massie had been killed during a duel with swords on Christmas Day 1817 by a Lieutenant Gustavus Drane after the two men had an argument about a card game.

The other soldiers said they avenged Massie's murder by getting Drane drunk and luring him into a dungeon where they chained him to the wall and sealed up the vault. In reality, Drane was court-martialed for the incident and acquitted. Poe will also have come into contact with other tales that featured people being walled up, such as Honoré de Balzac's 'La Grande Bretèche' published in the *Democratic Review* in 1843, or his friend, George Lippard's *The Quaker City; or The Monks of Monk Hall* of 1845.

There is little doubt that the story was written in response to his arguments with Thomas Dunn English. There are specific references in 'The Cask of Amontillado' to English's novel, *1844*. For a start, English's book is, like Poe's story, a tale of revenge, although a good deal more convoluted. The Masons that Poe's protagonist, Fortunato, mentions are similar to the secret society in English's book and the gesture that he makes is the same as the gesture of distress in it. The Montresor coat-of-arms is like the image of a hawk grasping a snake portrayed in English's work. A scene in *1844* takes place in a subterranean vault, much like 'The Cask of Amontillado'. But, Poe succeeded in creating a concise story that is extremely effective.

## EERILY REMINISCENT

The remainder of 1846 was squandered really, on a suggested collection of profiles called *Literary America: Some Honest Opinion About Our Authorial Merits and Demerits with Occasional Words of Personality*. He mooted the possibility of publishing it himself and reaping all the profits, but there was never a chance that he would be able to raise sufficient funds to see it to fruition. He was also unlikely to find a legitimate publisher because none of them was eager to antagonize the New York publishing world by setting Edgar Poe on them.

In their little cottage at Fordham, the Poe family was sinking deeper into poverty and December 1846 found them shivering and ill. Poe continued writing begging letters to friends and several, including Nathaniel Willis, did try to help. On December 30, an announcement in the New York *Morning Express*, placed by well-meaning friends, announced the perilous condition in which the Poes found themselves. It was eerily reminiscent of the notice posted on his mother's behalf shortly before her death.

> *ILLNESS OF EDGAR A. POE.—We regret to learn that this gentleman and his wife are both dangerously ill with the consumption, and that the hand of misfortune lies heavily upon their temporal affairs. We are sorry to mention the fact that they are so far reduced as to be barely able to obtain the necessaries of life. That is, indeed, a hard lot, and we do hope that the friends and admirers of Mr Poe will come promptly to his assistance in his bitterest hour of need.*

## WASTING AWAY

The story was picked up by the *Bostonian* which asked incredulously, 'Is it possible, that the literary people of the Union, will let poor Poe perish by starvation and lean-faced beggary in New York?' Some donations were made and Poe, although severely embarrassed by the announcement – especially as, of course, he was not 'ill with the consumption' – was glad of what little money he received.

He wrote to Nathaniel Willis: 'That my wife is ill then, is true. That I myself have been long and dangerously ill, and that my illness has been an understood thing among my brethren in the press, the best evidence is afforded by the innumerable paragraphs of personal and literary abuse with which I have been latterly assailed. This matter, however, will remedy itself ... I am getting better.'

Virginia was not, though, getting better. She was, as a friend reported towards the end of the year, wasting away. Poe was desperate and in a letter to his wife – the only one that survives – he urges her to:

> *Keep up your heart in all hopefulness, and trust yet a little longer. —In my last great disappointment* [the Broadway Journal debacle], *I should have lost my courage but for you—my little darling wife you are my greatest and only stimulus now to battle with this uncongenial, unsatisfactory and ungrateful life.*

Steel engraving by F. T. Stuart. Originally reproduced as the frontispiece to George E. Woodberry's *Edgar Allan Poe*, published by Houghton Mifflin, Boston in 1885.

# THE CASK OF AMONTILLADO

The narrator intimates that he has been pushed as far as he will allow and now must take revenge on Fortunato. He explains that Fortunato is a person to be respected and even feared but he has a weak point – his firm belief that he is a connoisseur of wine. The narrator claims that he too knows his Italian wines.

One evening during the carnival season, the narrator meets Fortunato who is wearing a costume and has been over-indulging, even a little drunk. The narrator tells him he has been in receipt of a pipe, or cask, of the Spanish sherry, Amontillado. Fortunato can hardly believe him and the narrator apologizes for buying it without reference to him for advice on the price, but he had been unable to find him. Fortunato has doubts that it actually is Amontillado and the two decide to make their way to the narrator's wine cellar to establish the nature of the wine.

He hands Fortunato a torch and carrying another himself they pass through the rooms of the palazzo before arriving at a long, winding staircase. They descend to find themselves in the damp catacombs of the narrator's family, the Montresors. Fortunato, drunk, is unsteady on his feet and as they enter the tunnels he begins to cough. The narrator offers to return as he obviously has a bad cold but the other man refuses the offer.

The narrator pours each of them a glass of Medoc to warm them up and they walk on, passing 'walls of piled bones, with casks and puncheons intermingling, into the inmost recesses of the catacombs.' Once again, the narrator offers to return to the warmth of the palazzo. Again Fortunato declines and they have another glass of Medoc. When Fortunato makes an odd gesture, it transpires that he is a member of the Masons and the narrator says that he, too, is a Mason. He jokingly produces a trowel from beneath his clothing.

They continue along the passage, arriving at a deep crypt in which the air is foul. They find a niche within which, Montresor tells Fortunato, is the Amontillado. Fortunato enters, by this time completely drunk, but the narrator suddenly grabs him and chains him by the wrists to the wall. The narrator begins to wall up the entrance to the niche with Fortunato inside.

Fortunato quickly sobers up when he realizes what is happening and tries to break free of his chains. As the bricks approach the top of the niche, the narrator holds his torch up to see inside.

*A succession of loud and shrill screams, bursting suddenly from the throat of the chained form, seemed to thrust me violently back. For a brief moment I hesitated—I trembled. Unsheathing my rapier, I began to grope with it about the recess; but the thought of an instant reassured me. I placed my hand upon the solid fabric of the catacombs, and felt satisfied. I reapproached the wall; I replied to the yells of him who clamored. I re-echoed—I aided—I surpassed them in volume and in strength. I did this, and the clamorer grew still.*

Fortunato now begins to laugh, pretending that he is the victim of a joke and that there will be people waiting for him. 'Ha! ha! ha!—he! he! he!—a very good joke indeed—an excellent jest. We shall have many a rich laugh about it at the palazzo—he! he! he!—over our wine—he! he! he!' However, as the narrator begins to put in place the topmost row of stones, Fortunato begins to plead with him, 'For the love of God, Montresor!' but the narrator replies only 'Yes, for the love of God!' Before he puts in place the last stone, he pushes a burning torch into the niche and then bricks it up completely.

*There came forth in reply only a jingling of the bells. My heart grew sick on account of the dampness of the catacombs. I hastened to make an end of my labor. I forced the last stone into its position; I plastered it up. Against the new masonry I re-erected the old rampart of bones. For the half of a century no mortal has disturbed them. In pace requiescat!*

*Its walls had been lined with human remains, piled to the vault overhead, in the fashion of the great catacombs of Paris.* Illustration for 'The Cask of Amontillado' by Harry Clarke, 1919.

# POE'S TALES
## OF MYSTERY & IMAGINATION
### ILLUSTRATED BY
### ARTHUR RACKHAM

## DUST JACKET FOR POE'S TALES OF MYSTERY & IMAGINATION BY ARTHUR RACKHAM

In 1935, George G. Harrap & Co. published an updated edition of *Poe's Tales of Mystery & Imagination* which was illustrated by the prolific British artist, Arthur Rackham (1867 – 1939).

The new edition contained twenty-five of Edgar Allan Poe's best-known works and included twenty-nine new illustrations by Arthur Rackham who also designed the book jacket, with a stunning black and orange illustration (shown here).

The recipient of multiple awards for illustrations, Arthur Rackham was a diverse artist with a talent for both the fantastic and the intricacies of human nature. He was ideally suited to illustrate Poe's stories.

# PART 4

# THE FEVER CALLED LIVING

Thank Heaven! the crisis —
The danger is past,
And the lingering illness
Is over at last —
And the fever called 'Living'
Is conquered at last.

Edgar Allan Poe *from* 'For Annie'

# CHAPTER 10

# THE MYSTERIES OF THE UNIVERSE

Virginia Poe tried to be cheerful when friends came by, but the disease was drawing to its inexorable conclusion. She was often visited at this time by the women's health care advocate, Mary Gove Nichols (1810 – 84). Poe said she was 'a Mesmerist, a Swedenborgian, a phrenologist, a homoeopathist, a disciple of Priessnitz' but he found that in spite of 'her crackpot ideas,' she was sympathetic and kind-hearted and 'a very interesting woman.' Mary Gove Nichols provided a description of the Poe family at this time:

*On this occasion I was introduced to the young wife of the poet, and to the mother, then more than sixty years of age [Maria was actually only fifty-six]. She was a tall, dignified old lady, with a most ladylike manner, and her black dress, though old and much worn, looked really elegant on her. She wore a widow's cap of the genuine pattern, and it suited exquisitely with her snow-white hair. Her features were large, and corresponded with her stature, and it seemed strange how such a stalwart and queenly women could be the mother of her almost petite daughter. Mrs Poe looked very young; she had large black eyes, and a pearly whiteness of complexion, which was a perfect pallor. Her pale face, her brilliant eyes, and her raven hair gave her an unearthly look. One felt that she was almost a disrobed spirit, and when she coughed it was made certain that she was rapidly passing away. The mother seemed hale and strong, and appeared to be a sort of universal Providence for her strange children.*

*The cottage had an air of taste and gentility that must have been lent to it by the presence of its inmates. So neat, so poor, so unfurnished, and yet so charming a dwelling I never saw … There were pretty presentation copies of books on little shelves, and the Brownings had posts of honor on the stand.*

Mary Gove Nichols also documented how things were as the end approached for Virginia:

Mary Gove Nichols (1810 – 1884).

*Then fall came and Mrs Poe sank rapidly in consumption, and I saw her in her bed chamber. Everything here was so neat, so purely clean, so scant and so poverty-stricken, that I saw the sufferer with such a heartache as the poor feel for the poor. There was no clothing on the bed, which was only straw, but a snow white spread and sheets. The weather was cold, and the sick lady had the dreadful chills that accompany the hectic fever of consumption. She lay on the straw bed, wrapped in her husband's great coat, with a large tortoise-shell cat on her bosom. The wonderful cat seemed conscious of her great uselessness. The coat and the cat were the sufferer's only means of warmth, except as her husband held her hands, and her mother her feet.*

*Mrs Clemm was passionately fond of her daughter, and her distress on account of her illness and poverty and misery, was dreadful to see.*

## GIVING UP THE STRUGGLE

Poe's guilt must have been unbearable. Virginia could not, in any case, survive her illness, but there can be little doubt that the conditions in which she spent her last months must have hastened her demise. She made Maria promise that she would never leave her 'poor Eddy' and that she would always look after him.

On January 30, 1847, she finally gave up the struggle, aged, like Poe's brother Henry and their mother Eliza, just twenty-four. She was buried two days later, the family's landlord feeling so sorry for them that he offered space for her in his family crypt so that she would not end up in a pauper's grave.

Poe, understandably fell to pieces. He had watched his young wife slowly die for five years. He ceased to care whether he lived or died and on one occasion collapsed unconscious and had to be carried to the doctor.

## PROMINENT FEATURES OF HIS GENIUS

After a while, however, he started to fare better, helped by his victory over Thomas Dunn English in the libel case and the much-needed money that brought.

He was also cheered by the recognition Rufus Griswold gave him in his new book, *Prose Writers of America*. In Poe's mysteries, according to Griswold, 'a subtle power of analysis is his distinguishing characteristic.'

He was also making headway abroad, Parisians being amazed that his C. Auguste Dupin tales of ratiocination, set in Paris, were written by an American who had never set foot in their city. As Evert Duyckinck put it, he 'is pestered and annoyed at home by penny-a-liners whom his iron pen has cut into too deeply ... It is curious to contrast this with his position abroad, where distance suffers only the prominent features of his genius to be visible.'

## WITH LOVE IN HER LUMINOUS EYES

Although recovered greatly, he was still mourning deeply and not writing very much at all. One poem, 'To – – –. Ulalume: A Ballad', did appear. A eulogy to a dead love, written as an elocution piece, it focuses greatly on the sound of the words and phrases. It was written for the Reverend Cotesworth Bronson who had requested of Poe a poem he could read at one of his lectures on public speaking, asking for a piece that had 'vocal variety and expression.'

Ultimately, Bronson did not use the poem in his lecture and Poe submitted it to *Sartain's Union Magazine*. It was rejected but was eventually published anonymously in the *American Whig Review* in December 1847. Nathaniel Parker Willis then re-printed it in the *Home Journal*, again anonymously, with Poe requesting that Willis insert a note asking for the name of the author.

The poem is extremely daring, hypnotic and uses insistent repetition for effect. Most people really did not know what to make of it. Many have found 'Ulalume' just too rich. Aldous Huxley called it 'a carapace of jeweled sound,' citing it as an example of Poe being 'too poetic' while American poet Daniel Hoffman (1923 – 2013) said that 'Reading "Ulalume" is like making a meal of marzipan. There may be nourishment in it but the senses are deadened by the taste, and the aftertaste gives one a pain in the stomach.'

> And I said—'She is warmer than Dian:
>
>   She rolls through an ether of sighs—
>
>   She revels in a region of sighs:
>
> She has seen that the tears are not dry on
>
>   These cheeks, where the worm never dies,
>
> And has come past the stars of the Lion
>
>   To point us the path to the skies—
>
>   To the Lethean peace of the skies—
>
> Come up, in despite of the Lion,
>
>   To shine on us with her bright eyes—
>
> Come up through the lair of the Lion,
>
>   With love in her luminous eyes.'

## THE NATURE OF THE UNIVERSE

To a deeply shocked *Broadway Journal* colleague, Poe had once declared 'The Bible is all rigmarole,' but towards the end of 1847 he could often be seen standing on the porch of the cottage in Fordham, perusing the night sky, wondering to himself what it was all about. He would keep Maria up long into the night as he hurriedly scribbled down the thoughts that would become his prose poem essay, 'Eureka'. She recalled later:

*He never liked to be alone and I used to sit up with him, often until four o'clock in the morning, he at his desk, writing, and I*

*dozing in my chair. When he was composing 'Eureka', we used to walk up and down the garden, his arm around mine, until I was so tired I could not walk. He would stop every few minutes and explain his ideas to me, and ask if I understood him.*

'Eureka' was a work on the nature of the universe, subtitled simply 'A Prose Poem' although it had previously carried the subtitle 'An Essay on the Material and Spiritual Universe'.

Poe did not carry out any experimentation or calculation, nor any scientific work at all, in fact, to enable him to come up with the conclusions contained in his poetic treatise about the nature of the universe and man's relationship with God. It was received very badly, thought absurd, even by those who generally supported him.

## MYSTICISM FOR THE MYSTICS

To this day there is debate about 'Eureka's' intent, some comparing it to his fiction, especially stories such as 'The Facts In the Case of M. Valdemar' and wondering if, like that work, it is fiction dressed up as real science. Poe, on the other hand, insisted that it was the greatest work of his life and of huge scientific importance. He wrote to a friend: 'What I have propounded will (in good time) revolutionize the world of Physical & Metaphysical Science.'

Poe had been highly critical of the Transcendentalists mainly because of the lack of rigor in their thinking and beliefs, describing them as 'mystics for mysticism's sake,' but now he was being mystical himself – even more mystical than them it could be argued – and with a similar disregard for the disciplines of science.

The Preface suggested that in reading the book, reason and reality should be put to one side: 'according to the schools, I *prove* nothing. So be it:—I design but to suggest— and to convince through suggestion.' He was afraid that people might think he was mad, and probably with good reason.

## A MOUNTAINOUS PIECE OF ABSURDITY

On the night of February 3, 1848, people began to arrive for a lecture at the Society Library at Leonard Street and Broadway in New York. The cheap advert in the *New York Tribune* that day had said rather vaguely:

> Edgar A. Poe will lecture at the Society Library on Thursday evening, the 3d inst. at half past 7. Subject, 'The Universe', Tickets 50 cents—to be had at the door.

The press had turned out to see what Poe was up to now and amongst friends who came was Evert Duyckinck. The hall was pretty empty, however, with only around sixty people sufficiently curious to attend. Poe walked on stage and announced that the subject of his talk that evening was the nature of matter, the stars, the planets, gravitation and electricity, the beginning and the end of the universe and God.

He read from a letter of the year 2848 when there are trains traveling at 300 miles per hour, airships and 'floating telegraph wires.' The letter was taken from a new story he was writing, called 'Mellonta Tauta', but he neglected to tell his listeners this. Then he moved onto talking about cosmology. As he droned on, the audience grew restless and it was almost 10 p.m. by the time he finished. His last words were a futile request for money for *The Stylus* magazine which he was vainly trying to get off the ground.

Evert Duyckinck was horrified. He wrote to his brother after the evening: 'A mountainous piece of absurdity for a popular lecture. It drove people from the room, instead of calling in subscribers.' Undeterred, Poe made an appointment with the publisher George Putnam (1814 – 72) and Putnam agreed to print five hundred copies of 'Eureka' in book form.

## I AM POE

The bizarre conversation with George Putnam showed the delusional state of Poe's mind at this time.

The reviewers were, on the whole, confused but respectful, referencing Swedenborg and the bestselling speculative natural history work, *Vestiges of the Natural History of Creation*, published anonymously in 1844 but later revealed to have been written by the Scottish journalist, Robert Chambers (1802 – 71).

Poe was once again resolved to launch *The Stylus* and in the summer of 1848 traveled to Richmond in the hope of raising some money. He wrote to a friend: 'I am desperately circumstanced—in the very bitter distress of mind and body. My last hope of extricating myself from the difficulties which are pressing me to death, is in going personally to a distant connection near Richmond.'

Unfortunately, the trip turned into a disaster. For three weeks he got drunk, staggering from bar to bar, lecturing other drunks on 'Eureka'.

THE

*STYLUS*

A

Monthly Journal of Literature Proper The Fine Arts And The Drama.

Purtus aliquando STYLUS, ferreus aliquando.
Paulus Jovius

EDITED BY
EDGAR A POE

Poe's design for the cover of *The Stylus*.

# POE'S STRANGE MEETING WITH GEORGE PUTNAM

## [AS DESCRIBED BY GEORGE P. PUTNAM ESQ., PUBLISHER]

A gentleman with a somewhat nervous and excited manner claimed attention on a subject which he said was of the highest importance. Seated at my desk, and looking at me a full minute with his 'glittering eye', he at length said: 'I am Mr Poe'. I was 'all ears', of course, and sincerely interested. It was the author of 'The Raven' and 'The Gold Bug'! 'I hardly know', said the poet, after a pause, 'how to begin what I have to say. It is a matter of profound importance.'

After another pause, the poet seeming to be in a tremor of excitement, he at length went on to say that the publication he had to propose was of momentous interest. Newton's discovery of gravitation was a mere incident compared to the discoveries revealed in this book. It would at once command such universal and intense attention that the publisher might give up all other enterprises, and make this one book the business of his lifetime.

An edition of fifty thousand copies might be sufficient to begin with, but it would be but a small beginning. No other scientific event in the history of the world approached in importance the original developments of this book.

All this and more, not in irony or jest, but in *intense* earnest … I was really impressed—but not overcome, promising a decision on Monday … The poet had to rest so long in uncertainty about the *extent* of the edition—partly reconciled, by a small loan, meanwhile. We *did* venture, not upon fifty thousand, but five hundred … it has never, apparently, caused any profound interest to popular or scientific readers.

George Putnam (1814 – 72).

# CHAPTER 11

# A DANGEROUS POWER OVER WOMEN

Edgar Allan Poe was undoubtedly attractive to women. A friend described how 'His remarkable personal beauty, the fascination of his manners and conversation, and his chivalrous deference and devotion to women, gave him a dangerous power over the sex.' Of course, he was also a sensitive poet who was a mess, a mixture that appealed to the intellectual, sentimental woman who wanted to be the one to save him from himself and his self-destructive tendencies.

In the last years of his life, Poe embarked on three disastrous relationships with other women – Marie Louise Shew (1821 – 77), Annie Richmond (1820 – 98) and Sarah Helen Whitman (1803 – 78). He had once said: 'I daren't sit in the world without a woman behind me' and now he was anxious to fill the gap that Virginia had left.

---

## MARIE LOUISE SHEW

The first woman he became interested in following Virginia's death was Marie Louise Shew who had looked after both Virginia and Poe in the later stages of her illness. Married to a water-cure physician whom she later divorced, Marie Louise was unlike the other women that Poe pursued, in that she was not involved in literature and was, on the whole, comparatively unsophisticated. Deeply religious, she devoted her life to caring for the sick and the poor.

Poe started to write poems to her and letters filled with passionate sentiments. But within a year she became concerned at his behavior both towards her and in general. Her friend, the Reverend John Hopkins told this intensely religious woman that she was

putting her faith in danger by associating with the writer of 'Eureka'. Finally, she ended their friendship, but Poe responded by writing self-pitying letters to her:

> *Are you to vanish like all I love, or desire, from my darkened and 'lost Soul'?—I have read over your letter again, and again, and cannot make it possible with any degree of certainty, that you wrote it in your right mind (I know you did not without tears of anguish and regret) ... Unless some true and tender and pure womanly love saves me, I shall hardly last a year, alone! ...*

He was unable to persuade her to change her mind and responded by drinking heavily and getting into fights. He challenged John Daniel, the editor of the Richmond *Semi-Weekly Examiner*, to a duel in August 1848 and it was probably fortunate for Poe that the duel never took place. Daniel wrote of Poe following his death, praising his intellect and his writing but he was also critical of what he termed his 'Ishmaelite' character and his 'proud reserve, his profound melancholy, his unworldliness—may we not say *unearthliness*—of nature [that] made his character very difficult of comprehension.'

Daniel also mentioned a nasty rumor that the Baltimore journalist John Hewitt had promulgated, that the younger Poe had made amorous approaches to his adopted father's second wife. Poe's drinking did not go unmentioned: 'Thousands of us have seen him drunk in the streets of this city. In all his visits save the last, he was in a state approaching mania. Whenever he tasted alcohol, he seldom stopped drinking it so long as he was able ... His taste for drink was a simple disease—no source of pleasure or excitement.'

## ANNIE RICHMOND

Nancy Richmond – known to Poe as 'Annie' – was eleven years younger than him, was married to a wealthy paper manufacturer and had a daughter. He met her through another woman, Jane Locke, whom Poe had set his sights on but when he visited her was disappointed to discover that she was older than he thought and was married with five children.

Annie Richmond lived next door to Jane with her husband and Poe irritated his host by becoming more interested in her. Like Marie Louise Shew, she was not of a literary bent but the two became very close although their

relationship remained platonic. He behaved as he always did with a woman in whom he was interested – he wrote her a story, poems and passionate love letters.

## SARAH HELEN WHITMAN

But Poe was, by this time involved with still another woman – the poet Sarah Helen Whitman, known to her friends as Helen, who was six years older than him and lived in Providence. She was the reason that he had returned to New York from his drunken rampage through the bars of Richmond when trying to raise money for *The Stylus*. He had been planning on a fund-raising tour of the south but when he received a couple of stanzas of poetry from Whitman, he abandoned it.

Poe's relationship with Helen Whitman had begun with poetry, as had his relationship with Fanny Osgood. Attending a Valentine's Day party at the home of the poet Anne Lynch, she read out a poem 'To Edgar A. Poe', although Poe was not at the party.

It later appeared in the *Home Journal*. Poe was told about it and replied with his poem 'To Helen'. Whitman did not respond, possibly because she was unaware that it had been sent by Poe himself.

Three months later, Poe composed a new poem entitled 'To Helen' that recalls the first time he had seen her in 1845. He had been attending a lecture by Fanny Osgood with whom he walked past Whitman's house. Whitman was standing in her rose garden but when Osgood offered to introduce him, he declined. Whitman was already a fan of Poe's work, writing to a friend:

> *I can never forget the impressions I felt in reading a story of his for the first time ... I experienced a sensation of such intense horror that I dared neither look at anything he had written nor even utter his name ... By degrees this terror took the character of fascination—I devoured with a half-reluctant and fearful avidity every line that fell from his pen.*

Annie Richmond (1820 – 1898).

## HELEN OF A THOUSAND DREAMS

Poe turned up at Whitman's house in Providence on September 21, and spent four days with her. By the beginning of October he was writing her lengthy love letters: 'As you entered the room, pale, timid, hesitating, and evidently oppressed at heart; as your eyes rested appealingly, for one brief moment, upon mine, I felt, for the first time in my life, and tremblingly acknowledged, the existence of spiritual influences altogether out of the reach of reason. I saw that you were *Helen—my* Helen—the Helen of a thousand dreams—she whose visionary lips so often lingered upon my own in the divine trance of passion.'

The couple had early on – after one day – made it clear that they were in a relationship, as one of Helen's friends who was present at a gathering at Helen's house on September 22 has written:

> *Of a sudden the company perceived that Poe and Helen were greatly agitated. Simultaneously both arose from their chairs and walked toward the center of the room. Meeting, he held her in his arms, kissed her; they stood for a moment, then he led her to his seat. There was a dead silence through all this strange proceeding.*

### DIVINE DESPAIR

Poe proposed marriage to Helen and she promised that she would answer him in a letter. By the end of September, however, she had heard about Poe's other amorous liaisons, with Annie Richmond and his childhood sweetheart, Sarah Elmira Royster.

Her friends and family were against the relationship with Poe and she was personally in a difficult situation, dependent on her mother and sister and with a responsibility towards them. She also had to consider her age and the fact that she had a weak heart. She said no to his proposal, but Poe would not accept it, writing to her on October 1, in an attempt to change her mind:

> *I have pressed your letter again and again to my lips, sweetest Helen—bathing it in tears of joy, or of a 'divine despair' ...*
>
> *All thoughts—all passions now seem merged in that one consuming desire—the mere wish to make you comprehend—to make you see that for which there is no human voice—the unutterable fervor of my love for you ...*
>
> *If throughout some long, dark summer night, I could but have held you close, close to my heart and whispered to you the strange secrets of its passionate history, then indeed you would have seen ... (that only you could) surround and bathe me in this electric light, illuminating and enkindling my whole nature—filling my soul with glory, with wonder, and with awe.*

### ROMANTIC ONSLAUGHT

In the letter, he tried to deal with her doubts and he tried again on October 18. It was a romantic onslaught but still she would not agree to marry him. On November 4, he returned to Providence in a bad way. He had no money and was in a severe depression. He was in such a state that he decided to end his life. That morning he took a stroll that led him past a pharmacy where he purchased a quantity of laudanum.

Without returning to his hotel, he boarded a train to Boston and wrote a suicide note addressed to Annie Richmond, reminding her, rather melodramatically, that she had promised to come to his bedside to comfort him when the day came. Arriving in Boston, he swallowed an ounce of the drug and walked to the nearest post office to post his farewell note. But it all went wrong.

> *Before I reached the Post Office my reason was entirely gone, & the letter was never put in. The laudanum was rejected from the stomach, I became calm, & to a casual observer, sane—so that I was suffered to go back to Providence.*

## POE'S VISIBLE DISINTEGRATION

Four days later, he had a daguerreotype taken by Edwin Manchester. In this iconic image Poe looks grim, older than his thirty-nine years. The French poet Baudelaire, a fan of Poe, said of it:

> ... he is very French: moustache; no sideburns; collar folded down. His brow is enormous both in breadth and height; he looks very pensive ... Despite the immense masculine force of the upper part of his head, it is, all in all, a very feminine face. The eyes are vast, very beautiful and abstracted.

Others have seen the ravages of the drunken binges. The American writer, Edmund Wilson, himself a drinker of note, wrote that '[Poe's] visible disintegration unpleasantly suggests an alcoholic patient.'

## SAVE HIM FROM PERDITION

On November 16, still in a very bad way, he wrote hysterically to Annie: 'But oh, *my darling, my* Annie, my own sweet *sister* Annie, my *pure* beautiful angel—*wife* of my soul—to be mine hereafter & *forever in the Heavens* ... I opened my whole heart to *you*—my Annie, whom I so madly, so distractedly love.'

Presumably to make her jealous, he dangled before her the news that he was actually seeing someone else at the time. '*Can* you, my Annie, *bear* to think I am another's? *It would give me* supreme—infinite bliss *to hear you say that you could* not *bear it.*'

On November 9, just as Helen Whitman was coming round to the idea of marrying Poe, he arrived at her door irredeemably drunk:

> He came alone to my mother's house in a state of wild & delirious excitement, calling upon me to save him from some terrible impending doom. The tones of his voice were appalling & rang through the house. Never have I heard anything so awful ...

> It was long before I could nerve myself to see him. My mother was with him more than two hours before I entered the room. He hailed me as an angel sent to save him from perdition. When my mother requested me to have a cup of strong coffee prepared for him, he clung to me so frantically as to tear away a piece of the muslin dress I wore ...

> In the afternoon he grew more composed, & my mother sent for Dr. A. H. Oakie, who, finding symptoms of cerebral congestion, advised his being taken to the house of his friend Wm. J. Pabodie, where he was kindly cared for.

Oddly, instead of dropping Poe like a hot potato, the incident warmed Helen to him and she finally agreed to marry him but only on condition that he stayed sober. If he would do that, she would make sure she obtained the permission of her mother. It was others, however, who would be Poe's undoing.

## AN IMPRUDENT MARRIAGE

Fanny Osgood was still upset at her humiliation, as she saw it, at Poe's hands and was also jealous that he was going to marry another. She stopped off in Providence to caution Whitman against the marriage. William Pabodie, to whose house Poe was taken when drunk, and who himself wanted to marry Whitman, also warned her about Poe. Even Maria Clemm had an opinion, preferring the more down-to-earth Annie and telling her: 'I so much fear *she* is not calculated to make him happy. I fear I will not love her. I *know* I shall never love her as I do *you*, my own darling.'

Matters got serious when, in the middle of December, Helen Whitman's mother gained sole control of the family estate to ensure that, in the event of the marriage taking place, Poe could not get his hands on any of it. Thus, if Helen were to marry Poe, she would be giving up everything. Nonetheless, she agreed to an immediate wedding arranged for Monday, December 25, Christmas Day.

# DAGUERREOTYPES

The only form of photography available in the United States during Poe's lifetime was the daguerreotype. The earliest and perhaps most beautiful of all photographic processes was introduced by Parisian artist Louis J.M. Daguerre in the summer of 1839. News of his discovery reached American shores the following fall. Like most Americans, Poe perceived the invention of these 'sun-drawn miniatures' as nothing short of the miraculous. In January 1840 he wrote: 'The instrument itself must undoubtedly be regarded as the most important and perhaps most extraordinary triumph of modern science ...' Before his death, Poe would sit for his daguerreotype portrait on at least six separate occasions.

Louis-Jacques-Mandé Daguerre (1787 – 1851) was a French artist and photographer, recognized for his invention of the daguerreotype process of photography. He became known as one of the fathers of photography. Though he is most famous for his contributions to photography, he was also an accomplished painter and a developer of the diorama theater.

# SARAH HELEN WHITMAN

Sarah Helen Power was born in Providence, Rhode Island. When she was just twelve her father went to sea, not returning for nineteen years. In 1828, she married the poet and writer, John Winslow Whitman who had been co-editor of the *Boston Spectator and Ladies' Album* in which he had published some of her poetry. He died in 1833 and by the time she met Poe she had been a widow for fifteen years, living with her younger sister and her mother, Anna, a forceful, domineering woman. Meanwhile, Whitman had developed a heart condition that she treated with ether, breathed in through her handkerchief.

She was a friend of the Transcendentalist writer, Margaret Fuller, as well as other New England intellectuals, but became interested in Transcendentalism after attending lectures by the movement's leading thinker, Ralph Waldo Emerson. Her interests were many and varied, however, and included mesmerism, science and the occult.

She was romantic in temperament, wore flowing draperies, lace scarves and shawls and is believed to have conducted séances in her house on Sundays. She met Edgar Allan Poe first in 1845, beginning a relationship with him three years later. They set a wedding date but the relationship ended when she was told that Poe had been drinking again.

Whitman's collection of poetry, *Hours, Life, and Other Poems* was published in 1853 and in 1860, eleven years after Poe had died, she published a book – *Edgar Allan Poe and His Critics* – that defended Poe against his opponents and especially Rufus Griswold.

Sarah Helen Whitman died in 1878, aged seventy-five.

But her friends still worried about the marriage and counseled her against it. Two days before the day of the ceremony, Helen and Poe were in a circulating library when she was handed a note. She later explained that 'a communication was handed me cautioning me against this *imprudent marriage* & informing me of many things in Mr Poe's recent career with which I was previously unacquainted. I was at the same time informed that he had *already* violated the solemn promises that he had made to me & my friends on the preceding evening.'

## SUFFERING INTOLERABLE INSULTS

She realized that it was going to be impossible to stop Poe from drinking and immediately canceled the wedding. Poe, of course, tried to change her mind, but Helen's mother sent him packing. She said that he 'left the house with an expression of bitter resentment at what he termed "the intolerable insults" of my family. I never saw him any more.'

He wrote to her again in January, blaming her mother and the effects of the ether that she took to treat her heart ailment but to which she was hopelessly addicted. He protested that he was never after her money and about the financial arrangements that she had been forced to accept by her mother – 'the suspicious & grossly insulting parsimony of the arrangements into which you suffered yourself to be forced by your mother.' He had also had enough of the bluestocking women with whom he had been associating: '... from this day forth I shun the pestilential society of *literary women*. They are a heartless, unnatural, venomous, dishonorable *set*, with no guiding principle but inordinate self-esteem.'

## THE EYES OF MY ANNIE

Poe now unashamedly turned his attention to Annie, telling her he was relieved at the parting of the ways with 'Mrs W.' In January,

he compared his feelings for her with what he had felt for Helen: '... there is *nothing* in this world worth living for except love—love *not* such as I once thought I felt for Mrs W. but such as burns in my very soul for *you*— so pure—so unworldly—a love which would make *all* sacrifices for your sake.'

In the background, however, the spurned Jane Locke was poisoning Annie's husband against Poe by telling him that Poe's love for Annie was more than spiritual. Poe severed his relationship with Annie for her sake:

> *It only remains for me, beloved Annie, to consult your happiness—which under all circumstances, will be & must be mine.— Not only must I not visit you at Lowell, but I must discontinue my letters & you yours. —I cannot & will not have it on my conscience that I have interfered with the domestic happiness of the only being in the whole world, whom I have loved, at the same time with truth & with purity.*

In response to this great disappointment, Poe wrote one of his finest poems, 'For Annie'. It deals with his suicide attempt – 'the lingering illness' – and how he had emerged from 'the fever called Living':

> *Thank Heaven! the crisis,*
> *  The danger, is past,*
> *And the lingering illness*
> *  Is over at last—*
> *And the fever called 'Living'*
> *  Is conquered at last.*

At the poem's conclusion – unusually upbeat for Poe – he says that his recovery is thanks to Annie.

> *But my heart it is brighter*
> *  Than all of the many*
> *Stars in the sky,*
> *  For it sparkles with Annie—*
> *It glows with the light*
> *  Of the love of my Annie—*
> *With the thought of the light*
> *  Of the eyes of my Annie.*

# CHAPTER 12

# THE SHADOW OF DEATH

Freed of the legion of women he had been pursuing and still unmarried, 1849 dawned with Poe, poverty-stricken as ever, having earned the princely sum of $166 during the whole of the previous year. Instead of writing and earning a living, he had spent much of it engaged in amorous pursuit, writing love letters instead of stories. He resolved to do better in 1849. 'I am about to bestir myself in the world of Letters rather more busily than I have done for three or four years past,' he told an editor.

He was as good as his word, entering a highly productive period. The vehicle for this was a new illustrated Boston weekly, *The Flag of Our Union*, that trumpeted itself as 'a paper for the millions.' Poe wrote about his latest story to Annie Richmond:

> *The 5 prose pages I finished yesterday are called—what do you think? —I am sure you will never guess—Hop-Frog! Only think of your Eddy writing a story with such a name as 'Hop-Frog'! ... It will be published in a weekly paper, of Boston, called 'The Flag of Our Union'—not a very respectable journal, perhaps, in a literary point of view, but one that pays as high prices as most of the Magazines.*

## POE'S REVENGE

It did, indeed, pay well and attracted a number of good writers even though a great deal of its content was not up to much. Poe contributed a number of stories to it including 'Hop-Frog', a story of revenge and cold-blooded murder featuring a dwarf who is a court jester.

It has been suggested that 'Hop-Frog' is Poe's revenge on Elizabeth Ellet, that she is the King and his seven ministers represent Ellet's circle of literary friends – Margaret Fuller, Hiram Fuller (1814 – 80), Thomas Dunn English, Anne Lynch Botta, Anna Blackwell, Jane Locke and Locke's husband.

Other biographical elements may be found in the fact that Hop-Frog is 'kidnapped from home and presented to the king,' the king in Poe's case being John Allan, and he is given another name, like Poe when he was adopted by the Allans. The escape at the end might have been him escaping all of that literary set and Trippetta might just be Annie Richmond.

## PALE, HAGGARD AND WILD

Soon, *The Flag of Our Union* was in financial trouble, closing down a useful source of income for Poe. Once again, he thought of launching his own magazine and there was a ray of light in that quarter because he had been in contact with a young investor, Edwin H. N. Patterson (1828 – 80).

The only problem was that Patterson wanted the magazine headquarters to be located in his home town, Oquawka, Illinois, and he wanted to call it the *Oquawka Spectator*. Poe was slightly put off by this, but departed on a tour of the East Coast to solicit subscriptions. As he left, he shouted back to Maria, 'Do not fear for Eddy!' They would be the very last words she would hear him say.

Maria had been worried about Poe's health and it was not without reason. A few days into his tour, he burst into the offices of John Sartain (1808 – 97), editor of *Sartain's Union Magazine*, looking 'pale and haggard' with a 'wild and frightened expression in his eyes.'

# THE FLAG OF OUR UNION

*The Flag of Our Union* (est. 1846) was a weekly story paper published in Boston, Massachusetts, in the mid-nineteenth century. In addition to news it featured works of fiction and poetry including contributions from notable writers such as Louisa May Alcott and Edgar Allan Poe. Publisher Frederick Gleason began *The Flag* in 1846, a 'miscellaneous family journal, containing news, wit, humor, and romance –– independent of party or sect.' Original stories, verse, and illustration appeared in the paper, as well as brief news items on local, national and international current events. Maturin Murray Ballou served as editor. In 1849, Gleason's office was located on the corner of Court and Tremont Streets in Boston. *The Flag* became quite popular. By some accounts it had 'the largest circulation of any papers in the United States,' *c.*1851. Around 1852, circulation reached 75,000, and shortly grew to 100,000.

He breathlessly explained to Sartain that he had heard some men seated behind him on a train plotting to kill him.

Poe said, he needed a razor to shave off his moustache and disguise his identity as they were pursuing him. Sartain did not have a razor to hand but offered to cut it off for him with scissors. When he asked him incredulously why anyone would want to kill him, Poe answered somewhat mysteriously that it was 'woman trouble.'

## THIS IS POE THE POET!

Sartain waited until he had calmed down a little, persuading him to go for a walk. Seated at a nearby reservoir, Poe admitted he might have been hallucinating. He told Sartain that he had been in Moyamensing prison which was close to Sartain's office and had seen a boiling cauldron and his Aunt Maria having her legs cut off bit by bit to torture him.

He said he had been put in prison for passing a counterfeit fifty-dollar note. Sartain suspected, however, that the prison stay, that had only been a few hours in duration, was actually for being drunk. Apparently, when Poe appeared in the dock in the courtroom, the magistrate had said, 'Why, this is Poe the poet!' and he had been freed.

It would not be the last time that the drunkard's nightmare – *delirium tremens* – would hit Poe. A week later, in a dreadful state he wandered through a cholera epidemic, penniless, starving, and wearing only one shoe before arriving at the door of the novelist George Lippard (1822 – 54). He was in despair, as a letter of the time to Maria testifies: 'It is no use to reason with me now; I must die. I have no desire to live since I have done *Eureka*.'

# HOP-FROG

Hop-Frog and his friend, Trippetta, both dwarves, have been captured in a far-off land and brought back to be used by the King as servants, Hop-Frog as a jester and Trippetta to work at arranging the decoration for social occasions. Hop-Frog is very deformed and even walking is painful for him while Trippetta is perfectly formed but just very small.

The King and his ministers are very obese and enjoy playing practical jokes which they do just about all the time.

*I never knew anyone so keenly alive to a joke as the king was. He seemed to live only for joking. To tell a good story of the joke kind, and to tell it well, was the surest road to his favor. Thus it happened that his seven ministers were all noted for their accomplishments as jokers.*

Poor Hop-Frog is often the butt of their jokes and he has been given that very nickname because of the awkward way in which his deformities force him to walk.

*In fact, Hop-Frog could only get along by a sort of interjectional gait—something between a leap and a wriggle—a movement that afforded illimitable amusement, and of course consolation, to the king, for (notwithstanding the protuberance of his stomach and a constitutional swelling of the head) the king, by his whole court, was accounted a capital figure.*

A masquerade ball is to take place for which Hop-Frog is expected to come up with costumes and invent a practical joke for the King and his ministers to play on the guests. He struggles to come up with something and the King, becoming impatient, makes him drink wine which Hop-Frog hates because 'he is susceptible to wine … when insulted and forced to drink [he] becomes insane with rage.' Trippetta tries to intervene on her friend's behalf but is knocked to the floor by the King who throws the wine in her face. Angered by this treatment of his friend, Hop-Frog comes up with a joke that the King and his Ministers can play on the guests.

The King and his ministers will dress as ourang-outangs and rush into the party terrifying the guests. The King loves it and Hop-Frog accordingly dresses them up in skin-tight costumes, paints tar on them and then sticks flax to it to look like hair. He then chains them all together. The King orders all the doors of the ballroom to be locked and the key is to be handed to Hop-Frog. When the guests have all arrived, he is to lock the final door so that the guests cannot escape.

Bang on the stroke of midnight, the door is unlocked and the King and his ministers, dressed as ourang-outangs run into the ballroom, creating chaos. Hop-Frog, as if taking part in the joke, attaches the chain to the hanging chain of a chandelier, the chandelier having already been removed under the pretence that the King did not want it to drip wax on to the costumes of the guests. Hop-Frog pulls the chained-up ourang-outangs into the air and with them hanging there, approaches with a flaming torch as if he is trying to find out who these creatures are. He says:

*'I now see distinctly,' he said, 'what manner of people these maskers are. They are a great king and his seven privy-councillors—a king who does not scruple to strike a defenseless girl and his seven councillors who abet him in the outrage. As for myself, I am simply Hop-Frog, the jester—and this is my last jest.'*

Hop-Frog sets them on fire, the highly combustible material burning ferociously. He climbs the chain to the ceiling and escapes through a small window onto the roof. Waiting there is his friend Trippetta. Together they leave the castle, the screams from the ballroom ringing in their ears.

Hop-Frog, Trippetta, the King and his ministers.
Illustration for 'Hop-Frog' by Arthur Rackham, 1935.

## THIS STRANGE AND STORMY LIFE

Lippard rallied some of Poe's friends to provide money so that Poe could continue with his journey and he also clothed and fed him, but he sensed a change in his friend and when Poe left him, Lippard later said, 'He held our hand for a long time, and seemed loth to leave us—there was in his voice, look and manner, something of a Presentiment that this strange and stormy life was near its close.'

Poe traveled on to his childhood home of Richmond, sweating in the summer heat while dressed in his dirty black clothes. Worse still, he had lost his lecture notes in Philadelphia and it was through these lectures that he hoped to raise money and subscriptions for his magazine.

Having arrived with only two dollars in his pocket, however, he was cheered by the sudden arrival of a fifty-dollar cheque from Edwin Patterson in Oquawka. He immediately spruced himself up and set out to find his childhood sweetheart, Elmira Royster who still lived in Richmond. The man that Elmira had married instead of Poe had died leaving her $100,000.

Elmira was getting ready for church one morning when there was a knock at the door.

> I was ready to go to church and a servant told me that a gentleman in the parlor wanted to see me. I went down and was amazed to see him—but knew him instantly. —He came up to me in the most enthusiastic manner and said: 'Oh! Elmira, is that you?' That very morning, I told him, I was going to church, that I never let anything interfere with that, that he must call again, and when he did call again he renewed his addresses. I laughed at it; he looked very serious and said he was in earnest and had been thinking about it for a long time. Then I found out that he was very serious and I became serious.

## THE POETIC PRINCIPLE

So, by the end of that morning, Poe had decided that they should get married. At first she thought he was joking, but soon realized he meant it and began to warm to the idea. Of course, the matter of his drinking had to be dealt with but he told a local doctor that he would stop and even joined a local temperance society. He re-wrote his lecture on 'The Poetic Principle' and delivered it to a packed house, delighting everyone at the end by providing a spirited rendition of 'The Raven'. He gave a second lecture the following month.

Poe's fiancée, Mrs Sarah Elmira Shelton (née Royster).

He was happy in Richmond that September of 1849, catching up with old friends and reacquainting himself with his little sister Rosalie who suffered from learning difficulties but followed him around like one of his cats. But, there was still work to be done on raising funds and subscriptions for his magazine, whatever it was going to be called.

## LEAVING HIS TROUBLES BEHIND

He and Elmira had reached an understanding about the marriage even though there were a number of obstacles. Her two children were very much against it and there were also financial issues. Her husband's will had stated that if she re-married, she would receive only a quarter of his estate. And, of course, Poe would have to consult with Maria.

In the meantime, he had found work paying a hundred dollars in Philadelphia where a piano manufacturer had asked him to edit some poems written by his wife. As he left Elmira, he was not well. She described their last evening together:

> *He came up to my house on the evening of 26th Sept. to take leave of me.—He was very sad, and complained of being sick; I felt his pulse, and found he had considerable fever, and did not think it probable that he would be able to start the next morning, as he anticipated.—I felt so wretched about him all of that night, that I went up early the next morning to enquire after him, when much to my regret, he had left in the boat for Baltimore.*

It had been one of the happiest interludes in Edgar Allan Poe's troubled life and he was reported by a friend to have left in a very positive mood: 'He declared that the last few weeks in the society of his old and new friends had been the happiest he had known for many years, and that when he again left New York he should there leave behind all the trouble and vexation of his past life.'

## HIS FINAL BINGE

In the early hours of September 27, Poe boarded a steamboat for Baltimore. He was eventually heading for New York to settle his affairs and then bring Maria back to Richmond with him but first, he had to spend some time working on the piano-manufacturer's wife's poems in Philadelphia. Arriving in Baltimore, he disembarked and went drinking. It would prove to be his final binge.

He met up with some old friends who insisted he join them in a glass of whisky. It was his first alcohol in three months and he had soon drunk himself senseless. For the next six days no one has any idea what became of him.

His cousin Neilson later wrote to Maria: 'At what time he arrived in the city, where he spent the time when he was here, or under what circumstances, I have been unable to ascertain.' It seems likely that, hopelessly drunk, he had spent those days gripped by the terrible hallucinations that had troubled him in Philadelphia.

On the afternoon of October 3, Poe was found by a young printer, semi-conscious and in a dreadful condition outside an Irish tavern named *Gunner's Hall*. An urgent note was sent to Poe's Baltimore friend, Dr. Joseph Snodgrass:

> *There is a gentleman, rather the worse for wear, at Ryan's 4th ward polls [an election was taking place], who goes under the cognomen of Edgar A. Poe, and who appears in great distress, & he says he is acquainted with you, and I assure you, he is in need of immediate assistance.*

Snodgrass reported that he found Poe dressed in ragged clothing obviously not his own:

> *His hat—or rather the hat of somebody else, for he had evidently been robbed of his clothing, or cheated in an exchange,—was a cheap palm-leaf one, without a band, and soiled; his coat, of commonest alpaca, and evidently 'secondhand'; his pants of gray-mixed cassimere, dingy and badly fitting.*

*He wore neither vest nor neckcloth, if I remember aright, while his shirt was badly crumpled and soiled.*

Poe was, as he recalled, unconscious and did not resemble the man he remembered:

*The intellectual flash of the eye had vanished, or rather had been quenched in the bowl ...*

*He was so utterly stupefied with liquor that I thought it best not to seek recognition or conversation ... So insensible was he, that we had to carry him to the carriage as if a corpse. The muscles of articulation seemed paralyzed to speechlessness, and mere incoherent mutterings were all that were heard.*

## DRENCHED IN PERSPIRATION

Poe was taken immediately to Washington College Hospital where he was examined by Dr. John Moran. Like the other patients who were in hospital because of alcoholism, he was given a bed in a turret of the old building, in a room that had bars on the window. The doctor reported that 'when brought to the hospital he was unconscious of his condition—who brought him or with whom he had been associating.'

For the next ten hours, Poe would remain thus but then the hallucinations began. He had a 'tremor of the limbs, and at first a busy, but not violent or active delirium—constant talking—and vacant converse with spectral and imaginary objects on the walls. His face was pale and his whole person drenched in perspiration.' It would take two days for these hallucinations to pass.

## LORD HELP MY POOR SOUL

When he awoke on October 5, he was very confused, believing, for instance, that Virginia was still alive. He was horrified at what had happened and said that 'the best thing his friend could do would be to blow out his brains with a pistol.' Moran knew that he was in a perilous condition, even though conscious.

He had his body sponged with warm water with spirits added, mustard plasters were applied to his stomach and feet, cold compresses were applied to his head and he was given a 'stimulating cordial.' It looked bad, however, and another doctor from the hospital was certain Poe was about to die from 'excessive nervous prostration and loss of nerve power, resulting from exposure, affecting the encephalon, a sensitive and delicate membrane of the brain.'

His last few days, including a very uncharacteristic religious exhortation, were recalled by Dr. Moran:

*When I returned [later on Friday] I found him in a violent delirium, resisting the efforts of two nurses to keep him in bed. This state continued until Saturday evening (he was admitted on Wednesday) when he commenced calling for someone called 'Reynolds' which he did through the night up to three on Sunday morning. At this time a very decided change began to affect him. Having become enfeebled from exertion he became quiet and seemed to rest for a short time, then gently moving his head, he said 'Lord help my poor soul' and expired.*

Edgar Allan Poe died at 5 a.m. on Sunday, October 7, 1849. He was forty years old.

## HYPOGLYCAEMIA AND LIVER DISEASE

So, who was 'Reynolds'? Perhaps he was Jeremiah Reynolds (1799 – 1858) whose *Address on the Subject of a Surveying and Exploring Expedition to the Pacific Ocean and South Seas* he had reviewed in January 1837 and whose book he used as a source for *The Narrative of Arthur Gordon Pym*. One biographer has suggested that Poe may have conflated Jeremiah Reynolds with the spectral figure at the black hole at the end of that story.

It is possible that Poe had been suffering from hypoglycaemia – low blood sugar – that could have been a product of liver disease. That might also explain his hallucinations and it would have made it difficult for him to tolerate alcohol. All the symptoms that he displayed in his last days would indicate this.

## COLD-BLOODED AND UNCHRISTIAN-LIKE

Poe's cheap coffin was interred at 4 p.m. on October 8, in the Poe family plot at Baltimore's Presbyterian Cemetery. Around the grave was just a scattering of mourners, amongst them Poe's aunt, Elizabeth Herring, and her husband, cousin Neilson Poe, Joseph Snodgrass, his former schoolmaster Joseph Clarke and Zaccheus Collins Lee (1805 – 59), a Baltimore lawyer who had been at university with Poe.

The ceremony, conducted by Reverend William Clemm, a cousin of Virginia, was brief, lasting just three minutes and carried out in a 'cold-blooded and unchristian-like' manner, as one mourner put it. Joseph Snodgrass remarked on the cheapness of the casket:

*'Into this [grave] the plainly coffined body was speedily lowered, and then the earth was shoveled directly upon the coffin-lid.'*

### The Whitman Daguerreotype
#### November 13, 1848

'This picture of mine has been hidden away all these years because I thought it did not represent him truly, but many persons who have seen it lately think it has the best expression of any picture yet taken of him,' wrote Sarah Helen Whitman in 1874.

*This was so unusual, even in the burials of the poor, that I could not help noticing the absence of not only the customary box, as the inclosure for the coffin itself, but even the commonest boards to prevent direct contact of the decomposing earth with it.'*

Tragically, when, a few years later, Neilson Poe ordered a tombstone Poe's luck turned out to be bad even in death – a freight train derailed and crashed into the stone-mason's yard destroying the stone.

## NEWS TRAVELS FAST

The news of Poe's death spread quickly, the *Baltimore Sun* noting that it 'will cause poignant regret among all who admire genius, and have sympathy for the frailties too often attending it.' Newspapers along the East Coast picked it up and all acknowledged his genius, if at the same time remarking on the difficulties he experienced. Writing in the *New York Daily Tribune*, Rufus Griswold, provided a dreadful obituary, using the pseudonym 'Ludwig'.

Griswold remarked that few people would be saddened by Poe's death because 'he had few or no friends' and described him as 'at all times a dreamer—dwelling in ideal realms—in heaven or hell—peopled with creations and the accidents of his brain.' Poe had often lampooned Griswold and now, it seemed, Griswold was taking his revenge.

He described Poe as cynical, envious and arrogant and that he 'walked the streets, in madness or melancholy, with lips moving in indistinct curses.' Poe had 'no moral susceptibility,' he claimed, 'and what was more remarkable in a proud nature, little or nothing of the true point of honor.' The problem was that Griswold, a respected figure, carried a great deal of authority in literary matters and his views were listened to, and believed to be true.

## VILIFIED FOR YEARS TO COME

A number of Poe's friends rallied to his support in the weeks following, associates such as George Lippard, Lambert Wilmer, Henry Hirst, Nathaniel Willis, George Graham and John Neal. However, Griswold's barbed comments were more likely to sell newspapers and it was those that were promulgated. Poe was vilified then and for a number of years to come.

Rosalie, his heir, was unable to administer his estate which passed instead into the control of Maria Clemm. Rosalie would end her days as a beggar, selling portraits of her brother on the streets. Admitted to a shelter in Washington D.C. in 1870, she died four years later aged sixty-four.

Poe had named Rufus Griswold as his literary executor and Maria gave Griswold her support, even noting in the Preface to Griswold's 1850 edition of Poe's works: '[Poe] decidedly and unequivocally certified his respect for the literary judgment of Mr Griswold, with whom his personal relations, on account of some unhappy misunderstanding, had for years been interrupted.'

## THE ANGELS ARE JEALOUS

It seemed strange that Poe had stipulated Griswold as his literary executor, but, given Griswold's literary credentials, it was in reality a canny move. Poe had hardly been in the ground a week before Griswold was compiling a collected edition of his works.

Meanwhile, Poe's last complete poem, the much-loved and much-adapted 'Annabel Lee' was hurried into print. Composed in May 1849, it explores the death of a beautiful woman with whom the narrator was in love and his love for her remains even in death. His love for her is so great that the angels are jealous of it:

*But we loved with a love that was more than love—*

*I and my Annabel Lee—*

*With a love that the wingèd seraphs of Heaven*

*Coveted her and me.*

## MEMOIR OF THE AUTHOR

Griswold published the poem two days after Poe's death as part of his scurrilous obituary and it appeared in the *Southern Literary Messenger* in November.

Griswold received no payment for compiling Poe's work which took him just six weeks. Maria, for her part, was given a few free sets that she tried to sell. On January 10, 1850, *The Collected Works of the Late Edgar Allan Poe* arrived in bookshops. It was in two green, clothbound volumes, the first *Tales*, the second *Poems and Miscellanies*, together amounting to a thousand pages. It proved a popular publication, selling 1,500 sets a year for a number of years.

Griswold's 'Memoir of the Author' that was printed in it was an extended version of his scathing obituary and for years Poe was measured by his words and viewed by readers as a drunken, depraved, amoral wastrel. Griswold added many falsehoods to the memoir, suggesting that Poe had been expelled from university and had deserted from the army. He dragged up the old rumor about Poe trying to seduce John Allan's second wife and accused him of drug addiction.

## DRUNKENNESS AND INCEST

Griswold even falsified passages in Poe's letters to him to make it appear that the dead man had admired him. He exaggerated Poe's drunkenness – although, frankly, little exaggeration was needed – by inventing a story about the police having to be called the night before Poe's projected marriage to Helen Whitman, a story that Whitman flatly denied. She insisted that Poe was, as many others had testified throughout his life, 'essentially and instinctively a gentleman, utterly incapable, even in moments of excitement and delirium, of such an outrage as Dr. Griswold had ascribed to him.'

Griswold's character assassination continued unabated. '[He] exhibits scarcely any virtue in either his life or his writings. Probably there is not another instance in the literature of our language in which so much has been accomplished without a recognition or a manifestation of conscience ... Irascible, envious—bad enough, but not the worst, for these salient angles were all varnished over with a cold repellent cynicism, his passions vented themselves in sneers.'

Griswold claimed that, if he had married Elmira, he would have insisted on living close to Annie Richmond whom he would have taken as a mistress. But, most disgusting of all, he reported that Poe had had an incestuous relationship with Maria Clemm.

## DEFENDING POE TO THE DEATH

Poe's women came to his defense. Helen Whitman opposed Griswold's views in *Edgar Poe and His Critics*, published in 1860, praising 'his devotion to his wife, his courtesy, his rare gifts as a conversationalist, his social charm, and his innate rectitude.' Annie Richmond invited Maria Clemm to live with her and when her husband died in 1873, she changed her name legally from Nancy to Annie which was what Poe had always called her. She died, aged seventy-eight, in 1898.

Griswold's efforts to besmirch Poe had the opposite effect to the one he intended because the public not only enjoyed reading Poe's works but also got an extra frisson from thinking that they were written by a man who was truly evil. The cult around Poe even stretched to Virginia whose bones were acquired by an early Poe biographer, William F. Gill. He put them in a box that he kept under his bed to show to visitors. Eventually, they were placed alongside her husband's remains at the Presbyterian Cemetery.

PART 5

# DOWN AMONG
# THE DEAD MEN

Don't put on any airs
When you're down on Rue Morgue Avenue
They got some hungry women there
And they really make a mess outta you.

Bob Dylan *from* Just Like Tom Thumb's Blues

# CHAPTER 13

# LIVING AN EXTRAORDINARY AFTERLIFE

Edgar Allan Poe's life was strange and unremittingly miserable, but his afterlife has been extraordinary. He was, arguably, the first American writer to achieve international recognition, and is now read and revered across the world and translated into countless languages. His influence is profound and ongoing, reaching into music, film and art as much as literature. There have been more than a dozen film versions of his story 'The Fall of the House of Usher', for instance. Meanwhile, his works have also inspired composers ranging from Claude Debussy to Lou Reed.

## A BRILLIANT DAZZLING ELECTRIC LIGHT

The restoration of Poe's reputation after the efforts of Griswold to besmirch it forever began with a number of his friends, but really got into gear in 1874 with the first significant biography, written by John Henry Ingram. A memorial ceremony organized by Sara Sigourney Rice in Baltimore in 1875 also helped. Of great interest was a volume of letters, reminiscences and speeches by a number of literary lions on the subject of Edgar Allan Poe.

Amongst those who contributed were John Greenleaf Whittier, William Cullen Bryant, Henry Wadsworth Longfellow, Oliver Wendell Holmes, Alfred, Lord Tennyson and Algernon Swinburne. Americans were amazed to see in what high regard Poe was held in Europe. Indeed, Swinburne was a particularly avid fan, writing to Poe's biographer, John Ingram: 'America should do something to shew public reverence for the only one (as yet) among her men of genius who has won not merely English but European fame.'

American poet Walt Whitman attended the ceremony. He had briefly met Poe in 1845 at the *Broadway Journal* offices and was a fan of Poe's virtuosity and praised his 'intense

Robert Louis Stevenson (1850 – 1894).

faculty for technical and abstract beauty,' but famously thought that although Poe could be named 'among the electric lights of imaginative literature, brilliant and dazzling,' there was 'no heat.'

## ACCLAIMED AS A GENIUS

It was left to the English poets who came to the fore after Swinburne to focus on the beauty of Poe's poetry, and distance themselves from the claims that he displayed a lack of 'moral principle' in his work. In this camp were those of the Decadent, Aesthetic and *fin-de-siècle* traditions, such as Ernest Dowson, Oscar Wilde and, to some extent, W.B. Yeats.

In fact, Poe was acclaimed as a genius in many books published in England between 1880 and 1930 while he was little appreciated in the United States and between 1880 and 1900 British publishers were responsible for around thirty-five separate editions of his works.

## STEVENSON AND KIPLING

British novelists also championed Poe and borrowed heavily from him. Robert Louis Stevenson borrowed themes from Poe's work and made them even more accessible to a popular audience. Thus, was 'William Wilson' plundered for the hugely successful *Dr. Jekyll and Mr Hyde* of 1886. 'The Gold Bug' provided a source for *Treasure Island* and he expressed his gratitude in the Preface of that book: 'I broke into the gallery of Mr Poe ... No doubt the skeleton [in my novel] is conveyed from Poe.'

Rudyard Kipling acknowledged the influence Poe had on him: 'My own personal debt to Poe is a heavy one.' He borrowed many technical effects from Poe such as the inclusion of poems within tales and re-worked a number of Poe's tales of revenge and the supernatural as demonstrated by his story 'The Phantom Rickshaw' in which, as in Poe's 'Metzengerstein', a horse is the vehicle of retribution. He even wrote a story in which an ourang-outang is the murderer, as Poe did in 'The Murders in the Rue Morgue'. A number of his stories of the supernatural similarly repeat Poe's themes.

## CHARLES BAUDELAIRE

It was in France, however, that his flame was really kept burning. The French poet, Charles Baudelaire, was largely responsible for the success of Poe there with translations of his fiction published between 1848 and 1864 at the expense of his own creative work. To the Poe-obsessed Baudelaire the American writer was the forerunner of the artistic and literary Decadent movement. But he was also a tragic artist figure, destroyed by the industrial thrust of American modernity.

Charles Baudelaire (1821 – 1867).

The truth was that the more people like Griswold turned Poe into a monster, the more the rebellious Baudelaire was attracted to him. '*Mon semblable, mon frère*' (My double, my brother), he called him. He believed that he had conceived ideas for works that Poe had already written before he encountered his work.

> *I found poems and stories which I had thought about, but in a confused, vague and disordered way, and which Poe had been able to treat perfectly ...*
>
> *The first time I opened one of his books I saw, to my amazement and delight, not simply certain subjects which I had dreamed of, but sentences which I had thought out, written by him twenty years before.*

## THE LITERATURE OF THE FUTURE

French writers who followed Baudelaire took their line from him. The Goncourt brothers, Edmond and Jules, acknowledged the influence that Poe's work would wield in the century to come.

> *After reading Edgar Allan Poe. Something critics have not noticed: a new literary world, pointing to the literature of the future twentieth century. Scientific miracles, fables on the pattern A + B; a clear-sighted, sickly literature. No more poetry, but analytic fantasy. Something monomaniacal. Things playing a more important part than people; love giving way to deductions and other sources of ideas, style, subject, and interest; the basis of the novel transferred from the heart to the head, from the passion to the idea, from the drama to the denouement.*

Paul Valéry, who even liked 'Eureka', also came under the spell of Poe, praising the originality on display across all his work:

> *It is not astonishing that Poe, possessing so effective and sure a method, should be the inventor of several different varieties, should have offered the first and most striking example of the scientific tale, of the modern cosmogenic poem, of the novel of the criminal investigation, of the introduction into the literature of morbid psychological states, and that all his work should manifest on every page an intelligence which is to be observed to the same degree in no other literary career.*

## NIETZSCHE AND KAFKA

In Germany, although not quite as adoring as in France, there were expressions of admiration from writers and thinkers such as the philosopher Friedrich Nietzsche who, like Baudelaire, responded to Poe's outsider status, 'often lost in the mud and almost in love with it,' as he put it. In *The Will to Power* he writes of the type of artist who is at

Franz Kafka (1883 – 1924).

war with himself as much as with the society in which he lives: 'A certain catholicity of the ideal above all is almost sufficient proof in the case of the artist of self-contempt, of 'Morass': the case of Baudelaire in France, the case of Edgar Allan Poe in America, the case of Wagner in Germany.'

The Bohemian-born writer, Franz Kafka, also responded to the work of Poe, identifying with his escape from the unpleasant reality he inhabited into the world of the imagination:

> *Poe was ill. He was a poor devil who had no defenses against the world. So, he fled into drunkenness. Imagination only served him as a crutch. He wrote tales of mystery to make himself at home in the world. That's perfectly natural. Imagination has fewer pitfalls than reality has ... I know his way of escape and his dreamer's face.*

## THE FIRST DETECTIVE

The list of writers influenced by Edgar Allan Poe is long and varied, including everyone from Agatha Christie to Richard Brautigan, Stephen King to Vladimir Nabokov and Fyodor Dostoevsky to Clive Barker. But, it is often as the inventor of the detective story that he is remembered most.

When he published the first ever detective story – 'The Murders in the Rue Morgue' – he set the rules for the genre that would occupy bestseller lists for the foreseeable future – an impossible crime; an eccentric but dazzlingly brilliant detective who analyzes the clues; a narrator who is the not-so-clever partner of the detective to explain to us the complexities of the detective's mind and the details of his solution to the crime. C. Auguste Dupin proved so popular that Poe himself provided two sequels to Rue Morgue, one of which – 'The Mystery of Marie Rogêt' – was the first detective story actually based on a real-life crime.

## SIR ARTHUR CONAN DOYLE

Other detective writers would follow in Poe's footsteps, principal amongst whom was Sir Arthur Conan Doyle who once said: 'Where was the detective story before Poe breathed the breath of life into it?' Conan Doyle, of course, created the master detective, Sherlock Holmes, whose mind worked in a similarly byzantine way to Dupin's. He also had a slightly less clever sidekick in the dependable Dr. Watson.

Like the unnamed partner in Poe's tales of ratiocination, Watson provides a conduit for Holmes's thinking. Like Dupin, Holmes and his sidekick live in isolation. As the narrator

Sir Arthur Conan Doyle (1859 – 1930), most noted for his fictional stories about the detective Sherlock Holmes.

# Jules Verne
## (1828 – 1905)

Together, Edgar Allan Poe and Jules Verne helped craft an important part of today's science fiction. French author Verne was a lifelong fan of Poe, having read his stories as a boy, and was influenced by Poe's writing. Both sought to tell stories that could exist in the real world, while blending in speculative scientific situations. Photograph by Félix Nadar, *c.* 1878.

in 'Marie Rogêt' says: 'Engaged in researches which absorbed our whole attention, it had been nearly a month since either of us had gone abroad, or received a visitor, or more than glanced at the leading political articles in one of the daily papers.'

## INDEBTED TO POE

Neither Dupin nor Holmes appear to have any interest in anything other than the pursuits of the mind, seemingly disinterested in the trivialities of normal human interaction. They are also the intellectual superiors of the police officers with whom they come into contact, can deduce what a person does by aspects of their appearance or behavior and solve crimes with dazzling displays of mindpower. Lestrade, the policeman in the Sherlock Holmes books is a direct descendent of 'G—' the Prefect of Police in Poe's stories.

Conan Doyle always publicly acknowledged his profound debt to Edgar Allan Poe in his work and wrote in his 1924 autobiography *Memories and Adventures* that Dupin was one of his 'boyhood heroes.' He said at a banquet to celebrate the centenary of Edgar Allan Poe's birth: 'These tales have been so pregnant with suggestion, so stimulating to the minds of others, that it may be said of many of them that each is a root from which a whole literature has developed.'

## POE AND SCIENCE FICTION

Poe's efforts at science fiction do not involve flying saucers, aliens, laser guns or time machines. His work is limited in this area by the scientific understanding of the time in which he lived. The closest he came to that style of sci-fi would have been in 'The Unparalleled Adventure of Hans Pfaall' in which he describes 'a fantastical-looking city' that is occupied by 'a vast crowd of ugly little people' without ears and who use 'a singular method of inter-communication' that could be surmised to be telepathy.

The great science fiction pioneers, Jules Verne and H.G. Wells were heavily influenced by Poe. Jules Verne read Baudelaire's translations of Poe's work in various magazines and newspapers and was impressed by Poe's tales of ratiocination and the up-to-date scientific information with which Poe laced some of his tales.

The mathematical descriptions of machines such as in Poe's story 'Maelzel's Chess-Player' and 'The Pit and the Pendulum' made an impact upon H.G. Wells who said that 'the fundamental principles of the construction that underlie such stories as Poe's "Murders in the Rue Morgue" ... are precisely those that should guide a scientific writer.'

## JULES VERNE

Jules Verne's 'Five Weeks in a Balloon' was influenced by Poe's 'The Balloon Hoax' and 'Hans Pfaall'. His story 'The Sphinx of the Snows' could easily be a sequel to *Arthur Gordon Pym* and is even dedicated to Edgar Allan Poe. And *Around the World in Eighty Days* has the same basic idea as Poe's tale 'Three Sundays in a Week' in which a couple are told they cannot get married until there are three Sundays in a week. They use the crossing of the International Date Line to experience the desired number of Sundays.

Verne's most famous work, *20,000 Leagues Under the Sea* is very influenced by Poe. Nemo reminds us of Hans Pfaall, Roderick Usher and Auguste Dupin. Like them, he suffers silently and has no time for society and the trappings of everyday existence. At the end of the story, Professor Aronnax describes what he has experienced as like:

*... being drawn into that strange region where the foundered imagination of Edgar Poe roamed at will. Like the fabulous Gordon Pym, at every moment I expected to see 'that veiled human figure, of larger proportions than those of any inhabitant of the earth, thrown across the cataract which defends the approach to the pole.'*

# CHAPTER 14

# AMERICA'S EVIL GRANDFATHER

In America, meanwhile, Edgar Allan Poe's influence began to be felt in the world of literature. In the works of Nathaniel Hawthorne and Herman Melville can be found what one commentator has called 'the ambiguous opposition of good and evil' so predominant in American literature and originating in Poe's work.

Certainly, *The Narrative of Arthur Gordon Pym* influenced Melville's *Moby Dick*. The works of Joshua Reynolds were employed as a source by both Poe and Melville and the opening sentence of each book is strikingly similar – 'My name is Arthur Gordon Pym' and 'Call me Ishmael.'

As in the case of the detective stories, each lead character has the companionship of a fearsome, semi-wild comrade who also saves his life. And surely the mysterious, evil white figure seen at the conclusion of 'Arthur Gordon Pym' is reflected in the white whale that Ahab madly pursues.

## F. SCOTT FITZGERALD

It was perhaps not only in his writing that F. Scott Fitzgerald saw the works of Edgar Allan Poe reflected but possibly in his life as well. Both writers had fathers who failed and both had greater aspirations than they possibly should. Neither graduated from university and both had fairly undistinguished military careers. Even in marriage there were similarities, Virginia dying from tuberculosis when she was just twenty-four years old, Zelda Fitzgerald being diagnosed as a schizophrenic, aged just twenty-nine and incarcerated in a psychiatric clinic for much of the remainder of her life.

Both Poe and Fitzgerald were forced by circumstances to write for whoever was paying and neither ever had any money, having to borrow constantly from friends and associates. They were also, most importantly, both alcoholics whose drinking ultimately killed them. They both antagonized those who could have given them work – Poe literary editors and other writers, Fitzgerald Hollywood film producers. Each of them

F. Scott Fitzgerald (1896 – 1940).

died with their literary reputations in tatters but each of them was re-evaluated a long time after their deaths.

Fitzgerald's story 'The Diamond as Big as the Ritz' parallels Poe's 'The Fall of the House of Usher', even the name of Fitzgerald's protagonist, Unger, is similar to the name Usher. The plots are alike with the two main characters – a young man in Poe's, a naive schoolboy in Fitzgerald's – being invited to visit a childhood acquaintance. Each observes strange behavior in the large houses they visit.

Each family is trapped, or even imprisoned, in these houses, the Ushers by the doom that surrounds the family and the Ungers by the pointless wealth they have accumulated. There is much else that is similar, including the doomed sister figure – Madeline Usher in Poe's account and Kismine Washington in Fitzgerald's, each of whom is briefly glimpsed. Finally, both houses are in the end destroyed but the young visitors manage to escape.

## VLADIMIR NABOKOV

Also influenced by Poe was Vladimir Nabokov, the Russian writer who fled with his family to the United States in 1940. He uses Poe's tragic life in a short story, 'A Forgotten Poet', written in 1944 in which a poet who has died at the age of twenty-four in 1849, suddenly re-appears aged seventy-four in 1899 demanding the money that has been raised for a memorial to him. It is no coincidence that the year of the death of his protagonist, Perov, is also the year of Poe's death. Both had died poor but the reputation of each had grown after death.

Nabokov's notorious novel *Lolita* has numerous allusions to Poe and his work, including the name of the main character Humbert Humbert's first love – Annabel Leigh, taken from Poe's poem 'Annabel Lee'. Their relationship is described, in fact, in phrases that are taken from Poe's poem and Humbert's relationship with the underage Lolita reminds us of Poe and Virginia.

## TOM WOLFE

Tom Wolfe calls a chapter in his bestselling *The Bonfire of the Vanities* 'The Masque of the Red Death'. In the same way that Prince Prospero in Poe's story is corrupt and his state is uncaring and cruel, so too, Wolfe suggests, is the New York of the wealthy elite. The ball of Poe's tale is replaced by a dinner party where a distinguished English poet, Lord Buffing, who is dying of AIDS, addresses the guests about literature and the failure of poetry – 'we poets no longer even have the vitality to write epics. We don't even have the courage to make rhymes ... rhymes of the sort Edgar Allan Poe gave us.' He goes on:

*Poe, who lived his last years just north of here, I believe, in a part of New York called the Bronx ... in a little cottage with lilacs and a cherry tree ... and a wife dying of tuberculosis. A drunk he was, of course, perhaps a psychotic—but with the madness*

Vladimir Nabokov (1899 – 1977).

## Poe's Number One Fan
## Howard Phillips Lovecraft
### (1890 – 1937)

'Poe has probably influenced me more than any other one person. If I have ever been able to approximate his kind of thrill, it is only because he himself paved the way by creating a whole atmosphere & method which lesser men can follow with relative ease.' H.P. Lovecraft, 1931.

*of prophetic vision. He wrote a story that tells us all we need to know about the moment we live in now.*

Buffing is himself the Masque of the Red Death who has broken into a world that has cut itself off from the realities outside. The rich denizens of New York attending the dinner party have no idea about the poverty that exists on their doorstep. And the Red Death in this case is, of course, AIDS.

## H.P. LOVECRAFT

Perhaps the biggest fan of Poe was the American writer of weird fiction, Howard Phillips Lovecraft. Lovecraft discovered Poe's work in 1898 and was profoundly influenced by it for the remainder of his life. 'To him we owe the modern horror story in its final and perfected state,' he wrote in his essay 'Supernatural Horror in Literature'. He was not averse to imitating Poe's style in his own stories: 'Since Poe affected me most of all horror-writers, I can never feel that a tale starts out right unless it has something of his manner. I could never plunge into things abruptly, as the popular writers do. To my mind it is necessary to establish a setting and avenue of approach before the main show can adequately begin.'

He particularly responded to the distance Poe created between himself and the action of his stories, what he called his impartiality. He said that he:

*... perceived the essential impersonality of the real artist; and knew that the function of creative fiction is merely to express and interpret events and sensations as they are, regardless of how they tend or what they prove – good or evil, attractive or repulsive, stimulating or depressing, with the author always acting as a vivid and detached chronicler rather than as a teacher, sympathizer, or vendor of opinion.*

In Lovecraft's greatest work, *At the Mountains of Madness*, published in the magazine *Astounding Tales* in 1936, he cites *Arthur Gordon Pym*:

*Danforth has hinted at queer notions about unsuspected and forbidden sources to which Poe may have had access when writing his Arthur Gordon Pym a century ago. It will be remembered that in that fantastic tale there is a word of unknown but terrible and prodigious significance connected with the antarctic and screamed eternally by the gigantic, spectrally snowy birds of that malign region's core. "Tekeli-li! Tekeli-li!"*

## STEPHEN KING

Lovecraft stands in a direct line of descent from Edgar Allan Poe, and in turn his influence has fanned out across modern science fiction and horror writing to authors such as Neil Gaiman, Clive Barker, Colin Wilson and Stephen King.

In a recent speech, Stephen King said of Poe: 'Poe was the first guy to write about main characters who were bad guys or who were mad guys, and those are some of my favorite stories.'

He added that Poe had inspired a number of his favorite authors, including Robert Bloch, H.P. Lovecraft and Ray Bradbury. 'I came along and read all those guys, so you can say that we were all twisted by our evil grandfather.'

King has even created his own version of Poe's 'The Tell-Tale Heart' in a story he characteristically re-named 'The Old Dude's Ticker'. In King's story the narrator is a Vietnam veteran suffering from combat fatigue.

When giving a reading of the story, he once said: 'Everything in the story that I'm going to read to you is in Poe's story, so if you get grossed out or if you get scared or if you go "Yuk!" or something like that, don't blame me, blame it right on Poe. And you can't get at him, he's dead.'

# CHAPTER 15

# POE'S LEGACY TO THE PEOPLE

Edgar Allan Poe has not only had a significant influence on literature; his work has also inspired numerous film and television adaptations – so many, in fact, that it would be impossible to list them all here. One website lists an incredible 254 titles based on his work. Its enduring presence on cinema and television screens is perhaps a tribute to the atmospheric, highly visual nature of his stories and the incredible power of his story-telling.

## POE GOES SILENT

Probably the first film that had anything to do with Poe was a short film made in 1909 by the famous silent movie director D.W. Griffith. *Edgar Allan Poe*, while not strictly biographical, was based on his caring for Virginia and his extreme poverty. In the film, he writes *The Raven* after seeing a raven perch on a bust of Pallas at their little house. He receives ten dollars for it from a publisher and buys food and medicine for Virginia. But it is too late. When he returns home he finds her dead and collapses melodramatically across her bed.

## THE RAVEN AND THE SILVER SCREEN

In 1935, horror mavens, Bela Lugosi and Boris Karloff, starred in *The Raven*. Lugosi plays Dr. Richard Vollin, a mad surgeon who expresses his passion for the work of Edgar Allan Poe by having a torture chamber filled with implements based on Poe's stories, such as a pit, a pendulum with a scythe attached, a room whose walls close in and so on. The raven, he claims, is his talisman. At the end of the film, the guests at a dinner party hosted by Vollin are caught in the Poe-inspired torture traps one by one.

This film, with its themes of torture, disfigurement and grisly revenge proved too prurient for 1935 tastes and failed at the box office. It also led indirectly to a temporary ban on horror films in Britain. Horror went out of fashion and ghoul *extraordinaire* Bela Lugosi fell on hard times. Interestingly, Boris Karloff would also appear in Roger Corman's version of *The Raven*, made twenty-eight years later and co-starring Vincent Price, Peter Lorre and a young Jack Nicholson who was a regular performer in Corman films early in his illustrious career.

## THE MOVIES OF ROGER CORMAN

Amongst the most notable of the film-makers who have turned to Poe for inspiration is Roger Corman, one of the most prolific film-makers in the history of the movies. He has directed fifty-five films and produced three hundred and eighty-five in a career spanning more than fifty years.

Amongst this mountain of celluloid are no fewer than eight adaptations of works by Edgar Allan Poe – *House of Usher* (1960), *The Pit and the Pendulum* (1961), *The Premature Burial* (1962), *Tales of Terror* (1962), *The Raven* (1963), *The Haunted Palace* (1963), *The Masque of the Red Death* (1964) and *The Tomb of Ligeia* (1965).

Seven of these films starred the doyen of the horror film, Vincent Price, while Ray Milland took the lead in *The Premature*

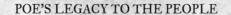

Poster for the 1935 Universal movie *The Raven*, starring Boris Karloff and Bela Lugosi.

*Burial*. *The Haunted Palace* (included above) is often regarded as one in Corman's series of eight Poe films, but, although marketed as *Edgar Allan Poe's The Haunted Palace*, confusingly the film actually derives its plot from *The Case of Charles Dexter Ward*, a novella by H.P. Lovecraft. The title, *The Haunted Palace*, is simply borrowed from a poem by Poe published in 1839.

Corman managed to persuade his studio, American International Pictures (AIP), to provide a bigger budget than he was used to and for the first of his Poe films, *House of Usher*, he was able to film in widescreen and in color and use more lavish sets than he normally had.

The success of this film led to the financing of further Poe movies, although the budgets were still limited, leading to the same sets being used again and again and even to scenes from one film being used in others, such as the burning of the roof of the Usher mansion which appears in several of the other films. This creation and use of stock footage plus the fact that the stories were, of course, in the public domain, rendering them royalty-free, made them extremely cost-effective.

## THE EMBODIMENT OF EVIL

The last of Corman's Poe adaptations was *The Tomb of Ligeia* in which Vincent Price plays a deranged aristocrat pursued by a raven-haired wife who has died and been buried. This film is different to Corman's earlier efforts. A lot of the dark humor is absent and, rather than a conventional horror story, it is a tale of obsessive love. It is beautifully shot, Corman having taken his cameras out of the studio and into the English countryside in Norfolk. He characteristically saved money by using the sets that had been built the previous year at Shepperton Film Studios for the lavish Burton-O'Toole costume spectacular, *Beckett*.

Corman made an interesting portfolio film of Poe's stories in 1962. *Tales of Terror* was said to feature three of Poe's stories,

but there were actually four as 'The Cask of Amontillado' and 'The Black Cat' were rolled into one. The others were 'Morella' and 'The Facts in the Case of M. Valdemar'. Vincent Price, Basil Rathbone, Maggie Pierce, Leona Gage and Peter Lorre starred. Although 'Morella' is disappointing, Price and Lorre bring superb ghoulish humor to 'The Black Cat' and Rathbone is the embodiment of evil in 'The Facts in the Case of M. Valdemar'.

## RE-ANIMATING POE

In 1953, James Mason narrated the animated film, *The Tell-Tale Heart*, which was nominated for an Oscar. It was the first cartoon to be rated X, indicating that it was only suitable for adult audiences. Surreal imagery in the film brilliantly conveys the narrator's descent into madness.

In 1968, three great directors – Federico Fellini, Louis Malle and Roger Vadim – each brought a Poe tale to the big screen in *Spirits of the Dead* (*Tales of Mystery* in the UK). Jane Fonda does an excellent job replacing the male protagonist in *Metzengerstein* which Vadim directed. *William Wilson*, is directed by French director Louis Malle and stars Alain Delon and Brigitte Bardot. *Toby Dammit*, based on the story 'Never Bet the Devil Your Head' stars Terence Stamp and is directed by Fellini.

*The New York Times* wrote that *Toby Dammit*, the first new Fellini to be seen here since *Juliet of the Spirits* in 1965, is marvelous: 'a short movie but a major one. The Vadim is as overdecorated and shrill as a drag ball, but still quite fun, and the Malle, based on one of Poe's best stories, is simply tedious.'

C. Auguste Dupin was brilliantly brought back to life by George C. Scott in the 1986 TV movie, *The Murders in the Rue Morgue*. A young Val Kilmer plays Dupin's godson and, bizarrely, Dupin has a daughter, played by Rebecca De Mornay. The inept Prefect of Police is expertly portrayed by Ian McShane.

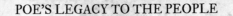

**Even on her wedding night she must share the man she loved with the "Female Thing" that lived in the Tomb of the Cat!**

AMERICAN INTERNATIONAL

*presents*

**VINCENT PRICE**

ELIZABETH SHEPHERD

STARRING IN

EDGAR ALLAN POE'S

**TOMB of LIGEIA**

IN

COLORSCOPE

Screenplay by ROBERT TOWNE · From the Story by EDGAR ALLAN POE · Produced and Directed by ROGER CORMAN

Film poster for *Tomb of Ligeia* (1965), starring Vincent Price.

## POE BIOPICS

Poe's life – and especially his death – has become a source of fascination for all and film-makers are no different. The 2008, film *Poe: Last Days of the Raven* made by actor-director, Brent Fidler and Eric Goldstein, paints a psychological portrait of Edgar Allan Poe as he lies dying in his hospital bed. It explores the things that shaped Poe's imagination – his dreams and nightmares and the deaths of his loved ones. The film's tagline reads 'His death was his greatest mystery!'

In 2012, James McTeigue brought *The Raven* to the big screen in a film starring John Cusack, Brendan Gleeson and Alice Eve. Again, it is a fictionalized account of the last days of Edgar Allan Poe's life but this time he spends them pursuing a serial killer whose murders resemble the murders in Poe's stories.

One oddity features Vincent Price simply sitting in various chairs and reading Poe's stories. In *An Evening of Edgar Allan Poe* (1970), Price is simply superb, his haunting voice adding chills to 'The Tell-Tale Heart', 'The Sphinx', 'The Cask of Amontillado' and 'The Pit and the Pendulum'. Highly recommended for Price's bravura performance, this film can be found online.

A Poe film that has never been made is Sylvester Stallone's biopic of the writer. The star of *Rocky* and *Rambo* has long wanted to make this film, saying of it: 'What fascinates me about Poe is that he was such an iconoclast. It's a story for every young man or woman who sees themselves as a bit outside the box, or has been ostracized during their life as an oddball or too eccentric. It didn't work for him either.'

## THE SIMPSONS AND SOUTH PARK

Television has also served Poe well. His work has featured in a variety of programs from *Futurama* to *Sabrina, the Teenage Witch*. The ever-popular *The Simpsons* has featured him a number of times. In the 'Treehouse of Horror' episode, velvet-voiced James Earl Jones reads 'The Raven' with Homer Simpson playing the narrator, Marge as Lenore and Bart as the raven. 'The Tell-Tale Heart' appears in 'Lisa's Rival' in which Lisa Simpson competes against another girl who recreates a scene from the story.

Poe's tombstone turns up in 'Saturdays of Thunder' in which it is being cleaned by Dr. Nick Rivera, and the House of Usher is seen

John Cusack in *The Raven* (2012).

exploding in the episode 'Lisa the Simpson' as part of a fictional Fox television show, *When Buildings Collapse*. Finally, in 'Homer's Triple Bypass', Homer rams a truck carrying a house. The sign on the house bears the legend 'birthplace of Edgar Allan Poe.'

*South Park* also got in on the act. In the episode named 'Goth Kids 3: Dawn of the Posers', the Goth and Vampire kids summon the ghost of Edgar Allan Poe who appears as a Goth, to help stop an invasion by Emo kids.

## U.S. CRIME DRAMAS

Poe has also been name-checked in countless programs. The hugely popular cop show *The Wire* is set in Baltimore where, of course, Poe once lived. In the program, the public housing estates where drugs are a unit of currency, and where violent, nasty, Gothic things happen are called the Poe Homes. *CSI: Crime Scene Investigation* brought together 'The Tell-Tale Heart' and 'The Cask of Amontillado' in its 2006 episode 'Up in Smoke' in which a body is found badly burned in a chimney.

## CLASSICALLY COMPOSED POE

Poe's work and life have long inspired musicians in a variety of genres. A number of classical musicians have, for instance, used his work in their compositions.

In 1909, French composer and conductor André Caplet wrote two works based on 'The Masque of the Red Death' – *Conte fantastique* for harp and string quartet and the orchestral symphonic study, *Le Masque de la mort rouge*. In 1997, Finnish composer, Einojuhani Rautavaara, based his haunting choral fantasy, 'On the Last Frontier', on the final two paragraphs of Poe's *The Narrative of Arthur Gordon Pym*. Several operas have been written based on his stories – *Ligeia*, a 1994 work by Augusta Read Thomas and *The Tell-Tale Heart* by Bruce Adolphe. French composer, Claude Debussy, failed to finish an opera based on 'The Fall of the House of Usher'.

## POPULAR MUSIC

Popular music has taken Poe to its heart. In 1957, Frankie Laine recorded a version of his poem 'Annabel Lee' and country music superstar Jim Reeves recorded it in 1963 on an album of poetry. In fact, 'Annabel Lee' has been recorded by numerous performers including Fleetwood Mac singer Stevie Nicks and folk queen Joan Baez on her 1967 album *Joan*.

U.S. folk singer Phil Ochs brilliantly set Poe's poem 'The Bells' to music for his debut album *All the News That's Fit to Sing*, his guitar chiming out the sound of bells while the greatest folk singer of them all, Bob Dylan, famously made use of Rue Morgue in his song *Just Like Tom Thumb's Blues* from his *Highway 61 Revisited album*:

> *Don't put on any airs*
>
> *When you're down on Rue Morgue Avenue*
>
> *They got some hungry women there*
>
> *And they really make a mess outta you*

## THE BEATLES

The Beatles referred to Poe a couple of times. The artist Peter Blake was responsible for the collage of notable people that served as a backdrop to the band on the sleeve of probably their greatest album, *Sergeant Pepper's Lonely Hearts Club Band*. The fact that Edgar Allan Poe's face from the famous daguerreotype can be seen in the center of the top row demonstrates just how much he had become a part of our cultural furniture by the 1960s. He was mentioned again in John Lennon's surreal masterpiece *I Am the Walrus* in which Lennon sings wryly the lines:

> *Elementary penguin singing Hari Krishna*
>
> *Man you should have seen them kicking Edgar Allan Poe.*

## ROCK AND POP

In 1976, the progressive rock band The Alan Parsons Project released an album, *Tales of Mystery and Imagination*, based entirely on Poe's stories and poems. Songs on the album draw on 'The Raven', 'The Cask of Amontillado', 'The System of Doctor Tarr and Professor Fether' – a Top 40 hit – and 'To One in Paradise'. There is also a rock symphony in five parts called *The Fall of the House of Usher*. A member of the band, Eric Woolfson wrote a stage musical entitled *Poe* in 2003.

Somewhat incongruously, Britney Spears named her 2001 – 2002 concert tour *Dream Within a Dream* after the Poe poem and lines from it and other work by Poe were incorporated into her show. The garage rock duo The White Stripes reference 'The Masque of the Red Death' in their 2002 single *Red Death at 6.14*.

Meanwhile, 2003 saw Lou Reed, formerly of The Velvet Underground release a concept album called *The Raven* consisting of musical and spoken-word interpretations of Poe's short stories and poems. The album featured contributions from Laurie Anderson, David Bowie, Antony Hegarty, Steve Buscemi and Willem Dafoe. It was Reed's final solo outing and featured tracks such as *The Conqueror Worm, Old Poe, Edgar Allan Poe* and *The Fall of the House of Usher*.

The album's producer, Hal Willner, had previously overseen a Poe tribute album, *Closed on Account of Rabies*, featuring a galaxy of stars reading Poe's works, including Marianne Faithfull, Christopher Walken, Iggy Pop, Dr. John and Debbie Harry. The spooky cover art was by Gonzo artist Ralph Steadman.

Cover of The Beatles 1967 album *Sergeant Pepper's Lonely Hearts Club Band*. Edgar Allan Poe can be seen in the center of the top row

## HEAVY METAL

A number of heavy metal bands have used Poe in their music. The American gothic instrumental duo, Nox Arcana, who have also written music based on the works of H.P. Lovecraft, produced *Shadow of the Raven* in 2007, paying tribute to Poe. Track titles include *Masque of the Red Death, Murders in the Rue Morgue, The House of Usher, The Tell-Tale Heart* and *The Raven*.

*Murders in the Rue Morgue* is the title of a song recorded by Iron Maiden for their 1981 album, *Killers*; Grave Digger's 2001 album *The Grave Digger* is dedicated to Poe and his work forms the basis of several of the songs on the album; there is a thrash metal band called Nevermore and a plethora of other metal bands – including Stormwitch, Agathodaimon, Annihilator and Crimson Glory, to name but a few – have recorded Poe-related material.

---

## MUSICAL THEATER

Not forgetting musical theater, a musical has recently been written about the life and death of Edgar Allan Poe. Written by Jonathan Christenson, *Nevermore: The Imaginary Life and Mysterious Death of Edgar Allan Poe* is described as a 'Gothic fantasia'. The *New York Times* has described it as 'Exquisitely stylish and excessively bleak.'

---

## EDGAR ALLAN POE IN GAMING

There are a number of games based on the work of Edgar Allan Poe. *The Dark Eye* was a horror computer game – a point-and-click adventure game – released in 1995 that has since achieved cult status. It features the gravelly voice of the author William S. Burroughs as one of the characters, Edwin, but he also provides the voiceovers of two slide-show sequences that illustrate Poe's short story 'The Masque of the Red Death' and the poem 'Annabel Lee'. Another of Poe's

tales, 'The Premature Burial' is to be found while reading the newspaper in the telling of 'The Tell-Tale Heart' and the poem 'To Helen' is also in the game.

---

## THE DARK TALES FRANCHISE

Big Fish created a series of games based on Poe's stories under the *Dark Tales* name.

*Dark Tales: Edgar Allan Poe's Murders in the Rue Morgue* is a Hidden Object and Adventure game in which the player works with C. Auguste Dupin to solve the murder in the famous fictional Paris street. The *Dark Tales* series also includes *Edgar Allan Poe's The Black Cat*, another adventure with Dupin. Monsieur Mark Davies' wife Sara has gone missing and the object of the game is to track her down and solve the mystery. The Black Cat helps to discover the hidden clues.

Other Poe stories are featured in *Dark Tales* games. In *Dark Tales: Edgar Allan Poe's the Gold Bug*, an acquaintance possesses a golden scarab-like bug, which he insists will lead him to treasure buried by the pirate Captain Kidd. The player has to help him decipher the puzzles that hide the treasure, and protect him from a mysterious individual who seems to want the investigation stopped at all costs.

In *Dark Tales: Edgar Allan Poe's The Premature Burial*, the objective is to help a distraught young man investigate the sudden death of his beloved. Big Fish have also published *Midnight Mysteries: The Edgar Allan Poe Conspiracy* in which the player has to help solve an ancient homicide and find Poe's murderer. The player is led through a series of Poe's classic tales, collecting clues, interviewing witnesses and trying to solve the mystery.

ERS Game Studios, the same company that published the Dark Tales franchise, produced in 2014 a free-to-play spin-off from that franchise known as *Nightfall: An Edgar Allan Poe Mystery*. C. Auguste Dupin returns to lead players through the mysterious streets of Paris, solving crimes.

A movie poster for *The Premature Burial* (1962), directed by Roger Corman. Ray Milland stars as a man so obsessed with his fear of being buried alive that he builds a special coffin that springs open at the slightest movement of a body inside. He believes his father was also buried alive and he could hear his father's cries as he tried to fight his way out.

D HAPPEN!

OU ARE THERE IN
UDDEN DARKNESS
WHEN THE HEART
BEAT STARTS...

Will YOU be the
first to crack?

ND in EDGAR ALLAN POE'S

ATURE BURIAL

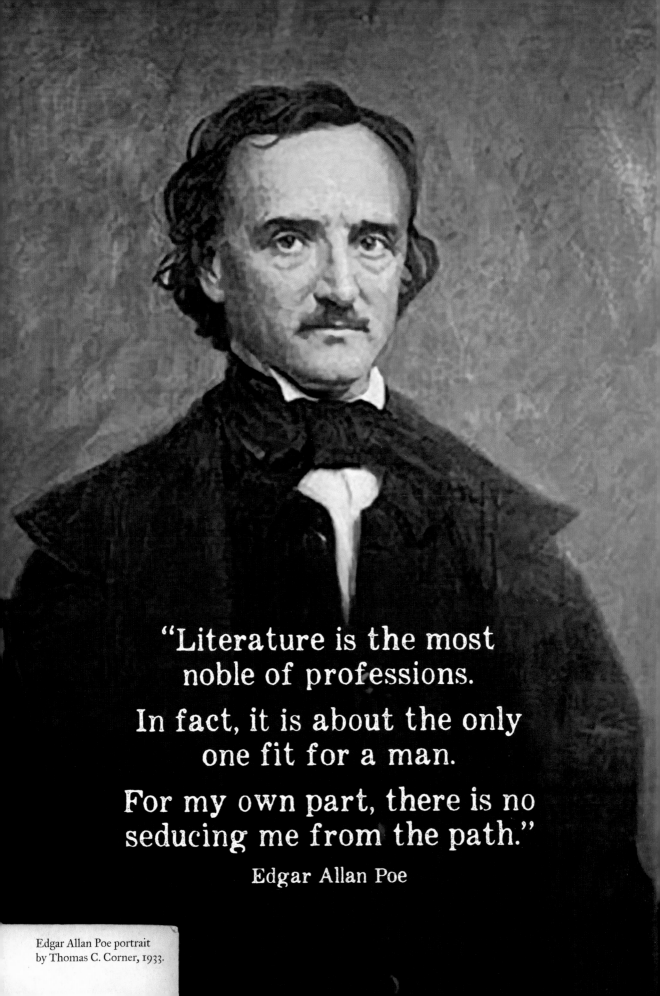

"Literature is the most noble of professions.

In fact, it is about the only one fit for a man.

For my own part, there is no seducing me from the path."

Edgar Allan Poe

Edgar Allan Poe portrait
by Thomas C. Corner, 1933.

# FURTHER READING

Ackroyd, Peter (2008) *Poe: A Life Cut Short.* London: Vintage.

Barnes, Nigel (2009) *A Dream Within A Dream: The Life of Edgar Allan Poe.* London: Peter Owen.

Beaver, Harold (1976) *The Science Fiction of Edgar Allan Poe.* London: Penguin Classics.

Budd, Louis J., & Cady, Edwin H., eds. (1993) *On Poe.* Durham, NC: Duke University Press.

Carlson, Eric W., ed. (1996) *A Companion to Poe Studies.* Westport, CT: Greenwood Publishing Group.

Corben, Richard (2014) *Edgar Allan Poe's Spirits of the Dead.* [Graphic Novel.] Milwaukie, OR: Dark Horse Comics.

Frank, Frederick S., & Magistrale, Anthony (1997) *The Poe Encyclopedia.* Westport, CT: Greenwood Publishing Group.

Hayes, Kevin J., ed. (2002) *The Cambridge Companion to Edgar Allan Poe.* New York: Cambridge University Press.

Hutchisson, James M. (2005) *Poe.* Jackson, MS: University Press of Mississippi.

Kane, P., & Prepolec, C., ed. (2013) *Beyond Rue Morgue Anthology. Further Tales of Edgar Allan Poe's 1st Detective.* [New Dupin stories by modern authors.] London: Titan Books.

Kennedy, J. Gerald, ed. (2001) *A Historical Guide to Edgar Allan Poe.* Oxford: Oxford University Press.

Kennedy, J. Gerald, ed. (2006) *The Portable Edgar Allan Poe.* London: Penguin Classics.

Meyers, Jeffrey (2000) *Edgar Allan Poe His Life and Legacy.* New York: Cooper Square Publishers.

Ocker, J. W. (2015) *Poe-Land: The Hallowed Haunts of Edgar Allan Poe.* [Travelogue of Poe's homes, artifacts and memorials.] Woodstock, VT, Countryman Press.

Poe, Edgar Allan (2002) *Edgar Allan Poe Complete Tales & Poems.* New York: Castle Books.

Poe, Edgar Allan (2009) *The Complete Tales & Poems of Edgar Allan Poe.* Knickerbocker Classics Slip Edition. New York: Race Point Publishing.

Poe, Harry Lee (2008) *Edgar Allan Poe: An Illustrated Companion to His Tell-Tale Stories.* New York: Metro Books.

Quinn, Arthur Hobson (1997) *Edgar Allan Poe: A Critical Biography.* Baltimore: Johns Hopkins University Press.

Whitehead, Dan, ed. (2007) *Nevermore. A Graphic Adaptation of Edgar Allan Poe's Short Stories.* [Graphic Novel.] London: SelfMadeHero.

## Poe Returning to Boston

Among the modern-day traffic in central Boston, Edgar Allan Poe rushes down the street in his flowing overcoat, with a giant raven bursting out of his briefcase. The literary giant returned from the dead to his birthplace in October 2014 as a bronze-based figure, created by artist Stefanie Rocknak. Ironically, Poe was never exactly fond of his hometown—!

# INDEX

Note: Page numbers in italic refer to pictures and illustrations.

## PICTURE CREDITS

Cover © ClassicStock / Alamy / © 19th era / Alamy/ © The Art Archive / Alamy

Internal 6/7 © AF Fotografie / Alamy / 20/105/120 © Interfoto / Alamy / 33 © Georgios Kollidas / Alamy / 35/37/119 © Lebrecht Music and Arts Photo Library / Alamy /125 © World History Archive / Alamy / 175/180 © Pictorial Press Ltd / Alamy/ 178 © Pioneer Pictures / The Kobal Collection/ Archive photographs and documents courtesy of Library of Congress Prints and Photographs Division

This edition published in 2015 by
Chartwell Books
an imprint of Book Sales
a division of Quarto Publishing Group USA Inc.
142 West 36th Street, 4th Floor
New York, New York 10018
USA

ISBN-13: 978-0-7858-3334-5

Printed in China